When God Took Sides

When God Took Sides
Religion and Identity in Ireland—Unfinished History

MARIANNE ELLIOTT

OXFORD
UNIVERSITY PRESS

OXFORD
UNIVERSITY PRESS

Great Clarendon Street, Oxford OX2 6DP

Oxford University Press is a department of the University of Oxford.
It furthers the University's objective of excellence in research, scholarship,
and education by publishing worldwide in

Oxford New York

Auckland Cape Town Dar es Salaam Hong Kong Karachi
Kuala Lumpur Madrid Melbourne Mexico City Nairobi
New Delhi Shanghai Taipei Toronto

With offices in

Argentina Austria Brazil Chile Czech Republic France Greece
Guatemala Hungary Italy Japan Poland Portugal Singapore
South Korea Switzerland Thailand Turkey Ukraine Vietnam

Oxford is a registered trade mark of Oxford University Press
in the UK and in certain other countries

Published in the United States
by Oxford University Press Inc., New York

British Library Cataloguing in Publication Data

Data available

Library of Congress Cataloging in Publication Data

Data available

Typeset by SPI Publisher Services, Pondicherry, India
Printed in Great Britain
on acid-free paper by
Clays Ltd, St Ives plc

ISBN 978-0-19-920693-3

1 3 5 7 9 10 8 6 4 2

For Don Akenson

Preface

This book started out as the Ford Lectures, which I delivered in Oxford in 2005. I want to thank the electors and the many friends and colleagues who attended faithfully and hosted the attendant social events, most notably Roy Foster, Anne Laurence, Tom Paulin, Toby Barnard, Olwen Hufton, Mike Broers, Peter Bell, Richard English, Marc Mulholland, Ian McBride, Mary-Lou Legg, Senia Pešeta, Jan Spurlock, Don Akenson, Andrew Franklin, Maurice Keane, Jose Harris, as well as the many who sacrificed successive Friday evenings to attend.

The structure of the book largely follows the lectures, themed, rather than presented as a chronological sequence. My historian friends have been rightly perturbed by this, emphasizing a potential danger of which I am all too painfully aware: that it risks minimizing change over time. Owen Dudley Edwards made the point with characteristic wit: 'For Heaven's sake put in dates all over the place. You zoom through time like *Jimmy and his Magic Patch* in the *Beano* comic', adding somewhat gallantly, 'You may be too young to have profited by consultation of this valuable source'! My apology is that while the contexts may have changed (and where possible I try to indicate that), the ideas and prejudices have been enduring, selectively preserved in aspic by interested parties. This then is not a history of religion or religious conflict in Ireland or of the positive contribution of faith to people's lives in the past. There are other books to which the reader can turn for these.

Rather it is about politicized religion and how it came to shape the identities of people in Ireland.

I found the topics of the different lectures and chapters selecting themselves in a way that I had not anticipated. For I was dealing with stereotypes. The reader may well wonder why Protestant teachings and attitudes figure disproportionately. This is because the various Protestant denominations started out in reaction to the perceived failings of the Roman Church and these negative perceptions endured thereafter. Since the power structures remained predominantly Protestant for most of the period under discussion (*c.*1600–*c.*2000), such religious stereotypes had an enduring influence and Catholic identity was often developed in response, the one too often emphasizing what was most alienating to the other. 'When someone feels that his language is despised, his religion ridiculed and his culture disparaged,' writes Amin Maalouf in *On Identity*, 'he is likely to react by flaunting the signs of difference.'[1] And if I needed any further reminder about the continuing prevalence of such religious stereotypes, it came in the reaction of individuals in audiences to which I have spoken on these topics over the past three years, causing me often to reflect on the words of William Butler Yeats: 'peace comes dropping slow'.

My debts are large: to the British Academy and the Arts and Humanities Research Council, who funded much of the research; to my long-suffering family (Trevor and Marc), friends, and colleagues at the Institute of Irish Studies in Liverpool, notably Frank Shovlin, Maria Power, Diane Urquhart, Patrick Nugent, Kevin Bean, Ian McKeane, Linda Christiansen, Carmen Tunney-Harper, and Dorothy Lynch; to Peter Shirlow, Mervyn Gibson, Ian Adamson, Pauline Hadaway, Mervyn Smyth, and Malachi O'Doherty; to my publisher, Oxford University Press; to my copy-editor, Laurien Berkeley, and indexer, Oula Jones; to my agent,

Karolina Sutton, and her predecessor, Kate Jones, who died tragically young before she could read the completed book; to the staff of the libraries used, notably John Gray, Gerry Healey, and Alistair Gorden of the Linenhall Library; to those who read and commented on earlier drafts of chapters: Roy Foster, Ian McBride, Diarmaid McCulloch, Alan Ford, Martin Maguire, Pat Nugent, Edna Longley, and most of all Owen Dudley Edwards and Don Akenson, who read the entire work, interrupting holidays and other important schedules to turn it around at speed. The book is dedicated to Don Akenson, who led the way in his research on this topic and whose friendship and scholarship have enlivened my life over many years.

M.E.

Contents

List of Plates

I

Irish Christians *Again*

Here you are born one thing or the other, Protestant or Roman
Catholic, just as you are born a boy or a girl.

(George A. Birmingham, *The Seething Pot*, 1905)

In 1977 *Punch* magazine published its humorous (if somewhat
condescending) cartoon on the Northern Ireland Troubles: 'Oh
dear, not the Irish Christians Again' (Plate 1).[1] This book too is
about the historic divisions between Ireland's main religious communities. In my choice of topic I had before me the formidable
precedent of earlier Ford Lectures delivered by F. S. L. Lyons in
1978. These were later published in his influential *Culture and
Anarchy in Ireland, 1890–1939*. Leland Lyons was speaking in the
worst decade of the Northern Ireland Troubles and there is a
pessimistic fatalism running through his lectures. He was an Ulster
Protestant, working in England before returning to Ireland in 1974
to become Provost of Trinity College Dublin. It was the year that
the power-sharing executive in Northern Ireland was brought
down by the Ulster Workers' Strike, the year that saw the worst
atrocity of the Troubles in the Republic (the Dublin and Monaghan bombings killing thirty-one and injuring 100). He would have
been aware of the profoundly negative impact of the northern
Troubles on the Irish Republic, which had eroded the liberalism of
the 1960s and revived extreme nationalism, anti-Englishness, and

anti-Protestantism. His lectures were largely about the efforts of the Protestant Anglo-Irish to attain a 'fusion of cultures' in Ireland, and their ultimate failure. Protestant Ireland, representing less than 5 per cent of the southern population and falling, seemed doomed.

It was doomed, he thought, because it was really England that the new Catholic nationalism was against and the Protestants were caught in between. It is not surprising that Lyons—like so many writers before him—was still concerned with the 'national' question: the role of England. 'I have not a book to turn to', complained Sean O'Faolain in his influential 1947 book *The Irish*, 'which is not either preoccupied with the national ego and a delusion of its self-sufficiency, or else a cursive record of political events.'[2] In both parts of Ireland we are still living through the consequences of socialization through the national stories. Narratives conveyed through school textbooks continue to inform people's views of the past, privileging 'memory' of historic rights and wrongs, even though, when tested, they often bear no validity in local contexts.[3] It was this which stunted the development of Irish sociology, ending the British empirical tradition of the nineteenth century. 'Social reform based on...empirical analysis', write the editors of *Irish Society: Sociological Perspectives* (1995), 'had little place within official nationalist and unionist thinking.' The South promoted a form of 'Catholic sociology', the North avoided empirical social research almost completely before the 1960s, and both were mentally confined to Irish–British comparisons.[4]

Colonizing processes, such as that which happened in Ireland, usually involve the preference of one group and the negative stereotyping of another. It was the Protestantism of England, the conquering power, which came to define 'loyalty', and its contempt for Gaelic ways translated into latter-day Protestant perceptions of Catholics as inferior. Popular resentment at past condescension is still a sub-current of Irish Catholic thinking, easily played upon by extreme nationalists. It provided independent Ireland with a safety valve to blame the old enemy for everything that went wrong, and Ireland's Catholic Church with its main theatre of 'missionary' activity. Irish Catholicism considered itself particularly virtuous; English Catholics were deemed lesser Catholics because of their Englishness.

In fact, England's relevance to this topic—once the Reformation had happened—is marginal. This book will be about communal relationships between the two 'master' faith systems in Ireland: Catholicism and Protestantism.[5] It looks behind the national story to its roots in religion and religious stereotyping. That the Protestant Reformation failed in Ireland is accepted by historians. Why it failed is still open to debate. Nicholas Canny has argued that it could not be pronounced as such until the second half of the nineteenth century, when the Catholic Church finally reorganized itself along the lines set out by the Council of Trent in the sixteenth century. Roy Foster, somewhat tongue-in-cheek, thinks it finally arrived in Celtic Tiger Ireland.[6] There was, however, a pre-existing religious culture in Ireland, thoroughly integrated into a daily life which Protestantism considered barbarous. It was not England which was to prevent the fusion of cultures— though it sometimes played them off against each other—but the two mainstream religious communities themselves. Conversion was not high on their list of priorities and they developed what D. H. Akenson has called mutually agreed 'separate boundary maintenance systems' to keep the others out. Only by such segregation, he comments, 'was it possible for the two groups to develop and perpetuate entirely incompatible social cosmologies and grossly inaccurate views of each other'.[7]

This book is not a history of religion in Ireland. Nor is it an analysis of formal religious beliefs per se. Indeed it is more often about what R. Scott Appleby calls the 'religiously illiterate', whose 'deep emotional currents' are easily exploited.

> Extremist religious or nationalist demagogues excel in [manipulat-ing] . . . ahistorical discourse about the inevitability of 'ancient eth-nic hatreds' . . . in an audience drawn from a religious but religiously illiterate population. The ritualized reenactment of a tragic injustice suffered by the community in the near or distant past often accomplishes the desired result . . . and serves to demonize 'the other' . . . and to extend a sacred canopy over the whole dubious process.[8]

It is about how negative stereotypes were developed in Ireland at a time of heightened religious conflict and political upheaval; how they were perpetuated and entrenched; and how they defined communal world-views and determined political outcomes. Above all it is about how Irish Protestants' and Irish Catholics' sense of self was conditioned by their views of each other.

Sectarianism

It is, of course, absurd to think that religious and national identities take primacy over others in deciding human behaviour. Yet in modern Ireland political identity has often taken a sectarian and negative route and sectarianism always has a religious element.[9] Sectarianism was there before modern nationalism developed, and the political division of Ireland was the consequence of such sectarianism, rather than the cause of it. If sectarianism had not been so deep-rooted, the Northern Ireland Troubles would not have happened. They happened because both sides acted as the stereotypes said they would.

Sectarianism operates at many different levels, and people can sustain sectarian systems and pass on sectarianism to their children without ever recognizing it in themselves. It is a 'distorted expression' of the very basic human needs of belonging and identity.[10] It has also stood in for class struggle in Ireland and usually destroyed any effort at socialist alliance. In the terrible economic conditions of the 1930s, Peadar O'Donnell, the prime left-wing thinker of the IRA, believed that only the sectarianism of northern republicans prevented them from winning working-class Protestants to their cause. He recalled attending a commemoration rally in Belfast for the 1916 rising—traditionally held by republicans at Easter. He persuaded some Protestants to come along. But when stopped by the police, 'the whole republican procession flopped down on its knees and began the rosary. My Orangemen could have afforded to risk getting their heads cracked with a baton, but they couldn't kneel on the Belfast streets to say the rosary.' The Belfast IRA, he concluded, was no more than 'a battalion of armed Catholics'.[11]

It is an argument which has been repeated during the recent Northern Ireland Troubles, though it is not one which republicans or nationalists generally would accept. Rather they argue that their problem has always been with the state and that Protestants alone are bigots. At first sight this is a plausible claim, since the fears of northern Protestants are often expressed in religious terms. Protestants have long seen the Catholic Church itself as the enemy, a belief which is reflected in the abusive terms 'papist' and 'Romanist'. It is why, within Ireland, the prefix 'Roman' to 'Catholic' is one of the stereotypical cues identifying the speaker as Protestant, even though it is usually not used abusively. But it often has been. It is the subject of Seamus Heaney's 1975 poem 'Whatever You Say, Say Nothing'. Heaney's poem has still not been surpassed in capturing that instinctive search for clues to religious identity which has made of Northern Ireland 'a land of password, hand-grip, wink and nod'. Although 'Religion's never mentioned here', 'You know them by their eyes', and hold your tongue.[12]

There are, of course, good reasons why sectarianism has been more blatant in the North. However, as I hope to show, sectarianism was not as confined to the northerners as the rest of Ireland would like to think. I see Northern Ireland rather like geologists see exposed rocks, as providing an insight into the past. Freud also applied the 'narcissism of minor differences' to space and territory: 'it is precisely communities with adjoining territories, and related to each other in other ways as well, who are engaged in constant feuds and in ridiculing each other'.[13] This idea can be applied also to England's and Ireland's mutual stereotyping of each other through history. But for the future it is more important to understand how it has bedevilled relations within Ireland. Even the best of Irish historians from the Republic of Ireland have tended to exclude Ulster. As Joe Lee argued in his 1989 history of twentieth-century Ireland: 'The Irish contemporary historian finds himself in the unusual position of being simultaneously insider and outsider. He cannot pronounce on both Northern Ireland and the Republic from the same perspective ... Southern Irish historians, like myself, are likely to be as ambivalent toward the North as are citizens of the Republic in general.'[14] Social attitude surveys bear this out, with the English scoring more favourable ratings than the Northern Irish and over half of those asked in 1988–9 thinking North and South two different nations.[15]

Identity: Living in the Perception of Others

The term 'identity' is enormously problematic, not least because it has become a modern obsession. It is often associated with the presumed characteristics of groups or communities, and sociologists and anthropologists are rightly concerned by its exclusive and negative connotations. They attack 'essentialism'—the idea that groups might have a single, homogenous culture and 'the popular tendency to freeze cultural differences between groups'.[16] Although we would have difficulty describing our own identity, which we know is multi-layered and apt to change in time and context, often we do not reflect that understanding onto others. We see them as different, make 'sweeping judgements' and ascribe to them collective guilt. However, as Amin Maalouf points out in his compelling study of identity, despite the many elements contributing to it, one's identity is 'singular', not a 'loose patchwork'. 'Touch just one part of it, just one allegiance, and the whole person will react, the whole drum will sound.' The aspect attacked then becomes uppermost and 'invades the person's whole identity'. Then the perfect stage is set for 'agitators' to take over, emphasizing all the crimes and humiliations of the past and making ordinary people capable of committing savage atrocities. 'The emotions of fear or insecurity don't always obey rational considerations' and the prevalent 'tribal' concept of identity facilitates distortion. 'It's a concept inherited from the conflicts of the past, and many of us would reject it if we examined it more closely. But we cling to it through habit, from lack of imagination or resignation, thus inadvertently contributing to the tragedies by which, tomorrow, we shall be genuinely shocked.'

It is this notion of identity that sees one side as 'ours' and allows often the most intolerant and fanatical members of 'our side' to define it and denounce as traitors those who do not accept the extreme definition. Atrocities are then explained away as self-defence, and 'the eternal sceptics' declare that things have always been thus and will never change. It is the fear of dilution or even destruction of that identity which produces excessive displays, often of its more extreme aspects.[17]

This cultural defensiveness—while more obvious among Irish Protestants—has been more long-standing and influential in Catholic Irish identity, which was developed in response to English and Protestant negative stereotyping. Secure identities—personal and national—tend to be low-key. The sociologist Fr Micheál Mac-Gréil applied a 'patriotic esteem scale' in his attitude survey of Irish thinking in the mid-1990s and concluded that there was a 'xenophobic sense of superiority *vis-à-vis* other nationalities and cultures'—high percentages of people believing Ireland better than most other countries, expressing pride in Irish history, and being defensive of Irish customs. 'The national respect . . . verges on the ethnocentric. It could be interpreted as indicating a quasi-superiority complex, which may be a reaction to being so long kept under the thumb of their colonial master.'[18] Here he describes the common traits of an inferiority complex. And in Ireland insecurities have often been the backdrop to aggressive and exclusive displays of heritage and culture.

The idea that group identity lies in difference then produces a disproportionate emphasis on those differences and a fear of dilution or loss of status. Here again we have Freud's idea that it is the small differences between people who are otherwise alike which are the source of hostility and group identity, any threat of loss creating the potential for violence, but also for cohesiveness within that community.[19]

Irish identity has been remarkably streamlined. The ideal type, the Irish 'properly so called' in the words of Wolfe Tone,[20] were expected to be Catholic. How Catholicism and Irishness became identified, and how that identity was moulded from themes of persecution and poverty, is a key theme of this book. People in today's more confident Republic of Ireland believe that they have left all this behind and the gulf between themselves and those in the North has widened. Indeed, the prolific Catholic writer and controversialist Desmond Fennell proclaimed in 2003 that he had decided to move permanently to Rome because of his dissatisfaction with the 'post-nationalist condition' in Ireland. The Irish nation had in both cases 'abolished itself', he thought, because it had stripped itself of its 'distinguishing religion, namely Catholicism' and he saw nothing to fill the gap.[21]

He had a point, and while old-style Catholicism is not generally lamented, many Irish people are worried about the crude materialism and loss of values with which it has been replaced. But he was premature, and since he has now returned, he undoubtedly recognized this. For such post-nationalist confidence sits uneasily with the continuing exploitation of a perceived collective suffering and victimhood, to which Protestants cannot really belong, for they were deemed the perpetrators. All the local historians in Henry Glassie's 1982 ethnographic study of County Fermanagh are Catholic. Protestants do not study Irish history, he was told, because 'Irish history is filled with the mistreatment of Catholics.'[22] Irish Protestants had much to say about such Catholic claims to victimhood and had a highly developed one of their own, drawing on biblical explanations to develop an entire philosophy of 'God's people', perpetually battling evil.

Identities come with a whole ragbag of assumed traits, one's purity determined by how one measures up to them. For those with full marks they can be comforting. But they can also be imprisoning, suffocating, and exclusive: 'not having the freedom to be oneself', as the poet Gerry Dawe describes the process.[23] In a very funny autobiographical sketch of his Irish upbringing in Waterford, the doyen of 'imagined' national identity,

Benedict Anderson, explained the dilemma of being caught in between. 'I grew up in that remote era [the 1940s] when people associated the word "identity" with algebra and formal logic.' But people knew what religious group they belonged to, and the children translated prejudice into actual attacks, separate schools, different accents easily identifying the Other. 'In the Waterford of my youth,' he recalled, 'the walls between the religious communities had grown very high.' Since neither he nor his parents had actually been born in Ireland, proof of Irish ancestry was required for an Irish passport. It took him down two stereotypical routes, one Gaelic–Catholic Irish, the other Anglo–Protestant Irish. In his anthropological research he was quite accustomed to the concept of selective ancestry. But his search for the height of Irish national purity—the anti-English Catholic Gaelic rebel—was to prove just how selective that definition of Irishness actually is. He found enough ancestors to fit the stereotype of the Catholic Gael—some rebels, exiles, Catholic, or nationalist campaigners—to give a veneer of Gaelic respectability. But he also found 'mixed marriages', Gaels who Anglicized their names, became English officials and soldiers, and, even when exiled for their religion, remained steadfastly elitist—not much sign of the poor downtrodden Gael of the Irish Catholic identikit among these Catholic ancestors.[24]

Irish History: Whose History?

Irish history itself then is seen as divisive. Protestant schools in independent Ireland complained that the 'official' version in school textbooks excluded their traditions and were permitted to supply their own. In the 1990s some Catholic schools in Northern Ireland stopped teaching Irish history because of this perception; while young Protestant sixth-formers felt they needed to know more. In the mid-1970s a republican mural in Belfast proclaimed: 'The victors write the History'. But in Ireland nothing could be further from the truth. These chapters will show that Irish Catholics were indeed on the losing side politically for a very long time. But their version of history has had equal longevity and historians who question it are denounced. This challenging of 'things you thought of as constants', Sinn Féin leader Gerry Adams told Fionnuala O Connor in 1993, is 'like a family trauma, like discovering you've been adopted'.[25] Community remembering sees history from the point of view of the losers, the victims, each new perceived hurt ratcheting up the memory of preceding ones, and you are not allowed to forget them. I have been struck when using folklore and oral sources how incidents of presumed betrayal in the past were still being used against descendants of the culprits centuries later, and how such 'remembering' depended on constant reminding. It has been such selective communal remembering of Ireland's faith communities which has shaped national identities and made the northern crisis so difficult to resolve.[26]

The main Northern Ireland churches launched an investigation into sectarianism in 1991. The report published in 1993 managed to reach agreement on every related issue besides history. But they could not agree on the history section and it was excluded, though written by the only trained historian of the group, Dr Joseph Liechty.[27] Sectarianism seems very obvious in Northern Ireland, but less obviously it has underpinned identities also in the South. It operates much as Colm Tóibín describes it in *The Heather Blazing* (1992), where the central character, a judge, raised in the prevailing Catholic nationalist ethos, when faced with a case which pitted that ethos against individual rights, instinctively opted for the former.[28] It is too early to write the obituary of Catholic Ireland, for national identity is still too bound up with it.

You cannot, however, write about Catholicism in Ireland without also looking at Protestantism, for one was shaped by how it was perceived by the other, not always negatively, but very often so. Chapters 3–5 look at Protestant identities through the centuries. Since Irishness became linked in people's minds with Catholicism, so Protestants were considered foreign 'blow-ins', settlers, planters, associated with the Big House and landlordism in the South, and the Stormont regime in the North. However hard Irish governments in post-independence Ireland sought to be inclusive, the emphasis on Catholic identity all but expelled Protestants from the 'nation'. In 1964 the Catholic Bishop of Cork, Cornelius Lucey, explained why Ireland was nervous about ecumenism.

> In Ireland the Protestant is for the Catholic not only a Protestant, but is associated with the dark past of the Ascendancy and penal times. Our immediate contribution to the ecumenical movement should be to forget the past and see our Protestant neighbours not as descendants of landlords, planters, and the rest, but as Irishmen like ourselves.[29]

In the 1960s attitudes were beginning to change radically. Even so, Bishop Lucey's claim would have been representative of how very many Catholics thought, particularly in rural areas.

Such attitudes, however, were not one-sided. Reformation theology (particularly the Calvinistic brand which established itself in Ireland) demonized Catholics, thought them simultaneously threatening and inferior, a different species altogether, the barbarians inside the gates. When Orangemen said as much, their insults had roots in the Reformation, and while it did not always colour government policies, Protestants held power and much of the land for over two centuries, and it often did. The resentful triumphalism of Catholic Ireland after independence, and the resentful defeatism of the Catholic minority in the North, need to be seen against a history of being deemed and often treated as inferior, just as the sensitivity and withdrawal of southern Protestants for much of the twentieth century had something to do with Catholics' perception of them as 'England's faithful garrison'.

The words are those of Sean Lemass in 1927, and since, several decades later, he was the politician who broke the mutual stalemate between North and South by travelling to Stormont, it is a token of how things can and have changed. Even so, Irish identities, to a considerable extent, have been fashioned by such religious stereotypes. It is what sociologists call 'labelling theory', whereby our self-perceptions are very largely shaped by the reactions of others.[30] The negative labels stuck. We were aware of them and ever sensitive to their use, and, as so many studies have shown, they often bubbled underneath prevailing good-neighbourliness. Arthur Clery noted this in his 1915 study of how denominational awareness operated in job appointments: 'all the friendliness is to a certain extent like the fraternisation of soldiers in opposing trenches ... a single shot, a blast on the trumpet, a tap on the drum, and they rush to take their places in the opposing firing lines'.[31]

Stereotypes

Thus do stereotypical perceptions of situations actually change them to become as we perceive them.[32] Even those stereotyped believe them and conform to them, looking for prejudice even if it is absent. You have 'a good Protestant face', John Gamble's Tyrone host told him in the early 1800s. Then he drew his chair conspiratorially close—so that his Catholic servants would not hear—gave a lurid commentary on the 'scarlet whore' of Rome, denounced 'thim' as 'varmin', and declared his Catholic servants ready to murder him in his bed, given half a chance. The stereotype of Catholics by Protestants—and one that can be traced over many centuries—is that of Catholics as genocidal rebels, their priests absolving murders of Protestants. So all Catholics were thought by a significant number of northern Protestants to have supported the IRA in the recent Northern Ireland Troubles, and random loyalist murders of Catholics had the same common thread: they were killing rebels. The word 'disloyalist' was often the excuse for discrimination. Contrary to myth, however, the Irish are not natural rebels, even if they subscribe to a culture which extols those who took up arms. This is not to say that some Protestant fears were not genuine, and IRA activities have tended to underpin the stereotype.

But Catholic sectarianism is no less real for being less easy to identify, and the belief that they have been history's victims puts Catholics in denial. It often takes the form of post-colonial speak: Protestant–planter–settler–colonial victimizer versus Catholic–native–Irish–Gaelic victim. The prize-winning novelist Lionel Shriver, when a young journalist in Northern Ireland, was commissioned to write a series of articles on the independent Opsahl Peace Commission of 1993. She attended all its public sessions and brought a wry sense of detachment to her task. She noted this new trend in republican discourse, 'American therapy-speak' and sociological jargon running through their statements like a computer virus. But the message was still old-fashioned nationalism: the only real option was for Unionists to 'join' the rest of Ireland, 'our' nation being the only legitimate one.[33]

Stereotypes, of course, have some foundation in reality, but they are stereotypes because they are distorted and the distortions then pass as fact, shaping perceptions, behaviour, and policies. Take, for instance, the very long-standing stereotype of Irish Catholics as an inferior breed, unwashed and untutored, a herdlike underclass, disinclined to work, their priests keeping them in ignorance of useful science subjects—the subject of Chapter 7. There is a long history connecting John Gamble's country squire's 'varmin' to David Trimble's 2000 outburst that Sinn Féin needed to be 'house-trained'.[34] Even nationalist heroes such as Henry Grattan and Theobald Wolfe Tone said much the same, if in less abusive terms. It has been noted in Northern Ireland that when Catholics moved into an area, Protestants often moved out, as much from the old fear of 'pollution' as for religious reasons.[35] It is a stereotype which kept Catholics out of government and out of jobs in the North after partition, and allowed Ulster Protestants to blame Catholicism for the economic backwardness of the southern state. This is caught in the 1970s poem by Patrick Williams, 'Cage under Siege':

> On our borders the known world ends sheer.
> We've pulled the sea around us like a shawl
> And heaved the mountains higher. The waiting
> South's bog-barbarians starve against a grand
> Squiggle on our map.[36]

Rescuing Ulster from the indolence of the 'bog-barbarians' became a standard justification of the seventeenth-century Ulster plantation. The denting of this stereotype by the economic transformation of the Irish Republic and the rise of a new Catholic middle class in the North is just one element in today's sense of confusion and defeatism in the Protestant working-class community. This perversely is causing irritation among Catholics, who feel that they alone were persecuted, they alone have been history's victims.

However, Protestants know they have to be careful about complaining too much, for that is another characteristic attributed to Catholics, giving rise to the stereotype of the 'whingeing mick'.

In 1965 Dr Kenneth Milne, representing the Church of Ireland General Synod, was invited to speak about the Protestant minority's viewpoint at a meeting of middle-class Catholics in Dublin. 'I am not here to wallow in self-abasement, but I want to be frank', was the general tone of the talk, and it was written up as such in the *Irish Times*. 'The tone . . . was frank without being churlish; it was neither an assault nor an apologia—and above all, it didn't whinge.'[37]

The ethos of each of the two Irish states has been permeated by such sectarian stereotypes. Swathes of people have fallen out of the national narratives because they do not fit the identikit, public figures, writers, artists, historians scrutinized 'for signs of allegiance or apostasy'.[38] The idea of 'selling out' has been a major feature of Irish nationalism and translated easily into 'informer' in times of conflict. The concept—if it can be so dignified—also exists in Irish Protestant tradition, but it is usually Britain rather than individuals which is so accused. 'In Ireland a man may be a Protestant or a Catholic,' reflected George Birmingham (the Revd J. O. Hannay) in 1919, 'a Nationalist or a Unionist, without suffering any serious inconvenience. He may choose his fold, but he must be a sheep', and those thinking outside the enclosure are thought 'eccentric' or worse.[39] Thus have 'the rich and varied syntheses of life'[40] been written out of single-identity histories in Ireland, which is why challenging them is so necessary.

The Northern Troubles and Communal Identities

A young person in working-class Northern Ireland has carried two histories in his head (for it was the young male who was most vulnerable): one for school assessment, the other the communal history to help him survive on the streets.[41] The street history was everywhere in conflict zones in Northern Ireland. Wall murals have reminded polarized communities of why they are polarized and urged them not to forget. Those in republican areas told of the true Gael, persecuted and despoiled and identified with the persecuted elsewhere. Those in loyalist areas linked Protestantism to truth and loyalty, the Bible, and the Crown, some harking back to an imagined time before the Gaels, to the ancient Ulaid, a pre-Gaelic ruling dynasty, dominant in 450 BC–AD 324, from whom the province got its name—the message: we were here before you. One of the most iconic figures throughout Irish history has been the mythical figure of Cú Chullainn. He is the hero of the ancient sagas known as the Ulster Cycle, first written down in the seventh century. Although best known for inspiring Patrick Pearse in the 1916 rising, Cú Chullainn had died defending Ulster from the rest of Ireland, and it is as Ulster's defender against the Irish that he has been assumed into modern-day loyalist street history.

The Belfast, or Good Friday, Agreement of 1998, though revolutionary at the time, is creating new problems: 'parity of esteem' is reinforcing single-identity politics, producing a hierarchy of victims, and deterring a proper critique of the different religious cultures. It is particularly noticeable on the republican side. As the influence of the Catholic Church declines, republicans are emphasizing their identity as a Catholic community and all manner of communitarian theory is being conscripted. It is, however, as Eamonn McCann has noted, a new form of sectarianism, with people 'even more aware now of the religiously-defined community from which they come and to which they think they belong'.[42]

Initially the northern Troubles fed into Catholic Ireland's national story of persecution. Catholicism had been a large part of many European countries' identity in the early part of the twentieth century and too often it was identified with Fascism. Ireland did not espouse Fascism, but as Catholic identity collapsed in other countries, Ireland was perceived as having one of the most illiberal Catholic cultures in Europe. We now know that the rumblings of discontent which would transform Ireland in the late twentieth century were already there. But they were muted by the northern crisis. Irish Catholic identity was still being attacked. As so often in the past, you closed ranks and emphasized your core values. In time, however, it was the Northern Ireland Troubles which brought the Irish Republic to rethink its underpinning Catholic nationalism.[43] 'If I were a Northern Protestant today,' wrote the Taoiseach, Dr Garret Fitzgerald, in September 1981, 'I cannot see how I could be attracted to . . . a state that is in itself sectarian . . . our laws and our constitution, our practices, our attitudes reflect those of a majority ethos [i.e. Catholic nationalist].'[44]

There are many similarities between the perceptions of Protestants in the Republic of Ireland and Catholics in Northern Ireland. Both were being punished for the sins of their ancestors, both kept their heads down, both were resentful, both could only integrate if the predominant religious culture weakened. Growing secularism has helped the religious minority south of the border to do so; there is still some way to go north of it.

In the summer of 2004 I watched a television interview with a Protestant family intimidated out of their home in Belfast. Defiantly they had festooned their enclave with Union flags and painted their kerbstones red, white, and blue, and they blamed 'Themins' for their plight. It was the same 'thim' as Gamble's country squire identified 200 years earlier. No further explanation was necessary. The term is used generically as shorthand for the other side. In this book I will be looking at nastiness and pettiness, rather than murderousness, but also trying to show how, from a range of choices, it was the negative more often than not which was emphasized. One of those geological layers mentioned earlier survives in a couple of dozen boxes of submissions, oral hearings, focus group reports, and a range of other meetings associated with the 1993 Opsahl Peace Commission in Ireland, on which I had the honour to serve. Its remit was wide and it privileged 'ordinary' people above the politicians and academics. It was a living history document as many of the themes outlined above were played out in people's lives. One day the room where the public sessions were held filled up more than normal for Sinn Féin's presentation, and as quickly emptied as the next presentation was made by two nervous women from a working-class housing estate. This is how the documents of history are often generated. The journalists had left to write up their stories of the extreme, but had not waited to hear about those ordinary syntheses of life. I am very conscious in this book that I will often be privileging the negative and the extreme, and my excuse is that this is because that is how religious identity has played out in Irish history, and the religion of one's upbringing continues to influence one's thinking, even if long abandoned. It is difficult to articulate confusion or to make everyday living, and the acts of neighbourliness it calls for, the stuff of drama, and too often the compelling simplicity of the one-story-fits-all has prevailed. Today the whole of Ireland—even the North—is hard to recognize from that of the 1970s, and there is an understandable wish to move on. I do not subscribe to the trite belief that if you do not understand the past you are compelled to repeat its mistakes. But I have always wanted to know why things are as they are and believe passionately that such knowledge is liberating. It is in this spirit that this book is presented.

2

Irishness at the Altar

> Catholic blood seemed to flow in every vein but ours...we
> knew in a vague sort of way that we were not considered 'the
> real thing', for we were Protestants and must only be playing at
> being Irish.

(Edith Newman Devlin, 2002[1])

This association of Irishness with Catholicism has been common
for a number of centuries. It lies behind many of the problems in
Anglo–Irish relations, informing the thought processes of successive generations of most Irish and British people and continuing to
bedevil the situation in Northern Ireland. Nor has this notion
been confined to Catholics. It was also proclaimed by Protestants,
often dismissively so. Modern Irish nationalism is built on an
inclusive myth. It was most clearly articulated by Theobald
Wolfe Tone in 1796. In this, all religious groupings are merged
in 'the common name of Irishman'. However, this ideal is
unachievable as long as Irishness remains so identified with Catholicism. Even Tone thought Catholics 'the Irish properly so-
called' and came to exclude his own kind (Church of Ireland
Protestants).[2] This chapter is about how Catholics became the
'real' Irish in common perception. As such, Irish nationalism
(particularly its republican variety) is deluding itself by underplay-
ing its exclusive and exclusionary religious roots and ethos. In this

I see Irish nationalism as another form of religion in disguise, one of the many ethno-religious nationalisms which have come to remind the modern world of the continuing force of religious-based identities.

Origins of the Catholic–Irish Identikit

At the 1993 Opsahl Commission's public hearings into the Troubles in Northern Ireland, I listened to a group of highly articulate Catholic grammar school boys explain why they opposed integrated education (religiously mixed schooling). It was not because they thought their *religious identity* would be weakened, but because their *Irish identity* would. Catholic schools all over Ireland have generally provided a 'package deal': Irish language, sport, culture, and history, along with religious instruction. And since Catholic schools in the North generally used textbooks produced in Dublin, there was in essence a common Catholic curriculum throughout the island, even after partition.

In essence the origin-myth of the Catholic–Irish identikit is that Catholics are the true descendants of the Gaels who were persecuted and dispossessed in the seventeenth and eighteenth centuries. A 1960s satirical song—on the mindset of northern nationalists—captured this perfectly:

> Come all you boys that vote for me, come gather all around,
> A Catholic I was born an' reared an' so I'm duty bound
> To proclaim my country's misery and express our Papish hope,
> To embarrass all the Orangemen an' glorify the Pope.
>
> Our allegiance is to Ireland, to her language and her games,
> So we can't accept the border boys, as long as it remains,
> Our reason is the Gaelic blood that's flowin' in our veins,
> An' that is why our policy is never known to change.[3]

The term 'Gaelic' is problematic. In strict scholarly terms it refers to the language spoken in Ireland (and Scotland), rather than to a particular race of people. Indeed prehistoric Ireland would have been quite a racial mix, sharing populations with Britain as well as continental Europe and Asia.[4] The arrival of the Anglo-Normans after the twelfth century introduced a further element in the mix. In addition, Ulster shared common cultural and linguistic ties with Scotland and the Isles—the Scottish influence increasing dramatically from the thirteenth century, with the introduction of large numbers of mercenaries by the Gaelic chieftains. Even after the Reformation the common language between Ulster and Scotland caused some interesting moments, not least when Scottish Protestants recently settled in Antrim, after the Williamite war, 'fell off to the Church of *Rome*', when they found only there could they attend services in Irish. A 1711 correspondent of the Revd John Richardson told of finding Irish-speaking Presbyterians also in Antrim ('Native *Irish* and *Highlanders*') drawn to Presbyterianism by an Irish-speaking minister.[5]

It is extremely difficult to assess popular mentality before mass literacy. In Ireland, the largely oral Irish-language culture survived well into the nineteenth century (and still later in north-west Ulster). Most people were illiterate, as we know the term, so this was an almost exclusively oral culture. Against this orality, the tiny elite (which included the Catholic clergy) possessed considerable power as opinion formers. The ruder verse and song beloved of the common people was deemed unfit for transcription by the elite-minded Gaelic scribes and therefore has disappeared. What *have* survived are the 'classical' writings of the dispossessed Gaelic elite. Irish-language sources need to be handled carefully, since those who transcribed them (the scribes) effectively decided what would survive and disproportionately selected those showing Catholicism the true religion of Ireland and associating Protestantism with England and foreign ways. On the whole, neither the Catholic hierarchy nor the Catholic middle class showed much enthusiasm for reaching out to the people in their own language, unless to combat Protestant efforts to convert Catholics through the medium of Irish.[6]

There is considerable disagreement between Irish-language scholars and most historians about the origins of Irish nationalism. Most of the latter subscribe to the view that Irish nationalism was a product of the late eighteenth and nineteenth centuries. This is undoubtedly valid for Tone's 'common name of Irishman' inclusive ideal, to which even Sinn Féin and the IRA pay lip-service. However, sectarian Catholic identity had its origins in the seventeenth century. It is normally traced to five political poems, composed between 1640 and 1660 by continental-trained Catholic clerics, and their message came to be disseminated very widely because they became popular ballads. Until then bardic poetry would have been incomprehensible to the vast majority of Irish people. But these poems mark a decisive shift towards the vernacular, and their imagery and ideas became stock elements in Irish-language verse and song thereafter—providing the slogans of later nationalism.

Of course, I am here condensing and simplifying a complex topic, and to suggest that the Catholic elite refused to accept the new Protestant power structure would be quite wrong. Ireland had its version of Gallicanism, whereby allegiance was given to the state, whatever its hue, and papal authority therein restricted. Surviving Catholic gentry would spend the next two centuries trying to prove that Catholicism was not incompatible with loyalty to a Protestant monarch. The failure to accommodate this old elite within the new culture would have very long-term consequences, for, as they were pushed down the social scale, it was their bitterness which informed Irish cultural identity.

The poems are highly politicized and propagandistic and reflect the extreme bitterness at the seventeenth-century land confiscations, particularly of the Cromwellian era. A notable feature is the many English loan-words associated with the legal system, which had led to 'the mangling of property'—a complaint about 'the English-speakers who defeated us with the law', which would resurface in succeeding centuries.[7] They probably reflect the elite's bitterness at loss of status more than the opinions of the common people. And, with the decimation of a Catholic landed class, increasingly the leaders of Irish peasant society were Catholic clergy, who stressed Catholicism as the ancestral religion.[8] In so doing they created the texts which fed into later nationalism, for Gaelic manuscripts were highly prized, frequently copied, widely circulated, and often memorized for recitation in public. By the time they came to be printed in the nineteenth century, their language and imagery had become stereotypical.

The most anti-Protestant of the five poems is *An Síogaí Rómhánach* ('The Roman Vision', *c.*1650). This may be due to its Ulster provenance, where larger numbers of Protestants resided as part of the Ulster plantation. In this poem, Protestants are referred to as the 'Saxon brood', the 'Lutherans', 'the heretics' who had 'scoffed at the Mother of the only Son'. Most English monarchs are denounced, with the 'lecherous' Henry VIII and the 'whorish' Elizabeth I to the fore. Their attack on the liturgical mass and the Irish language is singled out for particular scorn. The poem ends with a hope that the Gael will unite 'to drive out the strangers and set Ireland free'.

> Then none shall league with the Saxon,
> Nor with the bare-faced Scot,[9]
> Then shall Erin be freed from settlers,
> Then shall perish the Saxon tongue.

> The Gaels in arms shall triumph
> Over the crafty, thieving, false sect of Calvin.
>
> .   .   .   .   .   .
>
> True faith shall be uncontrolled;
> The people shall be rightly taught
> By friars, bishops, priests and clerics.

The association of Catholicism with Irishness, and the foreigner with the English-speaking 'churl' and 'Luther's' and 'Calvin's brood', marks a significant break with the literary past. This is the prototype anti-English, anti-Protestant poem, and its central message is that Protestantism is foreign. So the Irish word for foreigner, 'Gall', came to double for Protestant, and is usually placed in opposition to that for the Irish, 'Gael'. The modern equivalent appears as 'the Saxon foe' in the Irish national anthem.[10]

The most influential of these new-style political poems was *Tuireamh na hÉireann* ('Ireland's Dirge', *c*.1655), thought to have been composed in County Kerry by another Catholic cleric. As a rule, Gaelic scholars believe that ten surviving manuscripts of a work proves that it had entered popular tradition. This makes *Tuireamh na hÉireann*, which survives in 242 manuscript copies (to say nothing of the bilingual printed versions appearing from the mid-nineteenth century) one of the most popular Irish-language works of all time. While the poem traces the origin-legend of the Irish, its main concern is with recent events: the English-imposed Reformation and the defeat of the Catholic cause. 'Promiscuous Calvin and voracious Luther [were] a pair who abandoned their faith for harlots and wrote violently against the church. The princes of England— sad but true the story—Henry VIII and Elizabeth, and James, king of Britain and Scotland, they followed Luther and deserted the church', while Cromwell completed the 'conquest' (English in the original) of Ireland. Vincent Morley has found the most dramatic increase of manuscript copies in the first quarter of the nineteenth century, just when sectarian polarization was growing apace and a further Catholicizing of national identity was occurring during the campaign for Catholic emancipation. Among the subscribers to the bilingual printed versions of the 1850s were all four Catholic archbishops and twenty-seven other Catholic bishops.[11]

These poets do not mince words. Protestants are foreigners and heretics and Protestantism is the outcome of Henry VIII's whoring. A fairly general perception among Catholics has been the belief that the Reformation was caused by Henry's desire to marry Anne Boleyn. A much reported 1902 statement by a Dublin Jesuit held the Reformation to have happened 'because an apostate monk who lived with a runaway nun, and who boasted that he could tell the brew of any beer in Germany, chose to be rebellious as well as bad; and because in England a king, adulterer and murderer, wanted to put away his wife and marry his mistress'.[12] In the poetry, English names are mocked as so many 'Wullys' and 'Janes', 'bleating' their English tongue, 'a contemptuous brood' having placed 'in bondage the religion of the Gaels'.[13] Similar insult words are used for Elizabeth I, Calvin, Luther, and various other hate figures. The nineteenth-century translations—inspired by romantic nationalism—toned down some insults and created the image of sorrowful Erin mourning her lost sons. The mordant sectarianism of D. P. Moran, whose early twentieth-century *Leader* newspaper preached an Irish Irelandism which was Catholic and Gaelic, is mild by comparison. His barbed humour, insulting dismissal of Protestants as 'sourfaces', 'bigots', and 'foreigners', and of fellow-travelling Catholics as 'shoneens' (little Englishmen) and 'West Britons', echoed what was already there in Irish-language sources, and Conor Cruise O'Brien had a point when he described Moran's newspaper as providing the 'opportunity to look at Catholic nationalism with the lid off'.[14]

Protestant nationalists such as Thomas Davis (1814–45) found the Irish-language poetry too 'bitter and sectarian' for their all-inclusive nationalism, and looked instead to the United Irishmen.[15] It was their rebel songs which came to shape modern nationalism, pitting the defeated virtuous victim against tyrannical England. However, amidst such rebel songs collected by Denis Zimmermann in his classic *Songs of Irish Rebellion* (1967), there is the less polished ballad of 'The Banished Defender'. This was very popular in the early nineteenth century, composed *c.*1800, after the non-denominational United Irishmen had disintegrated and what was left of disaffection was largely lower-class Catholic Defenderism. Defenderism spoke the same anti-Protestant language as the Gaelic poetry–ballad tradition and its activities had already played a major role in alienating Protestants from the United Irishmen, with whom the Defenders had forged an alliance. 'The Banished Defender' addresses himself to the 'Poor Catholics of Erin', claiming to have been forced from his home 'for the sake of my religion'. He had fought at the battle of New Ross during the 1798 rebellion in Wexford, but 'for being a Roman Catholic I was trampled on by Harry's breed | For fighting in defence of my God, my country, and my creed'. 'Luther's breed and Calvin's seed' are scattered, for 'there's but . . . one true faith . . . one church and out of that none can be saved'.[16] Thus the confusion in Irish nationalism, or sectors of it: was it the English or the Protestants that it wanted rid of?—an ambivalence noted by generations of nervous Protestants. There is still a reluctance in the nationalist historiography of the events of the 1790s to accept Catholic sectarianism. The more obvious sectarianism of Orangeism, loyalism, and the Protestant ascendancy has allowed Catholics always to appear as the victim.

In the charged atmosphere preceding partition in 1921, the Belfast minister and future moderator of the Presbyterian Church in Ireland, the Revd William Corkey, attacked the language in Catholic school history books as sowing 'the seeds of sedition'. He pointed to the Christian Brothers' 1905 *Irish History Reader* (a very influential little book), and asked, how could the education commissioners permit historical primers which taught that

> the Protestant religion arose solely out of the sin of Henry VIII? ... No Protestant defends the conduct of Henry VIII.... Is it any wonder that almost all the Roman Catholic youth of Ireland know about the religion of their Protestant fellow-countrymen is expressed in the offensive, but unfortunately, familiar phrase, 'Protestantism was founded by an adulterer.' As long as the faith of Protestants is held up to such odium and scorn in the public schools there can be little hope for peace or harmony among the different religious communities in Ireland.[17]

Even though books used in the state-funded national schools had a distinctly Protestant ethos until late in the nineteenth century, Corkey was not wrong. The *Irish History Reader* did describe Henry VIII as rejecting papal authority because he 'grew tired of his lawful wife and wished for another'.[18] The sectarian Catholic reading of Irish identity was the core theme of such texts, dripfeeding anti-Protestant propaganda into modern nationalism and creating a common Protestant perception that Catholic schools taught biased history.[19] Corkey's anger was the greater since such concentration on Henry VIII denied even the existence of his own Presbyterianism, and showed no recognition that it was just as populist as Catholicism.[20]

The Catholic Old English: A Middle Nation

The defining of Irishness by Catholic clerics was in a long Irish tradition of churchmen moulding origin-legends in the interests of political and religious unity. The idea of an ancient Irish people was being created from at least the seventh century, and by the eleventh century learned men were already adept at marshalling stereotypes of 'the Other' (in this case the Vikings) to emphasize the virtues of the Irish.[21] There are, of course, flaws in the ethnic association of Gaelic Irishness and Catholicism. What about the many Catholics from elsewhere, most notably the Anglo-Normans and their descendants? The arrival of the Anglo-Normans in the twelfth century was denounced by later nationalists as the beginning of English rule in Ireland. Few took note of the 800th anniversary of their arrival, and a stone tablet erected at the beach where they landed was destroyed shortly afterwards.[22] The role of Pope Adrian IV in endorsing the invasion was sidestepped or attributed to Adrian's Englishness or the alleged forgery of the relevant papal bull, *Laudabiliter*.[23]

Yet this was not an invasion, but a common practice of one local lord calling on outside assistance against his rivals, and Gaelic Ireland scarcely registered it at the time. Contemporary sources reflected confusion about the ethnicity of the newcomers—not without reason, for they were quite a mix (Flemings, Bretons, Welsh, or Cambro-Normans (Anglo-Welsh)). The term 'Gall', or foreigner, was used to describe them collectively, not, it seems, in the later pejorative sense, but rather as foreigners residing in Ireland and generally understanding its language and culture, like the long-settled Hiberno-Norse. But what did they call themselves? Each century since their arrival produced legislation showing that they adopted Gaelic ways and language, and as late as 1541 a proclamation in English had to be translated into Irish for their descendants attending the Irish parliament. Even so, Stephen Ellis suggests that they referred to themselves as 'English', which finds some support in the later contest for Englishness between 'Old' (Catholic) and 'New' (Protestant) English. Indeed, the medieval historian Michael Richter has argued that the term 'Anglo-Norman' itself should be replaced by 'English', since the new arrivals were referred to as 'Angli' in contemporary sources.[24]

Given that there was considerable intermarriage and confusion about what to call the people actually inhabiting the area called England, historians came up with the unsatisfactory term 'Anglo-Norman' before 1216 and 'Anglo-Irish' thereafter—even though the latter does not appear in the records until the late fourteenth century. They were, concluded the historian James Lydon, a 'middle nation' who were 'neither wholly English, nor yet Irish, but something in between'.[25] Though very much a retrospective label, this Anglo-Irish hyphenated hybrid was to have a long and troubled history. Still, there were clearly tensions, as encapsulated in the comment of one fourteenth-century poet, Godfraidh Fionn Ó Dálaigh:

> There are two kindreds for whom poetry is composed in Ireland ... the Gaels ... and the English (*Goill*) ... In poetry for the English we promise that the Gael shall be banished from Ireland, while in poetry for the Gaels we promise that the English (*nGall*) shall be hunted across the sea.[26]

Whatever the modus vivendi operating between their descendants and the Gaelic Irish, the Anglo-Normans were proud of their English blood, and though technically members of the same religion, the cultural distinctions between them and the Gaelic Irish were reflected in the often hostile split between *ecclesia inter Hibernos* and *ecclesia inter Anglicos* which continued beyond the Reformation. Indeed, the most influentially negative account of the Irish was that written by the twelfth-century Cambro-Norman Catholic cleric Giraldus Cambrensis, *Topographia Hibernica* (*The History and*

Topography of Ireland). The threat from the Protestant English arrivals after the Reformation gave rise to the new name for the descendants of the Catholic Anglo-Normans, 'Old English', in which their English ancestry was emphasized in contrast to such parvenus. Through the political turmoil of the seventeenth century, the 'Old English' tended to follow a different agenda from those Catholics of Gaelic descent whom they called the 'Old Irish', who, like their ancestors, they deemed inferior.

Throughout much of the seventeenth and eighteenth centuries the 'Old English' and their descendants spearheaded the Catholic campaign for compromise with the Protestant state. They argued their continued loyalty to the monarch, when Protestantism was increasingly being seen as the main qualification for such. It was an association between Catholicism and disloyalty which the 'New English' (recent *Protestant* settlers) were aggressively promoting. This idea that subjects could not be loyal if not sharing the same religion as the ruler was a Reformation-inspired belief which still has some force. In the second half of the seventeenth century the state lost sight of the distinctiveness of the Old English, the terms 'papist' and 'Irishmen' now being used interchangeably.[27] The defeat of the Catholic James II involved the Old English and Old Irish in common ruin and, according to J. C. Beckett, 'all but eradicated the memory of any division between them'.[28] The merger in a common Catholic Irishness was further helped by another priest, the 'Old English' and thoroughly Gaelicized Counter-Reformation cleric Geoffrey Keating. Keating updated the pre-existing origin-legend of the Irish people to include the 'Old English', in what became the most influential of all the texts promoting the idea of the Catholic Irish nation, his *Foras Feasa ar Éirinn* ('Groundwork of Knowledge of Ireland', *c.*1634).[29]

Protestants and Qualified Irishness

If Catholicism came to be so identified with 'Irishness', how could Protestants also claim it? Catholic monopoly of the term 'Irish' has caused great resentment among Protestants, and a sense of being made to feel they did not belong. In Lennox Robinson's 1917 autobiographical novel *A Young Man from the South*, the central character exclaims: 'An Irish Protestant! The words, somehow, don't blend, do they?'[30] Historians struggle to describe Protestants' sense of Irishness, and the words 'ambiguous', 'inconsistent', 'hyphenated' are frequently used.[31] That it has been such an issue can be seen in the constant reminders of nationally minded Protestants that they too are Irish.

At the lower levels of Irish society in the past—particularly before the nineteenth century, when the different churches raised barriers—there was much fluidity, people often changing religion many times in their lives. But at the elite level Irishness came to be associated with popery and poverty, and as an identity tag the term was rejected by political Protestants. Among Protestants this rejection of Irishness tended to increase or diminish according to whether they felt threatened. Thus, in the late eighteenth century, as 'patriotism' blossomed among the Protestant political elite, an 'Irish' self or group identification was common. Then its use declined from the 1790s, as political Catholicism became more assertive. Much the same trend is discernible in the recent history of Northern Ireland; although 20 per cent of Protestants were happy to call themselves Irish in the 1960s, this had declined to 2 per cent by the 1990s.[32] And even if Protestants did accept an Irish identity in its geographical sense, they usually added something else to distinguish them from the *Catholic* Irish: from the 'Irish-born' but of 'English blood' (the 'Protestant [political] nation') of

Jonathan Swift and William Molyneux, to the 'imperial Irish' of the 1930s and 1940s. However, the term 'Anglo-Irish', with the same imputations of foreignness as the 'Gall' of the poetry, causes great resentment, particularly for those Protestants who can trace their Irish ancestry back many centuries.[33] The Ulster Unionist Prime Minister Terence O'Neill had more genuine Gaelic ancestry than most Catholics and resented the idea of a Catholic Irish nation, particularly when President Kennedy—whom he greatly admired—ignored Northern Ireland during his historic Irish visit of 1963.

The descendants of the seventeenth-century 'New English', like each successive generation of colonists, would develop a specific identity with Ireland and would eventually find that England herself denied the credentials of the 'Englishry' in Ireland. They responded in the eighteenth century with a form of Protestant patriotism, exclusive of the Catholic Irish, bringing new mutations and the return of the denomination 'Anglo-Irish', this time to describe the 'Protestant nation'. But the term 'Anglo-Irish' only came into general usage in the late nineteenth century and is increasingly being questioned. J. C. Beckett's classic 1976 study *The Anglo-Irish Tradition*, while continuing to use it for convenience, was defensive, pointing to its 'racialist' overtones, 'its essential purpose . . . to pick out one section of the population as less truly "Irish" than the rest'.[34] Written in the same period as Lyons's *Culture and Anarchy* (the worst decade of the Northern Ireland Troubles), Beckett's study is very pessimistic, concluding that this, his own tradition, was moving towards extinction.[35] The term was not widely used by Irish Protestants themselves in the period of their supremacy (1690–1801), and the move from seeing the defeated Catholics as 'the Irish' pure and simple to that of themselves as the 'nation' was hesitant and contradictory,

involving the same tendency as the Anglo-Normans and Old
English to call themselves anything but 'Irish'. Their failure to
adopt the term 'British' came from a reluctance to share an identity
with the Presbyterians, for whom they had a similar contempt.[36]
Regardless of the common bond of Protestantism felt by Irish
Protestants with the ruling power, it was England's tendency to
see everyone in Ireland as an inferior breed, which prompted the
fullest definition of the Janus-like concept of the Protestant nation
in Jonathan Swift's *Drapier's Letters* (1724–5). But their idea of a
nation going back to the twelfth century, which was purely theirs,
ignored the majority Catholic population (as well as everyone else
not part of the Church of Ireland).[37] 'They came to regard themselves as "the Irish Nation",' as J. C. Beckett concluded, but
'remained self-consciously English in tradition and culture.'[38]
And, like the Anglo-Normans before them, they resented England's tendency to class them together with the 'native' Irish.

Swift's Fourth Drapier's Letter, though addressed 'To the
Whole People of Ireland', deals exclusively with his own 'people',
Church of Ireland Protestants, 'the True English People of
Ireland'. Conceiving themselves superior to the Catholic masses,
they are incensed at being considered in the same category and
'stigmatized' by the English as papists 'ripe for Rebellion'. 'They
look upon us as a Sort of Savage Irish' talking of our 'insolence'
and 'our brogues and potatoes', he complained. Swift's arrogance
towards the 'native' Irish is recognized, even by his admirers. And
yet, however exclusive his language, however contemptuous he
was of the Catholic Irish, Swift's works fed into later Irish nationalism, not least in the separatist republican variety. Wolfe Tone, so
crucial to the later definition of that nationalism, readily acknow-
ledged his debt. Swift's writings reflected the dilemma of Irish
Protestants as a kind of middle 'nation' between the Catholic

Irish and the English, neither seeing them as equals. Though Irish-born, they considered themselves English by blood, and their resentment at not being treated as equal by the English produced in Swift some of the most brilliantly satirical literature in the English language. His *Holyhead* (1727), written while stranded on Anglesey as the boat to Ireland was delayed, speaks of his native land as one of slaves:

> Lo here I sit at holy head
> With muddy ale and mouldy bread...
> I never was in hast before
> To reach that slavish hateful shore...
> But now, the danger of a friend [Stella]
> On whom my fears and hopes depend...
> With rage impatient makes me wait
> A passage to the land I hate
> Else rather on this bleaky shore
> Where loudest winds incessant roar...
> I'd go in freedom to my grave,
> Than Rule yon Isle and be a Slave.[39]

The image of the 'Irish slave' became a favourite one with the United Irishmen. Why do we agree to live in slavery? was Tone's question in the 1790s. His answer: our, Protestant, fear of popery condemns us to live in resentful inferiority under English rule. Thus did Tone, the father of modern Irish nationalism, identify religious division as Ireland's core problem.

As the eighteenth century wore on, this 'colonial' or 'Protestant nationalism' developed into the 'patriot' movement of Flood and Grattan. It was still inspired by the resentment of the Protestant 'nation' (particularly its parliament) at England's treatment, and still excluded the Catholic Irish. Some, however, notably Grattan himself, did recognize the contradiction and became lifelong campaigners for Catholic emancipation. So too did those who progressed from these 'patriots' to found the Society of United Irishmen in the 1790s. However, as Ian McBride points out, the fragility of Tone's 'common name of Irishman' ideal 'did not replace traditional Protestant identities, but was awkwardly super-imposed on top of them'.[40] Grattan's 'patriot' parliament had added to Irish Protestants' vocabulary another term to describe their love of country without having to identify with developing and often aggressively Catholic Irish nationalism. 'It is because we are patriots', Archbishop William Conyngham Plunket told the Church of Ireland's General Synod in 1893, 'and because we love our country that we protest [against Home Rule]' which would bring ruin to 'our native land'. This geographic definition of Irishness was one frequently used by Irish Protestants.[41]

In fact Irish Protestants were not greatly concerned about 'national' identity until Britain started to challenge their ascend-ancy in the nineteenth century. Thereafter nostalgia for the eight-eenth century, as the high point of the Protestant 'nation', became central to their sense of 'nationality'. Samuel Ferguson, Isaac Butt, and W. E. H. Lecky all saw a return to leadership by the Anglo-Irish gentry as the way of preserving a sense of Irish nationality, while remaining part of the British empire. Indeed, in words reminiscent of their eighteenth-century heroes, they argued that Ireland was no mere colony, but an ancient nation. The Trinity-educated Irish Tories behind the *Dublin University Magazine* (1831–77) developed an intriguing rebuttal of the association of Irishness and Catholicism. It was members of the Church of Ireland who were the true representatives of Irishness. Presbyterians and Cath-olics pursued sectional interests, while popery was foreign, having been brought to Ireland by Henry II in the twelfth century.[42] Ireland's ills thereafter were attributable to English misrule and priestcraft. It was even suggested that the association of Irishness with Catholicism was one of England's many stratagems to keep Ireland divided.[43] There were suggestions that Ireland could forget her religious differences and unite in holding England to account. Isaac Butt, one of the founders of the *Dublin University Magazine* and its second editor, was very critical of English policies, particularly leading up to and during the Famine, and he supported the repeal of the Act of Union.

It was, however, a Protestant Irishness which largely celebrated historical figures from an Anglo-Irish past and defined its patriotism in much the same way as Swift had done over a century earlier. In the nineteenth century Church of Ireland Protestants continued to think of themselves as the natural leaders of Ireland, as they already were its major property owners. This attitude was just as sectarian as the Catholic 'democracy' which they decried.[44] Their denunciation of popery was accompanied by all the ultra-Protestant imagery discussed in the next chapter. They were defensive about the past, and while they applauded the end of religious penalization, they tortuously explained away the Penal Laws against Catholics and Dissenters as necessary so that the 'Protestant interest' could thrive and secure national independence under Grattan.[45] Even if they saw themselves as its natural leaders, however, their sense of nation was thoroughly Irish. Do not misrepresent our anti-popery for anti-Irishness, argued the Revd Tresham Gregg, and they were critical of their ancestors for holding themselves apart. 'You are an Irish Society', R. W. Nash told the Irish Metropolitan Conservative Society in 1836. 'Our Protestant ancestors . . . affected to think themselves English instead of raising their native country to a moral rank in which they might be proud to own themselves her sons.'[46]

But they could not shake off the imputation of being a foreign colony. The epitome of constitutional nationalism, Isaac Butt was to establish the Home Rule movement in 1870. He nevertheless sensed the trend in developing nationalism, after being denounced as an 'Englishman' by the young son of A. M. Sullivan, a friend, yet a formative force in developing the myths of that Catholic nationalism.[47] Irish Tories like Ferguson might use the term 'Anglo-Irish' to emphasize their Irishness, despite their ancestry, but that was not how it was perceived by Catholic writers. John Banim—one of the O'Connellite generation of Catholics beginning to breach ascendancy barriers—translated it as 'half-countrymen'.[48]

The Protestant Tory nationalists who wrote for the *Dublin University Magazine* were hardly liberal, and their writing was often extremely anti-Catholic and condescending. However, they did feel Irish, and, as Samuel Ferguson argued, if Protestants did not want to see a 'popish' establishment they should espouse cultural Irishness. Ferguson attacked the idea that Catholics had 'a monopoly of national Irish sympathies', his knowledge of the Irish language and scholarly interest in ancient Ireland giving substance to his complaints.[49] When the Gaelic League was founded in 1893, other Protestants also saw cultural Irishness as a way of surmounting religious divisiveness and providing an alternative to the growing power of the Catholic Church in Irish life. After all, in Douglas Hyde, the League *did* have a Protestant president, it *did* loudly proclaim its non-sectarian credentials, and, as a major new study by Tim McMahon shows, this was not mere rhetoric.[50] However, given the centuries of identification of Catholicism and Irishness, both positively and negatively, this was an unrealistic expectation, and so it proved.

The inability of the Irish to laugh at their pieties comes from a long history of having those pieties demeaned, and the story of

Protestant involvement with the Gaelic League contains an object lesson in how easily sensitivities could be aroused. Hyde's friend the Church of Ireland minister James Owen Hannay (and, under the pseudonym George Birmingham, a prolific fiction writer) had read the key works of the Irish revival and came to see the Gaelic League as a way of bringing all classes and creeds together. He himself struggled with the Irish language and later recorded, with some embarrassment, how in his enthusiasm he had their maid repeat his inadequate Irish phrases, only to discover that Irish was her first language and she had never actually spoken English until she went into service. He was not alone, for when another Gaelic League enthusiast visited Mayo, the local Irish-speaking populace thought he was Russian. The one thing the middle-class-led Gaelic League singularly failed to do was to enthuse those who actually spoke Irish as a first language in the often poorer western areas.[51]

Although efforts in Hannay's own Church were crowned by an Irish-language service in St Patrick's Cathedral, he found himself attacked by the *Church of Ireland Gazette*, which thought the League intolerant. But it was from some of the Catholic clergy that the main attack came. They considered his novels an attack on themselves and he was progressively forced out. Unionist papers took up his case and thought Hannay insufficiently alive to the propaganda potential of such victimization. In fact, he retained the support of a number of Catholic clergy, and his criticism of members of his own Church for behaving like chaplains to an English garrison was often more pointed. Hyde warned him against alienating the priests. 'They are, and will be for the next 50 years (unless a strong Home Rule Bill is passed) the dominating factor in Irish life. They are always on the spot. They have the women behind them . . . do nothing to frighten them off.'[52] Hyde knew what he was talking about, for there were constant tensions between the Catholic clergy and the Gaelic League as the League's ambitions of spreading the Irish language impinged on their jealously guarded control of the schools.[53] 'The cause of the [Catholic] Church was the cause of Ireland', Hannay himself had argued in his novel *The Seething Pot* (1905); and if you destroyed the priests' leadership, there would be no other, since the Protestant aristocracy had not given any, regarding the people as 'canaille'.[54]

'This Catholic and Irish Nation'[55]

By the time Hannay wrote the above (1905), the Catholic Church had become a visibly powerful institution, with apparent command over the lives of the bulk of Irish people. For much of the eighteenth century the Catholic Church, of necessity, kept a low profile. Later in the nineteenth century, however, clerical denunciations of Protestantism as an alien faith became more open. Canon Sheehan's popular novels (1895–1913) take Catholic nationhood as a given, though he himself was in favour of conciliation and cooperation with Unionists.[56] His Protestants are 'temporary fixtures', writes Catherine Candy, 'there to be converted, reformed and eventually nationalised'.[57] 'Irish Catholicism and Irish nationality are interchangeable terms', he wrote in 1899. 'The one means the other. So true is this, that English converts to Catholicity are known to their compatriots as Irish, so completely wound up is one idea with the other.'[58] And so indeed it seemed. By the end of the nineteenth century it was difficult to be considered a nationalist if you were not a Catholic, and a number of Protestant nationalists felt impelled to convert for this reason. Though initially a Young Irelander, espousing Tone's ideal of the Irish nation, the Ulster Presbyterian and influential republican John Mitchel described how his daughter converted to Catholicism because of 'her very strong Irish feeling...a kind of sentiment that one cannot be thoroughly Irish without being Catholic'.[59] Sheehan's novels are full of conversions, which were rare in reality, gentry suddenly becoming popular when they became Catholic.[60]

At its most basic, and in times of crisis, Protestant anti-popery saw Catholics as unthinking barbarians led by legions of crafty priests, ever ready to overwhelm the unwary. Millenarian prophecies and intermittent popular panics had re-enforced such views. These were particularly marked in the half-century before the Famine, a period of heightened sectarian tensions. This extreme Protestant stereotype, however, was far from the reality. After the Williamite victory, the Catholic bishops settled into a largely accommodationist approach to the Protestant state. By the end of the eighteenth century, as revolution engulfed Europe, the British Prime Minister, William Pitt, recognized the Catholic Church as a conservative ally in countering French-inspired subversion. But he could not convince the Protestant 'ascendancy' in Ireland of this, or, more importantly, the King, George III.

This anti-popery of successive British monarchs came as quite a shock to Catholics. Monarchy held a special aura for the largely rural Catholic population at this time, whatever the abstract anti-Englishness of the poetry. Certainly, given what was happening to the Catholic Church on mainland Europe—the French Revolution closing its seminaries and massacring its clergy—there was good reason why Pitt thought as he did. Indeed, the new Catholic seminary at Maynooth, set up in 1795 with government support, was largely staffed by clergy who had fled the Revolution. However, in the intense world-turned-upside-down atmosphere and violence of the 1790s–early 1800s—when eighteenth-century Ireland had not been particularly violent—sectarian stereotypes found new reasons to flourish. Foremost among these was the unrepresentative image of the rebel priest in the Wexford rebellion of 1798 and the forced conversion of Protestants to Catholicism before they were killed, often in brutal circumstances. Though this was formally condemned by the Catholic bishops, it was taken into Protestant folklore as another example of what might happen if popery ever regained power. In other words, popery, in Protestant perceptions, was always political and would always persecute. That is important; but it was wrong, and was largely based on old evidence from the seventeenth century. In the end, it partly created what it so feared: a powerful Irish Catholic Church.

In fact, the Irish Catholic Church was very nervous indeed about any political involvement and regularly condemned priests who became so involved. It particularly abhorred militant nationalist movements. The abusive term 'Fenian' for Catholics had little historical justification, for the Catholic Church condemned the Fenianism of the late nineteenth century and every other militant grouping, including the 1916 rebels and the IRA. However, a lot of things happened in the early nineteenth century to make the Church more openly anti-English and anti-Protestant. One was the failure to grant Catholic emancipation (restoration of Catholic rights to sit in parliament) until priests and people were mobilized in a vast and ultimately successful show of Catholic power. In the meantime, Britain had sought 'securities' in the form of a veto by the monarch over the appointment of Catholic bishops (and this when George III's anti-popery was public knowledge). The bishops were alarmed. Wasn't this what the French revolutionaries had done? Their accommodating attitude was further eroded by the proselytizing activities of evangelicalism's 'Second Reformation'.

No one until O'Connell had drawn the link between Irishness and Catholicism quite so publicly or so successfully, and he recruited the priests, despite their initial reservations. The lesson had already been learnt in 1792 that the Catholic Church provided the only really national popular network to reach the bulk of the people, and with its help O'Connell mobilized a vast, peaceful movement to win emancipation in 1829. O'Connell became a great hate figure for many Protestants, and the erection of his statue in Dublin in 1864 led to serious sectarian rioting in Belfast. But O'Connell, like the bulk of the clergy, was content to remain governed from England, provided Catholic denominational concerns were addressed. However, looking back from 1942, Elizabeth Bowen identified 1829 as the beginning of the end of Protestant political power in Ireland.[61] It was going to happen anyway as Britain extended the electorate and reformed local government. But the vast organization mobilized by O'Connell, and its policy of educating Catholics into their rights, meant that emancipation was just a beginning. Irish Catholicism had sensed its potential power and Protestants took note.

By the second half of the nineteenth century a resurgent (and resentful) Catholic Church was everywhere visible—even in Ulster, whose Catholic clergy had been the most accommodating of Protestantism. The appointment in 1850 of Paul Cullen as Archbishop of Armagh coincided with one of those periodic outbreaks of anti-Catholicism in Britain. The re-establishment of a Catholic hierarchy there had led to accusations of 'papal aggression', and an act was passed forbidding such bishops from using British place names in their titles. These events coloured Cullen's refusal to adopt any of the deference expected of his predecessors. He also set in train a vigorous programme of building, education, and spiritual renewal to restore the lost pomp of the Church. Numbers of clergy, nuns, and brothers increased; religious practice rose rapidly from low levels early in the century. And the 'ordinary'

Irish Catholics loved it, proud of the new prominence that their religious leaders had acquired and indeed at signs that they were finally gaining victory after victory from the Protestant state.

I will be stressing throughout this book that the various Churches reflected their faithful's attitudes and were often the led rather than the leaders. One of the new, and seemingly authoritarian, breed of Catholic bishops, Patrick Dorrian, of Down and Connor from 1860 to 1885, said as much when he responded to the Pope's denunciation of Irish land agitation by warning that if the clergy did not support their people in their complaints, they would lose all influence.[62] The Catholic Church may not always have been the prime mover in the narrow (and narrowing) identification of Irishness and Catholicism, and Protestant stereotypes about Catholics being led by the nose by their clergy were quite wrong. Nevertheless, Catholics saw the Church as part of that identity. Sean Connolly puts it well: 'If Irish Catholics freely adapted official doctrines...to their needs, it was nevertheless in the total triumph of their church over its rivals that they found a symbol for their aspirations.'[63]

In the decades preceding partition, sectarian awareness became more visible, not because it had intensified; rather because it had found a popular voice. The brilliantly acerbic journalist D. P. Moran is often blamed for this and credited with inventing a new vocabulary of insult words—which he partly did. In fact he simply brought them out of the closet, or rather made public what was Catholic 'in-talk', and a young generation of Catholics, finally coming up through education, loved it. Even so, in his *Philosophy of Irish Ireland*, and from 1900 in the columns of his newspaper *The Leader*, he conveyed the message that all Protestants were ascendancy palesmen (from the Pale, the area of English rule around Dublin in the sixteenth century). However much the Irish praised

Swift, Grattan, even Tone, he argued, they were not true Irishmen and their protest was an internal one between Britons.[64] 'The Pale got into the grumps' with England, and eighteenth-century patriotism was the product. The real problem for Ireland was not England but the relationship between its two civilizations, Catholic and Protestant.[65] Moran countered accusations that he was excluding Protestants from his 'Irish-Ireland' by arguing from numbers. Most Irish people were Catholic (*c*.75 per cent at that time). 'For an Irish-Ireland, as things stand, the Irish language is necessary, and also the recognition of Ireland as a Catholic country.'[66] If the numbers of Catholics and 'non-Catholics' should be reversed, then Ireland would cease to be a Catholic country. In fact, while the numbers argument remained a frequent one with those claiming an identification of Irishness and Catholicism, it was rather more than that and Moran knew it. Rather, the foreignness of Protestantism had long ago become part of Irish Catholic culture, and Moran's writings were fundamental to the further narrowing definition of nationalism as Catholic and Gaelic.

By the first years of independence after 1921, the gloves were off, and, as I will demonstrate in Chapter 8, the triumphalism of the Catholic Church for at least the next forty years was a resentful reversal of roles. After months of build-up to the celebrations for the centenary of Catholic Emancipation (1929), bold headlines in the Catholic press declared Catholics attending high mass in Dublin as the 'Whole Nation'. And, reversing past Protestant condescension, the Revd A. M. Crofts OP told his Dublin audience: 'Let us show the descendants of the minority, who fashioned so skilfully the unjust laws of oppression . . . that intolerance forms no part in the life of the Catholic people.' 'We have unconsciously sucked into our social life much that is anti-Catholic, alien, and Protestant . . . [but] the Irish Catholic people have survived, and once again have power to shape the destinies of this nation.'[67] And so they did. Eamon de Valera, after he came to power in 1932, denied that the real reason for the partition of Ireland was religious. The Ulster Unionists maintained that it was, and all the rhetoric about a Catholic nation heightened tensions in the North. Both were right. Visitors to the Free State were astonished at the high levels of Catholic practice and the absence of the anticlericalism of Continental Catholicism. This is because Catholicism *was* their national identity, national as well as communal life being structured by it. In speech after speech de Valera spoke of the rightness of the state reflecting majority opinion, which was Catholic.[68] Ulster Unionists responded with a similar majoritarian argument to defend their 'Protestant state'.[69] De Valera's 1937 constitution affirmed the Catholic Church's 'special position' 'as the guardian of the Faith professed by the great majority of its citizens', and, as with state legislation generally, it reflected Catholic social teaching on marriage and the family.

A few lone voices in the Dáil—including, ironically, the biographer of Theobald Wolfe Tone, Frank MacDermot, who, like his subject, called for a pluralist Ireland—argued that the constitution and the role it accorded the Catholic Church would alienate the Ulster Protestants and postpone reunification. And not for the first or the last time was the retort made that it was they alone, the northern Protestants, 'these objectionable religious bigots', who were the sole barrier to unity.[70] MacDermot's point was that while the clause did not give the Catholic Church a privileged position, it was likely to be interpreted as just that and hence should be omitted. In fact de Valera and his party, Fianna Fáil, were not in the pockets of the Catholic Church and worked very hard behind the scenes to prevent overt Church interference. Discussions had been held with all the other Churches, and diplomatic pressure exerted in Rome to block attempts by the Catholic Primate Cardinal MacRory to have the Catholic Church's special position given much more substance in the 1937 constitution.

With Catholicism and Irish national identity so intertwined, however, the Catholic social values reflected in the state were 'reflexive' rather than products of direct interference from the hierarchy. This is why, as Dermot Keogh presciently noted, the various referendum crises over divorce (1980s–1990s) would be part of a 'shift from confessional to consensus democracy', involving a change in 'the very definition of "Irishness"'.[71] He was writing before the clerical sex and paedophilia scandals of recent years, which, given the emphasis placed by the Church on chastity in the past, have considerably weakened the link between Catholicism and national identity. However, in today's fashionable scapegoating of the Catholic Church, Irish people ignore what amounted to national collusion in the scandalous concealment which allowed and perpetuated such abuse, particularly by the state, for it did not fit in with 'Ireland's national imagining'.[72]

Catholic Ireland—Protestant England

Finally I want to pose the question: if the Catholics had become the Irish, how Irish was Irish Catholicism? This question was the topic of a very unsatisfactory Irish television debate in 1964, which paid too much attention to the Italianate statues and holy pictures of the nineteenth-century devotional revolution and the supposed infusion of Victorian values to explain the notorious killjoyism of Irish Catholicism. What it entirely missed was this: Irish Catholicism was Irish because it was not English, and how it differentiated itself from Catholicism in the neighbouring island and one-time ruler says much about its inferiority–superiority complex.

To its faithful, Irish Catholicism was considered the pure proto-type. It was deemed peculiarly spiritual, as distinct from the threatening materialism of England. Countless sermons and publications sirened the fear that Irish Catholic emigrants to England would be lost. To some Irish minds Englishness and Catholicism seemed contradictions. Statements by the Irish Catholic clergy during the 1929 centenary of Catholic Emancipation took particular pride in reporting celebrations in the towns of 'Protestant England', but largely missed its significance for *English* Catholics, in what was treated overwhelmingly as an Irish issue. And so indeed it had been a century earlier, for English Catholics sought 'quietist assimilation' and disapproved of the threatening under-class of Irish Catholics beginning to flood the English towns.[73] England was considered a *pays de mission*, and the welfare of Irish Catholics going there (as much as those 'tripper–emigrants' bringing bad habits back) became a matter for national concern.

Nor were English Catholics living in Ireland considered the real thing. Although in the 1850s there were more fundamental issues underlying John Henry Newman's disputes with the Irish bishops in his role as Rector of the new Catholic University in Dublin, they were scandalized by his introduction of English ways and English staff.[74] The dangers of 'slippage' or 'leakage' from the faith by Irish emigrants to England was a frequent topic of Catholic debate, particularly from the 1940s, when England had become the main destination for Irish emigrants. A series in *The Furrow* in the 1950s thought those Catholics going to England often regarded it as 'a vacation from religious practice'. If they came back to Ireland, they might bring with them the easier ways of English Catholicism. With 'Such things as Evening Service—the very name itself is suspect', more suggestive of a concert than a religious service, and, with the attempts to introduce the liturgy in

English, English Catholicism was surely too close to High Anglicanism. All of which would 'give our average Irish Catholic the feeling that he had found in England a none-too-orthodox brand of Catholicism'.[75]

But if he stayed, the prognosis was worse. He might assimilate and become 'as English as the English themselves: beer at the local, Sunday morning *News of the World'*,[76] the dominant culture having become 'cannibalistic of the other'. So assimilation was not to be encouraged. Irish parish priests should inform their opposite number in England of parishioners moving there; specific Irish leisure activities should be arranged; and the Irish-founded Legion of Mary set up stalls in London's Euston and Paddington stations to meet the boat-trains from Ireland. There can be no doubt that many Irish going to work in England have welcomed the Church's help. However, it also contributed to the ghetto mentality of the Irish community there and further reinforced the association of Irishness with Catholicism.

Given that association, there were always going to be problems in relations with the English Catholic Church, itself a pillar of the establishment. Criticisms—such as that of England's Catholic leader, Cardinal Basil Hume, of the Irish hierarchy's failure to condemn as suicide the deaths of the republican hunger strikers in 1981[77]—were likely to be seen as just another example of English condescension. There were periodic worries by the Irish bishops that the papacy was over-susceptible to English influence. There had been tensions over the veto controversy in the early 1800s, English Catholics supporting the right of the monarch to veto Catholic ecclesiastical appointments, the Irish opposing.[78] The First World War saw further tensions when the head of the English Church, Cardinal Bourne, was given full responsibility by the Pope over Catholic chaplains to British regiments, even those which were predominantly Irish, when the Irish hierarchy were particularly sensitive about any suggestion of ecclesiastical superiority from Westminster.[79] As the Irish Revolution developed in these years, some Irish bishops, again suspicious of British influence on the papacy, vigorously thwarted a rumoured Vatican condemnation of Sinn Féin.[80]

At the Opsahl Commission's oral hearing in Derry in February 1993, a memorable exchange took place between Lady Lucy Faulkner, the Dublin-educated widow of the Unionist Prime Minister of Northern Ireland Brian Faulkner, and the leading nationalist Paddy Doherty. She said that she considered herself Irish but that it was difficult for her Protestant friends to espouse Irish identity when their people were being murdered in the name of Ireland. 'Congratulations on your clear statement that you're Irish', declared Paddy Doherty. Lady Faulkner was irritated: 'I don't need congratulations. It's just a fact.'[81] They were, in fact, talking about two different types of Irishness, under a genuinely held belief in the ideal all-inclusive type. It was a striking example of what I have been trying to show in this chapter. Protestants could not be Irish because Irishness was Catholic. Today's nationalists in Northern Ireland do not define their identity in anything other than cultural and political terms and are annoyed by outsiders who more accurately portray it as religious. This is because that religion was so successfully subsumed into Irish political culture over three hundred years ago.

3

Protestantism and the Spectre of Popery

Many Church of Ireland people . . . are now anxious to repudiate all kinship with the more vulgar, esoteric or intolerant of the Reformation's children . . . [but] we cannot do this without falsifying our pedigrees and invalidating the title-deeds of Irish Protestantism.

(Hubert Butler, 1953[1])

Recalling his schooldays in the 1930s and 1940s, the Belfast writer Robert Harbinson spoke of learning little history, except 'the Protestant story', 'over and over again'. 'On leaving school . . . I had no notion of the world's past other than a few prehistoric tales and dreary details concerning our Protestant faith and the unrelieved darkness of Rome.'[2] In looking at Protestant identity in Ireland I am aware of the dangers of homogenizing the different Protestant denominations, of assuming a shared religious culture between southern and northern Protestantism, and of minimizing changes over time. But one thing has united Irish Protestants in the past and to some extent still does, particularly in Ulster. That is anti-popery, the fear and dislike of the Roman Catholic Church as an institution and of popery as a system. Defined against the perceived horrors of popery, Irish Protestant identity has been

much more streamlined and much more political than that of
Catholics. So powerful has been this self-definition against the
Other that often it has negated Protestantism's proclaimed love
of liberty. As it exists in Northern Ireland today—indeed as it has
always existed—anti-popery ranges from quaint notions to murderousness, with fear and suspicion ingredients in all.

'It probably surprises Catholics', writes the Revd Dr John
Dunlop, former Moderator of the Presbyterian Church in Ireland,
'to know that Protestants are preoccupied about them in a way
that is not reciprocated.'[3] He goes on to describe the real problem
which Protestants have had with the Catholic Church: it is seen as
'threateningly powerful' and allied to a nationalist culture which
might prefer to see Protestants return from whence they came.
John Dunlop was a courageous Church leader during the
Troubles. He is more honest than most about Protestant perceptions of Catholics and the sense of being enveloped by a culture
which to outsiders seems more mellifluous and welcoming than
their own.

The Protestant Theological Case against Rome

Despite its perceived privileged status, the Church of Ireland was
much more fundamentally Protestant than its English counterpart,
its theological grounding dictated by its minority presence in a sea
of popery. Anglicans in England tend not to refer to themselves as
'Protestant'. Members of the Church of Ireland have no such
problem and dislike the term 'Anglican' as carrying a whiff of
incense. Although resentment at the Roman Church's monopoly
of the term 'Catholic' can occasionally be heard today, it was not
widely shared by Irish Protestants in the past. 'In Ireland,' wrote
George Bernard Shaw in the preface to *John Bull's Other Island*

(1904), 'Protestantism is really Protestant . . . all that the member of the Irish Protestant Church knows is that he is not a Roman Catholic . . . The clause in the Apostles' Creed professing belief in a Catholic Church is a standing puzzle to [Irish] Protestant children.'[4]

Despite the role of anti-Catholicism in British national identity, Britain's rulers were usually keenly aware of governing two religious communities in Ireland and were less opposed to toleration than Irish Protestants. However, the theological formation of Irish Protestantism came later than that of England, and, as Alan Ford has pointed out, skipped its Lutheran phase and developed instead against the Calvinist and Puritan climate of the early seventeenth century. In this Catholicism was considered a tyrannical system rather than just a religion, governed by the dictates of a pope who was the incarnation of evil as described in the Bible. This was enshrined in the 1615 Articles of the Church of Ireland, which were much more Calvinistic than the Thirty-Nine Articles of the Church of England. They even included the doctrine of double predestination, by which, in addition to the elect who were predestined to salvation, the reprobate were predestined to hell. At this time, Irish Protestants tended to view the Catholic Irish as already damned; condoning their religion risked divine punishment. As Archbishop Ussher preached in July 1620: 'as Jehu said to Joram, "What peace, so long as the whoredoms of thy mother Jezebel, and her witchcrafts are so many?" so I must say unto them: What peace can there be, as long as you suffer yourselves to be led by "the mother of all harlots".'[5] Although the Irish Articles were effectively replaced by the Thirty-Nine Articles in 1634, their spirit infused the teaching in Irish Protestantism's new seminary, Trinity College Dublin, and reflected the theological beliefs of Irish-born clerics as distinct from those brought in from England.

The Irish Articles were not actually repealed, but left to wither, and, while the Church of Ireland has moved a very long way indeed from its Calvinist beginnings, a pedantic critic could claim that it is still formally committed to the belief that the Pope is Antichrist.[6] The Calvinism of the 1615 Articles had allowed Presbyterian clergy to operate within the Irish Church and inspired Presbyterianism's central doctrinal statement, the 1643 Westminster Confession of Faith (with its article on the Antichrist). In this world-view popery was also political. It united a faith which was deemed superstitious and persecutory to threatening Catholic foreign powers, France, Spain, the papacy itself, and latterly—for northern Protestants—southern Ireland.

David Hempton has written extensively on this topic. He describes how, from Elizabethan times onwards, Protestant national identity was based on an 'apocalyptic ideology' which opposed 'a sinister and monolithic Catholic Church' to Protestant liberty. Protestantism was 'morally pure . . . providentially on the right side in the great cosmic battle between good and evil, between Christ and Antichrist. Roman Catholicism, on the other hand, was foreign, violent, morally corrupt, doctrinally erroneous, magical, devious, and was led by a standing army of Popes, Jesuits and priests'.[7] Anti-popery goes very deep. It was after all the foundation stone of the Protestant Reformation and was reinvigorated by the Enlightenment. The Protestant Archbishop of Armagh instructed his clergy in October 1745:

> You are to raise in your people a religious abhorrence of the Popish government and polity, for I can never be brought to call Popery in the gross a religion . . . Their absurd doctrines . . . their political government . . . [make] it impossible for them to give any security of their being good governors, or good subjects in a Protestant kingdom.[8]

Central to the theology of the main Irish Protestant Churches is the belief that the Bible is the only source of God's authority and as such people should be given direct access to it, without the mediation of priests or saints or devotional aids. This is the meaning behind the Open Bible symbol, a particular feature of Orange and Loyalist imagery in Northern Ireland. The National (and interdenominational) education system in the nineteenth century was attacked by Protestant clergy because biblical education was to take place outside school hours. Thomas MacKnight, the English newspaper editor, travelling from Dublin to Belfast in 1866, encountered a clergyman at Portadown who complained that religious instruction should not be so confined. 'God is everywhere. His religion ought to be taught everywhere. An open Bible, sir, or nothing.'[9] In the belief that Catholics were denied direct communion with God, because Catholic teaching required clerical interpretation of Scripture rather than lay reading, the Bible was something of a Protestant weapon. 'We used to stand to attention and draw our bibles from under our arms like swords', a Presbyterian friend told me of his Sunday-school days in 1970s Northern Ireland. 'For one particular crime we would never forgive the Mickeys,' recalled Harbinson, 'their hatred of the Bible. All Catholics were under orders, we were told, to burn any scripture they found'—a good example of the survival in folk memory of images from the 1641 depositions, discussed below.[10]

Whether one could or could not read the Bible would not have been of much concern to most people in pre-printing, largely oral-culture Europe, where literacy was confined to the elite and the clergy in the universities and the monasteries. But the invention of printing in the fifteenth century changed all that and suddenly created accessible vernacular editions of the Bible and a new interest in reading. Such increased availability of scriptural texts went on to produce the Reformation, rather than the reverse. This fundamental requirement to know the Bible ensured very high levels of Protestant literacy, particularly among Presbyterians.[11] The Open Bible symbol was 'the lowest common denominator' uniting all kinds of Protestants. A trend of speaking in biblical quotations was born. In Ireland this became particularly associated with Ulster Presbyterianism, its appearance in seventeenth-century Gaelic poetry, usually recording insults by Sassenachs against the Gael, indicating that arguments about the supposed unscriptural nature of the Roman Church were already being aired on the ground.

The belief is that the Roman Church forbids its adherents to read the Bible directly; rather it must be interpreted by the clergy. This was indeed the case in Italy, but not elsewhere, although in Ireland Bible-reading by the laity was discouraged until the late nineteenth century. The issue was that of accepting the Bible as the *only* source of the word of God. No, said the Council of Trent (1545–63); there were also 'unwritten traditions', handed down and preserved by the Catholic Church. Even so, it amounted to the same thing in Protestant thinking. This was Rome claiming to be the arbiter of God's word, and those 'traditions' were tested against the Bible and denounced as unscriptural. 'The motive which led to this publication', explained the influential Church of Ireland rector and editor of the evangelical *Christian Examiner* the Revd Charles Stanford, in his 1852 *Handbook to the Romish Controversy*,

> was an unfeigned desire to direct the mind of the Roman-catholic to the unscriptural and anti-scriptural character, tendency, and teaching of the Roman Church; and so to assist in the energetic endeavour to emancipate our Roman-catholic fellow-countrymen from the thraldom of a superstitious system, as fatal as it is tyrannical, and as deadly as it is dark, and to invest them with all the glorious privileges of that 'liberty wherewith Christ makes us free'.[12]

The *Handbook* was one of an outpouring of similar evangelical tracts in this period of deepening confessional division and evangelical 'ascendancy' in the Church of Ireland.[13] But its arguments were those of the Reformation, and in Ireland have been the basis of anti-popery since the sixteenth century. The Revd Stanford's pamphlet systematically tested Catholic doctrines, as set down by the Council of Trent, against the Bible and portrayed them as having no foundation in Scripture. Since the only true sacrifice was that of Christ on the Cross, the sacrifice of the Roman mass was illegitimate and the doctrine of transubstantiation and the idea that 'God could be eaten' absurd. As for penance and confession, only God has such powers and to claim such for any 'Romish priest' was 'the very spirit of Antichrist'.[14]

Besides the centrality of the Bible, the role of the Pope, Mary, the intercession of the saints, and the differing views on salvation (justification) greatly exercised Stanford, and have continued to inform political Protestantism. 'Roman Catholics need Mary and the saints; we communicate directly with God' was how Free Presbyterians summed up the difference in October 2006, on the eve of the first ever meeting between their Moderator, the Revd Ian Paisley, and the Catholic hierarchy.[15] The same point was made by the *Dublin University Magazine* in 1835: 'their religion chiefly consists in giving an unreasoning and unhesitating obedience to its [their Church's] dictates. They, in fact, only know the gospel through the church; whereas, Protestants only know the church through the gospel.'[16] All of these areas had been contentious in the Western Church even before the Reformation. But again it was Calvin who produced the starkest denunciation of sacred images and prayers to Mary, denouncing one as idolatrous, the other as blasphemous.[17] A religion of the word did not need images and so they were removed, destroyed, or painted over.

It was the logical conclusion of the belief in the direct communion of man and God. 'God alone is the object of prayer', Jesus alone the mediator. Indeed, almost a quarter of Stanford's entire work is devoted to this.[18]

Protestantism's complaints about Rome's micro-management of salvation produced the exclusivist doctrine of justification by faith. Luther, himself an Augustinian monk, had taken up Augustine's more pessimistic teachings about human salvation. Opting for a specific translation of key words in St Paul's Romans, Luther developed his idea that faith was entirely in God's gift through divine grace. He had, in essence, singled out an elect. The Roman Church taught that faith alone was not enough for salvation without good works, and that man had free will to choose his path to salvation. Luther also believed that very few would be chosen. Calvin took this a stage further to support the idea of predestination, a chosen few, God's elect.[19] It could also be applied to an entire people, a chosen or covenanted nation, much like the Israel of the Old Testament.

Not all reformers accepted such a narrow reading of Scripture, nor has it always translated into its logical conclusion that if some are saved, some also are damned and need no rescuing. However, it was reinvigorated by a specifically Irish brand of evangelicalism, particularly in the nineteenth century, and was core to both Orangeism and Paisleyism.[20] The concept of 'God's people' has been invoked through the centuries to explain the peculiar virtues of British Protestantism, the victorious emergence of the Irish Protestants from their life and death struggle with popery in the seventeenth century, the defeat of Home Rule in the nineteenth, and any number of narrow escapes in the twentieth. In the aftermath of the Anglo–Irish Agreement of 1985, loathed by many Ulster Protestants, Ian Paisley delivered a sermon addressed to

Prime Minister Margaret Thatcher. Musing on the prophecy of Micah about good and evil, he predicted ultimate victory for 'God's people'. 'You might laugh at their religion, laugh at their Bible . . . [but] God has a people in this province', who have been specially preserved by divine providence. Each time it seemed near disaster, God intervened to save 'this plant of Protestantism sown here in the north-eastern part of this island'.[21] After the brutal sectarian usages of predestination in the seventeenth century, the Church of Ireland moved away from the more pessimistic readings and in Archbishop William King produced a reinterpretation which rejected predestination and restored free will. But it remained an important element in Presbyterianism.[22]

The Church of Ireland dean Jonathan Swift considered Presbyterians just as guilty as the Catholics of distorting Scripture—and he had direct experience, having been minister in Kilroot, County Antrim, the most Presbyterian part of Ireland.[23] In his *Tale of a Tub* (1704) the father figure God leaves his three sons identical coats (Christianity) and in his will (the New Testament) he gave exact instructions on wearing and managing them. But after time the sons changed the primitive garment (religion) and attached every gold braid and frill that fashion dictated. Peter (popery) then locked away the will and declared some of these fashionable adornments canonical (traditions). Naming himself Lord Peter, he had not one but three crowns clapped on his head (papal). He purchased a huge continent (purgatory) and sold it over and over again throughout the world (indulgences). He then invented a new remedy for worms, which involved the patient in nonsensical contortions (penance), a whispering office (the confessional), 'hypochorical puppets and raree-shows' (processions), and pickle (holy water) 'to preserve houses, gardens, towns, men, women, children and cattle'. He sent away his own wife and those of his brothers (celibacy), and cut wine and meat from their diets by convincing them all were contained in the bread (transubstantiation). At length there was a rupture (the Reformation). The two brothers challenged Peter's attempt to keep them from their father's will (popery denying Scriptures). They were then expelled with the help of dragoons (popish power persecuting the reformers) and set about restoring their coats to their primitive state. Having pulled off the silver and gold lace (dogmas), unstitched the embroidered figures (worship of saints), Martin (Church of Ireland) concluded that any further ripping would damage the cloth and the 'substance' should be preserved (Church of Ireland offering the middle way). But Jack, indignant at Peter's tyranny, fell upon the coat with such zeal that little was left of the original. Jack the Dissenter is a slave of the people, unable to talk about the most basic things, even to the point of being unable to relieve himself, without recourse to the Bible. The Dissenters were 'Fanaticks' and 'Pretenders to Purity', whose scriptural language and affectations disguised their cant and hypocrisy.[24]

The Reformation's central argument of no intermediary between God and man also gave new life to an old claim that the Pope was the Antichrist of Scripture. Protestants were adamant that only through Christ could one be saved. All other intermediaries— saints, ministers, popes—were irrelevant. 'Daniel . . . and Paul . . . foretold that Antichrist would sit in the Temple of God', wrote Calvin. 'With us, it is the Roman Pontiff we make the leader and standard bearer of that abominable kingdom.'[25] The concept of the Antichrist was further developed against a backdrop of unusual millennial and apocalyptic excitement in the sixteenth century, the living models two exceptionally nasty, even 'lunatic', popes, Paul IV and Pius V, and, as Diarmaid MacCulloch argues, few thereafter lived up to the stereotype.[26] It became identified with biblical references to the sins and excesses of Babylon, popery as 'The Mother of Harlots and abominations of the earth' (Revelation 23: 5). The phrase 'Mother of harlots' has been the term used for the Pope in populist Protestant literature throughout the past four centuries. At its rawest the idea gave rise to a form of pornographic sectarianism. Robert Harbinson's recollections contain some hilarious, though disturbing, childhood adaptations of the 'Mother of harlots' description of popery. These Protestant children thought popes, like the mummy in the Belfast museum, were embalmed and displayed as moneyboxes and when filled were canonized as saints. At school they were grilled on the actions and misdeeds of the popes, and 'before we tumbled out of our cradles', they knew about the antics of the Borgias and the orgies of the papal court, where nuns acted as naked shepherdesses and 'Roman strumpets' burnt their bare bottoms on Vatican candles. 'No wonder our preachers referred in horror to Rome as the Scarlet Woman!'[27]

The concept of the Antichrist also figures in Presbyterianism's key doctrinal statement, the Westminster Confession of Faith: 'There is no other head of the Church but the Lord Jesus Christ. Nor can the Pope of Rome, in any sense, be head thereof; but is that Antichrist, that man of sin, and son of perdition, that exalts himself, in the Church, against Christ and all that is called God.' While many attempts have been made to soften the Confession's message, most recently in 1988, the concept of Antichrist remained relevant to many Presbyterians. The concept could, occasionally, be extended to authoritarian systems of government and has been shown to have determined some Presbyterians' involvement in rebellion during another millennial moment in 1798.[28] But in general it continued to be used in its original Reformation definition: the Church of Rome, exercising its influence in 'subtle' ways as the vehicle for the Devil in the battle between good and evil. It became for some a whole philosophy of life and another justification for keeping Catholics out of political power.

In 1782 the Monaghan Seceding Presbyterian minister the Revd John Rogers sought to dissuade the Volunteers from taking up the Catholic cause by reminding them that the Pope was the Antichrist, 'the Man of sin and son of perdition; who opposeth and exalteth himself above all that is called God'.[29] Three decades later John Gamble found the concept even more colourfully expressed by a County Tyrone squire. 'D—n the Pope,' said he, 'an outlandish vagrant, seated cross-legged on his seven hills, like a scarlet whore, as he is.'[30] It was extended to incorporate Daniel O'Connell as popery's new instrument in the Orange song 'Dan O'Connell in Purgatory', which is characteristic of many Orange songs in lampooning Catholic religious beliefs and practices. It sings of 'Rome, the mystic whore, | Who keeps the keys of Heaven's door', and satirizes Rome's teachings on celibacy, purgatory, devotional aids, 'scapulars, crosses, cords and beads', the indulgence prayers recited on All Saints' (All Souls') Day, supposed to release souls from purgatory. And though Dan damned 'Saxons' and heretics as having no right to Ireland for not eating 'the wafer god' or believing in purgatory, in the conflict between William of Orange and James II the Protestant victories of Derry, Aughrim, and the Boyne had freed them from any need to believe in such.[31]

The Persecution of 'God's People'

In this reading the Antichrist will always persecute 'God's people'. In September 2006 I spoke with a group of Ulster loyalists and members of the Orange Order who had just made something of a pilgrimage to the Protestant Martyrs' Memorial in Oxford. This was clearly a very important part of their visit to the city, particularly since the group included members of the Orange Lodge, whose banner also commemorates the same martyrs: Cranmer, Ridley, and Latimer, burnt at the stake in Oxford in the reign of the aptly named 'Bloody' Mary. Some three hundred perished in her short reign and their sufferings were chronicled by John Foxe in his *Book of Martyrs*, 'one of the cornerstones of English Protestant identity'.[32] In this Foxe reproduced Cranmer's last words: 'And as for the pope, I refuse him as Christ's enemy, and Antichrist, with all his false doctrine.'[33] This bloody baptism of British Protestantism was portrayed by Foxe as giving it a special place in the struggle against the Antichrist. Foxe's *Book of Martyrs* has never been out of print and was regularly updated with new examples of popish persecution, its woodcut drawings proving even more influential than the words themselves.[34]

A notable difference between Irish Catholic and Irish Protestant martyrology was the incorporation of English figures into the latter, but not the former. One reason was the absence of any Irish Protestant martyrs in Ireland's Reformation.[35] Another was the identification of England as a Protestant nation, Irish Protestants and Catholics alike assuming that Englishness and Catholicism were mutually exclusive. 'That many Catholics were living in London with our Protestant king', recalled Harbinson, 'seemed impossible. The idea of a papist cathedral near the gates of Buckingham Palace would have been laughed at with scorn.' Then came the rude awakening when the schoolchildren were issued with picture books of the coronation of George VI showing the Duke of Norfolk as Earl Marshal greeting the two princesses. How could this be, when the Duke had been cited as an example of subtle popish scheming in 'a blood-curdling Orange sermon'? The only explanation must be that provided by the 'Protestant story'.

Norfolk was scheming to win back the crown and return them all to the days of 'Bloody Mary'.[36]

Foxe prepared an English audience for the incorporation of the Irish into the story of popish persecution. From the later sixteenth century religious conflict in Europe entered a peculiarly savage phase and all sides were guilty of persecution. As Protestant and Catholic powers fought in the Thirty Years War, Europe was gripped by a peculiarly apocalyptic mood. Protestantism was in retreat in some of its earliest European homelands, its refugees eventually reaching Ireland to add fuel to the image of popish persecution. It was against this background that the main event in the story of the popish persecution of Irish Protestants occurred: the massacre of 1641.

'A false and idolatrous religion, does naturally produce bloodshed, barbarity, wasting and destruction', argued the Revd Ralph Lambert in his 1708 sermon commemorating 'the barbarous massacre committed by the Irish Papists' in 1641.[37] Against a background of extraordinary political instability, the lead-in to civil war in England and Puritan propaganda linking Charles I to a popish plot, the Ulster Catholics, many resentful at the loss of land and status in the Ulster plantation, captured the whole of Ulster in what was initially a bloodless coup. But then inferior leaders, some of them Catholic Scots escaping from the covenanting war in Scotland, turned on the Protestant prisoners and as many as 12,000 Ulster Protestants may have died (when the overall Protestant population was around 30,000). Much of the killing falls into the chilling 'intimate enmity' Rwandan type, rumours of retaliatory massacre prompting neighbours to pre-emptive murders, and Catholics too were murdered in the great fear of that year. But the barbarities were real, the main victims Protestant, and even today Ulster Protestants are reminded of it since one of the worst incidents (eighty to a hundred men, women, and children drowned in the river Bann at Portadown) is featured on the banner of Portadown's Orange Lodge. Given the violence of Europe's dynastic and religious wars of the seventeenth century, 1641 was not extreme.[38] What singles 1641 out as so crucial for identity formation is rather the way in which it was promoted by an extreme group to communicate Protestant solidarity at a time when Protestants were anything but united.

The memory of 1641 was successfully used to block any spirit of moderation and, in A. T. Q. Stewart's memorable phrase, acted as an 'occult force', informing Protestant consciousness, particularly in times of crisis.[39] But, as so many generations of Irish Protestants have discovered, England could be fickle and needed constant reminding of their sufferings against the common enemy. After 1641 it was the more extreme Protestant political leaders—in an effort to convince England of the danger in which they found themselves—who now determined the parameters of the myth; and their writings would be regularly reprinted as an antidote to any spirit of moderation towards papists.

In a series of lurid tracts and pamphlets, the figures of Protestants massacred rose to 600,000 (when there were fewer than 100,000 Protestants in the whole island), and salacious details were dwelt upon, informed by the timeless English stereotypes of the Irish. The Irish equivalent of Foxe's *Book of Martyrs* was Sir John Temple's *Irish Rebellion*. It portrayed Catholics as irredeemable and bent on the dispossession and massacre of Protestants if given the chance, and it went through many reprints in later centuries. Deeply influenced by his father, Sir William Temple, who had first-hand experience of Continental Catholic persecution of Protestants, Temple was part of a militantly Calvinist group which saw the whole Irish Catholic populace as infected by the murderousness of a few. And through the elder Temple—Provost of Trinity College Dublin, set up in 1592 as a seminary and Calvinist from the outset—they influenced successive generations of graduates and office-holders. Although denounced by London and its representatives in Ireland after the restoration of the monarchy in 1660, as increasing animosity between the Irish and the English, Temple had entered oral traditions through Church of Ireland liturgy and provided 'a precocious growth' to a common Protestant identity based on anti-Catholicism.[40]

Many of Temple's claims had been based on information gathered by Henry Jones, the Dean of Kilmore and agent for the impoverished Irish Protestant clergy who had fled to London. Jones had cleverly transferred guilt to Catholics generally, and was particularly influential in determining Cromwellian policy towards Ireland. He published his tracts in London and sent extracts on the atrocities to the English parliament in 1652, just as its policy of transplantation to Connaught was being finalized.[41] In Jones's work we have the archetypal image of popery:

> And out of that ancient hatred the Church of Rome beareth to the Reformed Religion . . . There hath been beyond all parallel of former ages, a most bloody and Antichristian combination and plot hatched, by well-nigh the whole Romish sect, by way of combination from parts foreign, with those at home, against this our Church and state; thereby intending the utter extirpation of the reformed Religion, and the possessors of it: In the room thereof, setting up that idol of the Masse, with all the abominations of the whore of Babylon.[42]

Although other Protestant propagandists had some difficulty reconciling all of this with the fact that most Irish Protestants joined with Catholics in a royalist alliance of 1649, the propaganda of Jones and Temple had already infused Irish Protestant thinking with the belief that Catholicism was the Antichrist, plotting the annihilation of Protestantism: 'they cannot propagate their Catholic doctrine but by our destruction: if the Protestants stand, Rome must fall'.[43] Jones's influence over developing Protestant identity continued through his appointment as Ireland's official historian and Provost of Trinity College. It was Jones too who developed the trumped-up case which would lead to the 1681 execution of Archbishop Oliver Plunkett, the Catholic bishop most well disposed towards England.

The importance of Foxe's *Martyrs* and Temple's *Irish Rebellion* to the development of English national identity is well recognized. The American scholar Raymond Tumbleson likens the presentation to that of early Hollywood's cowboy and Indian wild westerns. Just as the Indians deserve to be crushed because of their monstrous cruelties, so in Ireland the listing of atrocities (one account, deriving from Temple, containing a list twelve pages long) serves the same purpose. 'Dehumanizing the Irish into fiends against whom all measures are fair' was part of 'a programmatic desensitization to any pain in Ireland but that of the settlers.'[44]

The afterlife of the 1641 myth was ensured when in 1662 the government sanctioned special sermons, bonfires, and illuminations, and an Act of the Irish parliament decreed that all residents should go to their places of worship on 23 October each year to celebrate the discovery of the 'barbarous and cruel' plot 'to extirpate the Protestants'. The leading Protestant officials and gentry and members of corporations, as well as some Presbyterians, attended church on that day. It was finally dropped from the Church of Ireland's calendar in 1859—not, it seems, because of changing opinion in Ireland, but as a decree from the London parliament.[45]

The Revd Ralph Lambert's 1708 commemorative sermon opened with Isaiah 59: 7, 'Their feet run to evil, and they make haste to shed innocent blood', then singled out the most brutal images from Temple and Jones, detailing the ripping of fetuses from wombs and the tossing of infants on pikes. It argued that popery was 'a false and idolatrous religion, [which] does naturally produce bloodshed, barbarity, wasting, and destruction', and that 'the doctrine and practice of the Church of *Rome* do allow and justify such barbarous massacres'.[46] Temple continued to be reissued at times of tension right up to 1912. It still finds its way into local Ulster histories and ultra-Protestant web sites, including and predictably that of the Revd Ian Paisley.[47] It took on a new life particularly in the eighteenth century as part of Irish Protestants' resistance to growing tolerance in London, and was a factor in the upsurge of sectarian tensions in Munster in 1766 and the judicial murder of Father Nicholas Sheehy—one of the few incidents living up to the many myths surrounding the penal laws. It resurfaced after the 1798 rebellion, and during the nineteenth-century campaigns for Catholic emancipation and Home Rule it was cited as proof of the murderous potential of Catholic Ireland.[48]

The Revd Lambert's 1708 sermon also cited Isaiah in support of another stereotype of papists, their deviousness: 'there is no judgment in their goings; they have made them crooked paths'. Again, this may have been pioneered in Giraldus Cambrensis' views of the Irish: 'they are also treacherous and deceitful, using honeyed words, they do not blush to break bond and violate oaths, their wile more dangerous than their war, their friendship than their fire', 'expediency' rather than 'honour' their guide.[49] The Orange song 'Sons whose sires with William bled' keeps the warning alive (along with another enduring claim, that Catholics whinge and exaggerate their wrongs).

> Yield not now to Popish guile,
> Trust them least when most they smile...
> Loud and high their clamors rise,

> Of pretended miseries;
> The Papist creed is only lies,
> Which none but fools believe.[50]

'Northern Protestants believe that Catholics do not say what they mean', the former President of the Methodist Church in Ireland the Revd Sydney Callaghan told the Opsahl Commission in 1993; 'that they are profligate with words, past masters of the art of the fine point, the innuendo and the half-truth'.[51] Protestants in the Irish Republic pointed to a willingness by Catholics to bend the law or to turn a blind eye when the law was evaded, the à la carte nature of contemporary Irish Catholicism being but one feature of such a mindset. Even friendly gestures by Catholics can be interpreted as Garden-of-Eden-like serpent's wiles.

Once the idea had been established of a slavish mindset programmed by popery, every atrocity (however rare) became proof of popery's exterminatory intentions. 'When once an individual has been *tattooed*, as it were, into the system of popery, it becomes almost second nature.'[52] These were the words of a defrocked priest in 1836. Since the early seventeenth century converts from popery—particularly if former clergy of Italian or Spanish stock—fed the appetite of popular Protestantism. A favourite theme in the nineteenth century was that of nuns as sex slaves to lascivious priests, and there were repeated calls for searches of convents. Another work feeding the heightened anti-popery of the early to mid-nineteenth century was the 1836 *Awful Disclosures of Maria Monk*. This told sensational stories of a convent in Canada, where nuns were kept as such sex slaves to priests and the offspring subsequently murdered. Though quickly declared a hoax by a Protestant team who visited the convent, its sectarian pornography has helped keep it perennially popular. It is regularly advertised in fundamentalist Protestant publications and web sites, including loyalist news-sheets of the recent Troubles, and, perhaps more surprisingly, given best-seller ratings by mainstream web-based booksellers.[53] Unfortunately it was just such sensationalism which made Catholics so resistant to *any* criticism of their Church, particularly in those areas of sexual deviance that had traditionally titillated extreme Protestantism.

The Spanish Inquisition and the persecution of the Huguenots in France were other favoured topics. A parliamentary report into the sectarian riots in Belfast in 1857 highlighted the inflammatory preaching of the Revd Thomas Drew to the Sandy Row Orangemen. He told them of popery's 'detestable machinations of the Confessional, of Jesuitism, and of the Inquisition', and drew horrifying images of papal prisons drenched in blood and hair and villainous bishops dabbling in the gore of Protestant women who were being tortured on the rack.[54] The persecution of the French Huguenots, in particular, was a frequently cited example of what political popery could do and of how their industriousness was a peculiarly Protestant virtue. Not only had Huguenot refugees fought under William of Orange, but thousands had arrived in Ireland in the late seventeenth century, helping to kick-start Ulster's linen industry, among others. Thomas MacKnight's 'tall and solemn clergyman' quizzed him on Foxe's *Book of Martyrs*. 'Every Protestant ought to read it', he was told, and as the train passed through Lurgan and Lisburn he told of how the towns had been destroyed in 1641. 'That was a frightful time. It showed what Popery can do.' Then he talked of how the Huguenots had been driven out of France and of what they had done for the area's linen trade. 'You can yet see the tombstones of these Huguenots who were obliged to leave their native country. This will show you what the Roman Catholics are.'[55] Foxe, Temple, and various other popular works on popish perfidy would have been well known to every class of Protestant. John Gamble encountered such texts in his travels through Ulster. Sean O'Casey recalled them too from his poor evangelical Protestant background in Dublin as 'a regiment of theological controversial books...holding forth that the Bible, and the Bible alone, is the religion of Protestants...Foxe's *Book of Martyrs*, full of fire and blood and brimstone'.[56]

This fearful fascination with the apparent mystery and secrecy of Catholicism can be found at every level of Protestantism, even in the writings of Wolfe Tone. Ken Heskin noted it in his 1980 *Northern Ireland: A Psychological Analysis* as 'a vague, almost primitive uneasiness, with a body which to the Protestants is so full of mysticism, symbolism, clandestine activity (the Vatican, convents, monasteries, retreats, separate schools) and unworldly practices such as clerical chastity, monastic silence and so forth'.[57] Hubert Butler—with a candour as unusual as John Dunlop's—thought southern Protestants wrong to criticize Ian Paisley. They were deluding themselves in denying the anti-Catholicism at the heart of their faith and culture, an anti-Catholicism which was as much 'psychological as creedal'.

> Our affections and our aversions are emotional, not intellectual. We mostly have an atavistic horror of confessionals[;] the idea of whispering sexy sins to some dim figure behind a lattice...I think of stuffy bedrooms, where the poor lie dying under a picture of the Sacred Heart...the things from which we recoil link Ireland with Europe and with past generations. But our repugnance too has a history behind it.[58]

Butler's views did not go down well with fellow Protestants, but he was right in highlighting the way Protestants generally tried to whitewash their abhorrence of Catholicism. This after all is what the Reformation—particularly in its later stages—was about.

Loyalty and Liberty in a Protestant State

After the Restoration of the monarchy in England in 1660, there
was an uneasy peace in Ireland. But the uncertain religious identity of the state perpetuated Protestant nervousness. The return of
a Catholic monarch in James II did not immediately produce
Protestant revolt. Certainly it did not look as if he would be the
anticipated champion of the Catholic dispossessed when in 1689
he taunted the Catholic gentry, who wished to proclaim as rebels
2,000 named Protestants: 'What gentlemen, are you for another
"41"?'[59] With his Lord Deputy in Ireland systematically reversing
the policies of the past century, however, some Protestants did fear
bloody reprisals and Catholic repossession of their lost lands. Some
were imprisoned, some fled to England, their impoverished exile
stoking that determination to maintain the Protestant constitution
in Church and state which so influenced political thinking in the
eighteenth century. During the many popish scares, they had
always felt able to call on help from Protestant England. James II's
reign, however, showed how vulnerable they would be if the royal
court became completely Catholic. When James was overthrown
in 1688, although the rejection of a legitimate monarch caused
major soul-searching among Irish Protestants, one thing was
clear for the future: their loyalty was conditional on the monarch
being a Protestant. John Gamble's Orange country squire
boasted his loyalty to George III; but he had his doubts about
his heir, the future George IV, whom he thought far too pro-
Catholic, a fact he attributed to his relationship with Mrs Fitz-
herbert, the Catholic to whom he was secretly, if unconstitutionally,
married.[60]

The very concept of liberty as Protestant and embedded in
constitution and state was part of popular Protestant psyche

throughout Britain and Ireland. It was the natural outcome of the religious beliefs of Protestants' direct access to God and priestly powers over the Catholic mind, outlined above. This belief in the association between Protestantism and liberty can be found at every social level. Indeed, the more fundamentalist the spokesperson, the more the claim to religious and civil liberty.[61] It has also informed the belief that Protestant states were tolerant and Catholic ones were not. The Archbishop of Armagh's 1745 statement about 'popery in the gross' was part of an outpouring of propaganda by Protestant clergy arguing as much during the Jacobite scare of that year. While they show generally good intercommunal relationships in the 'penal era', they also display that inherent contradiction in Protestants' proclaimed love of liberty which is not always clear to Protestants themselves. The argument was that Catholics enjoy greater freedom under a Protestant government than they would under a Catholic one. 'Popery and tyranny are inseparable', argued the Lord Bishop of Clonfert, Kilmacduagh, and Kilfenora in October 1745. Were the popish Stuart pretender to succeed, 'A court of inquisition would probably be introduced', and then not only would Protestantism be suppressed, but any struggle by papists to achieve liberty would also expose *them* to 'the evils of that wicked tribunal'. Had not the papists enjoyed liberty of their persons and properties, under the existing constitution, equal rights to the courts, and 'free exercise of their religion'? Yes there had been penal laws introduced against them, but these were chiefly against their priests 'for the defence of the government against their dangerous principles and practices'; and, in an argument which would reappear frequently over succeeding centuries, the Bishop of Cloyne pointed out that to reject all these perceived benefits would be a mark of ingratitude. That year's commemorations of 1641 took on a particular significance, those at Youghal burning in effigy the Jacobite leader, Prince Charles Edward, 'a bundle of Rosarys (or Padareens) hung to his nose to shew his obedience to the Pope'.[62] And in 1770, long after there was any real threat of a Stuart restoration, riotous Protestant Steelboys who had destroyed property and intimidated juries still claimed to be 'loyal' subjects, defending 'his majesty's person and government against unjust attempts of all popish pretenders to the crown of these realms'.[63]

This proclaimed love of liberty, however, did not extend to civic rights for those deemed 'disloyal'. Catholics were penalized, not because of their religion, but their politics, their lands confiscated not because of 'heresy', but 'treason'. Just as in post-1921 Northern Ireland they were discriminated against, not because of religion, but their 'disloyalism'—a distinction Catholics did not themselves perceive. Huguenots could buy property in France, argued eighteenth-century Catholic campaigners against the penal laws. That was because they could be 'loyal' to the civil magistrate, countered Protestants, whereas Catholics were at best 'half subjects', their temporal allegiance divided with that to the Pope,

> Popery being little else than a mere system of politics, the foundation of which is allegiance to a foreign prince. Papists have no right to claim protection from the magistrate of any country, which does not belong to, or depend on that prince; and consequently they are not intitled to a toleration in Protestant states . . . Thus the question of tolerating Papists in Protestant states, is not a question of religion, but of politics.

And as such, the Penal Laws were 'the sacred Magna Charta of the Protestant constitution of this country'.[64]

Since the first allegiance of Catholics was to 'a foreign prince' (the Pope), it was argued that they could not be loyal to a Protestant monarch, particularly since Pope Pius V in 1570 had issued a

papal bull declaring Elizabeth I a heretic and absolving her subjects from their allegiance. The bull was considered a disaster at
the time—even by the Catholic Church itself, and the next Pope,
Gregory XIII, declared Catholics not bound by it. It was the last
time a pope declared such a sentence against a reigning monarch
and the unhappy precedent is thought to have influenced the
papacy in its reluctance to condemn Nazism in the 1930s.[65] But
there it was, formally enshrined in the third canon of the Fourth
Lateran Council of 1215, and cited as proof of 'the deposing power
of the Pope' and the papal claim to power to absolve subjects from
their allegiance to heretical rulers.

It was unlikely that the papacy could have enforced this in the
centuries after the Reformation, and France, officially Catholic
though it was, specifically rejected such powers in the Gallican
articles of 1682. Moreover, since most of the secular Catholic
clergy in Ireland (and in most of northern Europe) were educated
in France before the French Revolution, there was a distinct
Gallican flavour in their attitudes to papal power. But the fact of
the matter was that although Protestant extremists made more use
than justified of this old papal claim to depose and dispense with a
subject's loyalty, it does not appear to have been rescinded by the
Catholic Church. Frequent popish plots (real and imaginary),
French and Spanish wars, and Catholic support for the deposed
Stuarts (particularly by the Pope) and in twentieth-century
Northern Ireland for Irish reunification, have made the perceived
disloyalty of Catholics a refrain in anti-popery throughout the
centuries. The syllabus of the partially state-funded seminary at
Maynooth (founded 1795) was scoured by critics to see if it taught
such treason.[66] Mind you, if such critics could have read the
originals of the poems discussed in Chapter 2, they would have
had better fuel for such claims than in treacherous priestcraft. But

that is the point: the religion itself was deemed political, and therefore political allegiance could not be separated from it. Declarations against transubstantiation were required for public office, membership of parliament, and certain professions. This effectively barred Catholics from positions of power, some remaining closed far into the nineteenth century.

This was the problem which bedevilled the troubled history of finding a way in which Catholics could swear their allegiance to a Protestant monarch without rejecting papal jurisdiction. It had led surviving Irish Catholic gentry and a number of clergy in 1666 to sign up to a compromise devised by the Sorbonne, whereby the king's rights in temporal matters were accepted and the deposing power of the Pope rejected. But if the political wrangle over this formula underscored the huge uncertainty throughout Europe (even Catholic Europe) of where ultimate jurisdiction really lay, it also made more difficult the genuine efforts of the restored Stuart monarchy after 1660 to implement a policy of religious toleration. After the defeat of the Stuarts in 1690 the problem was more acute since there was widespread, if largely passive, Catholic support for the deposed Stuarts, and from 1715 to 1766 James II's son had power from exile in Rome to nominate Catholic bishops to Ireland. The issue of swearing allegiance divided Catholic clergy and laity, most accepting simple acts of allegiance, though hesitating over abjuration clauses requiring denial that the Stuarts had any right to the throne or the Pope to any temporal (civil) jurisdiction.

The wording of the oath required by the 1793 Catholic Relief Act shows little diminution of the fear of political popery, or any lessening of the idea of popish disloyalty, which had so exercised Irish Protestant MPs in the debates preceding it. The oath required specific denials of papal infallibility, of the right to murder or injure any person under the pretence of being a heretic, and of the claim to absolve 'any sin whatsoever'. In addition, qualifying Catholics had to swear to defend the current property settlement (much of it based on past dispossession), and to disavow any intention of subverting the Church establishment and substituting a Catholic one or in any way 'to disturb and weaken the Protestant religion and Protestant government in this kingdom'. The oath required by the Catholic Emancipation Act of 1829 was substantially the same, but with much clearer requirements to uphold the Protestant succession, Protestant religion, and Protestant government of the country. The belief that Catholics would not keep oaths with heretics is also reflected in the required declaration that the oath is taken 'without any Evasion, Equivocation or mental Reservation whatsoever' (taken word for word from the 1704 Act to prevent the further growth of popery).[67] In fact Catholics accepted such oaths from the 1770s onwards, up to and including that required by the Act of 1829.

The siren-like quality of the 1641 literature and the tradition which it inspired did not simply arise from Protestants' sense of vulnerability, isolation, and encirclement. They reflected a belief that they were God's chosen people, being punished for weakening in their mission to destroy popery. This is why 1690 came to be the main symbol of Protestant victory. Few cared to notice papal support for William. God's people had again been tested and had emerged victorious with William of Orange's defeat of James II and political popery. The state and constitution, the monarch, courts, army, and parliament, were all now Protestant, and papists firmly excluded (or about to be). The 'great ruler of all things decided in favour of our ancestors, he gave them victory and Ireland became a Protestant nation enjoying a British constitution'.[68] The year 1690 appears everywhere on gable walls in Protestant Ulster, the symbol of the continuing threat from political popery and a reminder of the need constantly to fight old battles.[69] 'The siege of Derry and the Battle of the Boyne', writes John Dunlop, 'continue as powerful symbols from the past, as well as interpretive models of the present, because they speak about the periodic threat of being overwhelmed by a majority.'[70] The lengthy disputes between Presbyterians and Anglicans, indeed the very fact that some of each had been reluctant resisters to James II, have long been forgotten. This was Protestantism's providential escape from popery and in Ulster is still the subject of annual commemorative marches and celebrations. It was proof that papists never changed their spots, 'where even the Principle of Religion instils a kind of Fierceness and Barbarity into their Nature', according to George Walker, who inspired Derry's resistance to the Jacobite siege and whose version of the siege came to be the accepted one.[71] Walker's account went through numerous editions and was particularly popular in England and Scotland, where the association of national identity with Protestantism was taking shape.

Evangelicalism and Anti-Popery

One of the main reasons for the continuation into modern times of these beliefs was the evangelicalization of all denominations of Irish Protestantism, particularly in the years of the so-called 'Second Reformation', early to mid-nineteenth century. John Wesley read accounts of 1641 to prepare himself for his missions to Ireland, twenty-one in all:

> I procured a genuine account of the great Irish massacre in 1641. Surely never was there such a transaction before, from the beginning of the world! More than two hundred thousand men, women, and children, butchered within a few months, in cool blood, and with such circumstances of cruelty as make one's blood run cold!

It is well if God has not a controversy with the nation, on this very account, to this day.[72]

In his earlier tours, large numbers of 'poor Papists' attended his sermons and there was as much opposition from members of the Church of Ireland and the authorities as from the Catholic priests. However, references to specific atrocities in 1641 are a refrain in his journals. He spent much time with the exiles from Continental Catholic persecution, Moravians, Huguenots, and Palatines, and the hostile Catholic crowds and those priests he did encounter confirmed him in his views of Irish Catholics. 'I was surprised to find how little the Irish Papists have changed in an hundred years', he wrote after a visit to a village near Castlebar in the west of Ireland. 'Most of them retain the same bitterness . . . and thirst for blood, as ever; and would as freely now cut the throats of all the Protestants, as they did in the last century.'[73] In the troubled decade after the 1798 rebellion, a later itinerant evangelist came up with the pragmatic strategy of positioning himself in front of apothecary shop windows to deter the all too frequent stoning.[74] Evangelicalism was particularly successful in those areas where the Ulster plantation had placed lower-class Catholics and Anglicans in competition for scarce land (south Ulster, most notably Armagh). It was no accident that Orangeism, which developed from the same homelands, was to have a strong presence in future evangelicalism.

No Church in the eighteenth century had a real conversionary policy, and separation preserved an uneasy peace. The intrepid American evangelical Asenath Nicholson travelled through Ireland in 1844–5, distributing tracts and bibles to the Irish poor. She had no desire to proselytize and rejected as too sectarian the pamphlets proffered by a Baptist missionary.[75] She found a genuine desire to hear 'the word of God' and ready audiences for her readings, and she often contrasted the welcome she received from Catholics, however poor, with the uncharitableness and snobbery that she encountered among Protestants, particularly the well-off. However, the proselytizing activities of many evangelicals awakened an alarmed Catholic Church, and a successful fight back in the South concentrated evangelical activities in Ulster. To avoid the hostility of the priests, the methods used by evangelical preachers seemed devious: individuals or small groups (and often they were children) were instructed behind haystacks or turf-clumps, giving rise to long-held Catholic folk-belief, still circulating in the early days of Paisleyism, that fundamentalist Protestant clergy kidnapped Catholic children to convert them.[76] Even more negatively influential was the exaggerated belief that evangelicals traded food for the conversion of Catholics during the Famine. The practice came to be known as 'souperism', from the soup kitchens distributing food to the starving people. So evangelical Bible groups were particularly unpopular in Catholic Ireland. As late as the 1980s the Dublin Christian Mission was accused of 'souperism' and picketed by the Legion of Mary.[77]

Most divisive was the various Bible societies' use of the Irish language. Because of the activities of the evangelicals in Kerry, Nicholson found the Catholic clergy unusually sensitive about the Irish-language material she was carrying.[78] It was the fear of proselytization which soon eroded previous cooperation in education, giving rise both to the strict educational segregation of modern times and to the Catholic Church's paranoia about mixed education. More particularly, it actually produced in Ireland what Protestants claimed had always existed: a powerful Catholic Church—the so-called 'Devotional Revolution', which, under Cardinal Paul Cullen from 1849 to 1878, created the authoritarian Irish Church of modern times. In alarm at the use of the Bible by the evangelical crusade of the nineteenth century, the Catholic Church rushed into print a Catholic edition, and some 308,600 Douay bibles were printed in Ireland between 1817 and 1852. Of course, the Second Reformation also coincided with Daniel O'Connell's mobilization of the priests in his campaign for Catholic emancipation, followed by a number of reforms dismantling the Protestant state, all of which fed Protestant fears that political popery was on the march. The progressive hardening of Protestant attitudes in the nineteenth century can be traced through these developments. In England the reforms proved unpopular, and existing anti-Catholicism was fortified by Irish evangelical preachers. The evangelical tradition of open-air preaching was particularly important in playing upon traditional fears of popery among the lower-class non-churchgoers and in convincing them that the undoubted prosperity of Ulster was conditional on its Protestantism and increasingly on its attachment to Britain and its empire.

The decline of the domestic textile industry in the first half of the nineteenth century affected Protestants and Catholics alike, and initially there was some cross-community support for O'Connell's repeal (of the Union) movement, on the understanding that the return of the Irish parliament might improve the situation.[79] But the idea that the downturn in economic prospects for Protestants might also be due to the rise in Catholic power, following Catholic emancipation, had the same effect that the sight of Catholics prospering always had: drawing Protestants together in their anti-popery. The Dublin Protestant Operative Association, established in 1841, was led by the evangelical minister the Revd Tresham Gregg, who blamed the economic depression on Catholic emancipation and the state's promotion of popery. This perceived threat of 'Romanization' was further heightened by the

Home Rule campaign in the 1880s, and, just as in the contempor-
aneous development of cultural nationalism, public figures were
increasingly measured against very extreme definitions of politico-
religious identities. Constructive Unionism was seen as selling out
to nationalism, and in 1900 the Liberal Unionist MP Horace
Plunkett lost his parliamentary seat in County Dublin for this
very reason.[80]

Orangeism and Loyalism

Such religious-based anti-popery found its most basic expression in
Orangeism and Ulster loyalism. The Orange Order proclaims
itself a religious organization, and so it is, in the sense of the
religious culture outlined above. 'Our purpose is the advancement
of pure biblical Christianity,' the Orange Grand and Deputy
Grand Chaplains, the Revd Ian Meredith and the Revd Brian
Kennaway, wrote in 1993, 'as opposed to the superstitions and
idolatries of Romanism.'[81] New members receive a copy of the
Bible and swear to 'strenuously oppose the fatal errors and doctrines of the Church of Rome, and scrupulously avoid countenan-
cing . . . any act or ceremony of Popish worship [and] . . . resist the
ascendancy of that church, its encroachments, and the extension
of its power'.[82] It is important to realize that Orangeism functions
at many levels and not only in the swaggering anti-popery sometimes displayed during 12 July celebrations. In Northern Ireland it
has played an important socializing role, its halls and social occasions replicating for Protestants what Catholic church halls and
activities provided for Catholics. It also acted as a kind of 'para-
church', offering missions, Sunday school, and other religious
activities to all denominations of Protestantism.[83] Nor should we
equate Orangeism generally with Protestantism. However, it has

been the most vocal representative of political Protestantism, its parades and pageants providing visual history of Protestantism's perceived mission to combat popery and preserve the Protestant state. Even non-members can identify with it, a 1993 survey of Presbyterian churchgoers in Belfast, for example, finding a 65 per cent approval rate.[84] John Dunlop describes it as follows:

> Perhaps the clearest linkage between Protestantism and the political system has been the Orange Order. Many Protestants in Northern Ireland have been influenced by the perspectives of the Order. This linkage makes it difficult for them to separate loyalty to Jesus Christ from loyalty to the Crown and Constitution. The Orange Order, with its associations between Protestantism and Unionism, provides the model of interpretation for a community's experiences.[85]

In Orange tradition a loyal Catholic is an oxymoron. Patrick Shea (one of the very few Catholics to reach the higher ranks of the Northern Ireland civil service) recalled arriving in Rathfriland, in south Down, as a 12-year-old in 1920, after moving from Athlone with his Kerry-born Royal Irish Constabulary father. In the North he found that his family's loyalty to king and empire was met with disbelief. Catholics were not supposed to be 'loyal'. He had watched that year's Orange parade pass by their door, men in navy suits marching four abreast, in Orange sashes and cuffs, decorated with Masonic symbols. 'There were bands by the dozen and large painted banners . . . depicting in a hundred different themes the benefits which Protestantism and Britain had brought to mankind', banners depicting bibles, Union flags, Queen Victoria, various Protestant martyrs, and Luther fixing his propositions to an iron-studded door. 'This was secular Protestantism soberly commemorating the Battle of the Boyne [and] . . . the Protestant succession to the English throne', and the 'whole Protestant community was involved'. Local Catholics were 'withdrawn and sullen', the reason for which he learnt afterwards when he read the words of the Orange songs and the newspaper reports of the speeches at the field, which seemed to suggest that 'the forces of Popery were about to seize the Crown of England'.[86]

Orangeism's self-perception has been of a Bible-based evangelical organization, and since its formation in 1795 it has provided a common base of fundamentalist Protestantism to an otherwise very divided tradition. Its origins lie in Protestant perceptions of Catholic disloyalty and of themselves as allies in protecting the Protestant state. That state was unthreatened in the eighteenth century, wrapped around by the penal laws and the voluble Protestantism of British national identity. It was signs of state weakening on these issues, and an assumption that the law ought to be on their side, which lay behind the formation of the Order in 1795. In addition, there always were enough Catholics resorting to violence against the state to underpin the belief that all were rebels requiring suppression. Under the Penal Laws, Catholics were banned from carrying arms, and lower-class Protestants regularly took it upon themselves to enforce this, even after the law had been repealed in 1793. In the crisis circumstances of the 1790s and until the end of the French wars in 1815 the state reluctantly accepted the Orangemen's loyal assistance. Thus were things restored to their natural order, at least in Orange perceptions, and it is noteworthy that Orange histories jump from 1690 to the late eighteenth century, when popery again was deemed to be on the rise and the safety of the Protestant state threatened. In the Orange story, popery's murderous intent is proved by selective coverage of two notorious incidents from this period, the barbaric attack by Catholic Defenders on Alexander Berkley and his family at Forkhill, south Armagh, in 1791,[87] and the Scullabogue massacre in Wexford during the 1798 rebellion, and they have been added to 1641 and 1688–9 in the condensed history of persecution on the Orange web site, among others.

In the early decades of the nineteenth century Orangeism was particularly strong, assisted by a significant number of Orange magistrates and landowners. Orange parades were banned in 1832, but this sense of being part of Protestant law enforcement often meant that proclamations against Orange marches were simply torn down and marches forced through police cordons. It was at this time that the event occurred which led to a further ban on parades and provocative flags and emblems, and the withdrawal of propertied Protestants from Orangeism until the 1880s. This was the clash in 1845 between Orangemen and Catholics after Orange marchers used a contentious route through the largely Catholic Dolly's Brae area near Castlewellan in County Down. They had been taunted on the route out by Catholic Ribbonmen, and, fired by the local landlord's call to defend the Protestant constitution, which he argued was under threat, their response to further provocation was a bloody attack in which thirty Catholics were killed and their homes burnt. The story is retold as a great Protestant victory in the consistently popular Orange song 'Dolly's Brae':

Just then two priests came up to us and to Mr Biers [the magistrate]
    did say:
'Come turn your men the other road and never cross Dolly's Brae.'
Begone, begone, you papish dogs, you've hardly time to pray
Before we throw your carcasses right over Dolly's Brae.

And when they came to that great hill they were ranked on every side
And offering up their papish prayers for to help to stem the tide

But we loosed our guns upon them and we quickly won the day
And we knocked five hundred papishes right over Dolly's Brae.

So now my song at last I'll end, my pen I will throw down,
And wish success to every man supports the British Crown
And generations yet unborn will mind this place of yore
For we named the spot King William's Ridge and Dolly's Brae
   no more.

This is the version currently selling in popular Orange songbooks in Belfast. The original version also had references to priests distributing the 'wafer God', and to papists worshipping images and being led blindly by the Pope.[88]

The background to the heightened sectarian tensions of the early nineteenth century was the success of Daniel O'Connell's Catholic emancipation campaign and his subsequent prominence in Westminster politics. The reality of popish wiles was argued to resist any moderation. Once you let them in, they would take over. The grant of Catholic emancipation in 1829 was the point of no return, the frequency of sectarian clashes in subsequent years a direct consequence. Orange songs—often dating from this period—incorporate all the same references to popes, priests, saintly worship, and other phobias of anti-popery outlined earlier. The revival of the Catholic Church in the second half of the nineteenth century, the growing power of the papacy, and increasing visibility of priests in political campaigns, all revived fears of political Catholicism and cemented that Orange–Unionist alliance which became so significant in the Northern Ireland state after 1920. For the next fifty years every prime minister of Northern Ireland was an Orangeman, as were all but a tiny handful of Unionist MPs. Orangeism was also pervasive in the forces of law and order, notably in the Ulster Special Constabulary, the B Specials. Once again the Protestant state seemed to be secure, at least in Northern Ireland.

Orangeism reprised the idea of Calvin's godly city on earth, its role to protect it against the darkness of Rome and be eternally vigilant for slippages by the rulers of the Protestant state. A Catholic in government was inconceivable in a Protestant state, and Orangeism has been opposed to every attempt at introducing any. Orangeism reacted in much the same way to the dismantling of the Protestant Irish state in the nineteenth century as that of the Protestant Ulster state in the twentieth, presenting an image of a persecuted people. The current web site of the Grand Orange Lodge of Ireland presents history as a series of highpoints in the persecution of the Ulster people. This is the mirror image of that origin-myth as victim which has long informed Irish nationalism.

Popular Orange historiography combines celebration of Protestant victories with commemoration of past persecution by Rome and Rome's agents, taking in all the Protestant martyrs of the sixteenth and seventeenth centuries, 1641, Forkhill, Scullabogue, 'witnesses of the past and warnings of the present', as Orangeism's leading historian, R. M. Sibbett, wrote in 1914, when once again they were fighting off Home Rule and reminding Britain of its debt to their ancestors. Sibbett argued vigilance, as popery was 'an enemy which never sleeps'.[89] Even though Ulster accounted for 90 per cent of lodges in the middle decades of the nineteenth century, those elsewhere exhibited the same fundamental belief.[90]

Orange songs and humour have also been vehicles for conveying the simple message instilled into the young Robert Harbinson. Nationalist songs tell of unjust authority and 'innocent' victims, and are often sentimental to the point of being maudlin. Orange songs are brisk and martial, celebrating victories over papists in many encounters. As noted earlier, they also lampoon Catholic religious practices, neutering the threat through ridicule. 'The Ould Orange Flute', a popular broadside ballad from the nineteenth century, has an Orange weaver and flute-player from Tyrone marrying a papist and becoming papist himself, fleeing to Connaught to avoid intimidation. But when asked by the priest to play at mass, the Orange flute, despite being dipped in holy water, refused to play anything but 'The Protestant Boys' (also known as 'Lillibulero', commemorating 1688), and 'Croppies Lie Down', commemorating 1798 (the two tunes played at most of the sectarian affrays in the late eighteenth and nineteenth centuries).

> At a council of priests that was held the next day,
> They prepared to administer auto-da-fay
> Sure they couldn't knock heresy out of its head,
> So they bought Bob another to play in its stead,
> So the ould flute was doomed and its fate was pathetic,
> 'Twas branded and burned at the stake as a heretic;
> While the flames roared around it they heard a strange noise
> 'Twas the ould flute still playing 'The Protestant Boys'.[91]

The evangelical Protestantism at the heart of Orangeism and Paisleyism did not always lead to hatred of Catholics as individuals, but when it did it coloured and justified it. 'As a young teenager I thought God was Protestant', a Portadown loyalist ex-prisoner told BBC Radio 4 on 14 August 2007, as he explained why he was able to murder Catholics. Why, asked the commissioner investigating the 1857 sectarian riots in Belfast, did Protestants feel the need to attack Catholics in a city where Protestants were in the majority? Similar complaints were made by British officials during the violence of 1920–2, which saw many Protestants killed, but a disproportionate number of Catholics. However, such comments missed the point. At times when Protestants appeared to be losing out, Catholics were not considered as individuals, but as part of a faceless system. The IRA during the recent

Northern Ireland Troubles were seen as Catholics reverting to type, however much they were condemned by constitutional nationalists, including the Catholic Church. The first issue of the *Loyalist News* (27 September 1969) treated the violence as a papist rising, orchestrated by the Catholic Church. 'Rome never changes [a recurrent phrase through the centuries], one word from their Cardinal would have ended the violence, the responsibility lies at the door of the papist Hierarchy[,] the Red Robes are [Bishop] Conway's and the[y] drip with innocent blood.' The killing of a loyalist resident in Londonderry during the September riots was carried out by the 'the sons of the "Holy Roman Church"', a deed 'typical of that system which set up the Inquisition . . . The responsibility for this deed lies at the door of that false church, the implacable foe to Ulster, whose teaching from cradle to grave fosters hatred of Protestants.' Similar sentiments were expressed in the Paisleyite *Protestant Telegraph*.[92]

In the 1970s loyalist newspapers spoke of past atrocities, such as the St Bartholomew's Day massacre of some 5,000 Protestant Huguenots in France in 1572, as if recent events.[93] The *Orange Cross* was the voice of the loyalist prisoners in Northern Ireland, its logo 'Their only crime was loyalty'. The present struggle was a continuation of 1641 (in which, it claimed, 154,000 Protestants were killed savagely, descriptions once again lingering on the images outlined earlier).[94] It was 'a continued attempt by Romanism to clear every Protestant off the soil of Ireland', the Common Market a 'wooden horse, with its treaty of Rome and papal nuncio and Spain the land of the inquisition' about to join.[95]

> Dare to be Protestant, Dare to stand alone,
> Dare to fight with purpose true against the Church of Rome
> Dare to stand beside those men preparing for the fray,
> Dare to fight the Priest, his witchcraft, his tool, the IRA.[96]

The nineteenth-century song 'Dare to be a Daniel' was infinitely adaptable. Robert Harbinson recalled another version being sung by temperance 'Salvationists' outside Moses Hunter's pub in Belfast.[97] All the anti-papist beliefs noted earlier are in these loyalist news-sheets: the same fascination with the confessional and convents, the unnaturalness of celibate clergy, priestcraft (particularly of the Spanish and Italian variety), 'Rome and her harlots',[98] the popular reading recommended, *Foxe's Martyrs*, the pornographic *Maria Monk*, and the pamphlets *The Papacy in Politics Today*, *Advance of Popery*, and *Convent Life Unveiled*,[99] and once again 'liberty' is defined as queen, flag, Bible, Ulster, and freedom from Rome:

> Freedom to live with courage and hope,
> To be able to live and not worship a Pope.
> To be Protestant, to be able to say
> We don't have to worship idols of clay.
>
> We don't have to pray to Saints or beads,
> We can talk straight to God of our doubts and our needs
> And know that though we, who soon may be gone,
> Can trust that our God will see ULSTER LIVES ON.[100]

Orangeism's and loyalism's view of the past, then, is that of evangelical Protestantism, and, as the Revd Patrick Mitchel's highly critical survey from within Irish evangelical thinking shows, declining numbers mask Orangeism's continuing potency. 'Orange identity remains a potent force. Its appeal for legitimacy, based on a 200-year-old quarrel, still corresponds closely enough with modern realities to attract continued support from a sizeable proportion of the Protestant population.'[101] Mitchel (a lecturer in Theology at the Irish Bible College in Dublin) is very critical of Orangeism's claims to be a religious institution based on evangelical Protestantism, its political ethos invalidating its religious. He finds that there is no real interest in evangelical theology in

Orangeism and that the Bible is 'often simply an ideological prop', its narratives commandeered 'to tell a story conducive to the goals of political Protestantism in Ulster'. He points out that although biblical symbols pervade the Order's culture, they are simply 'external rituals'. Indeed, the Presbyterian minister and Grand Master of the Orange Order Martin Smyth admitted as much in his comment to Frank Wright in the 1970s that the Shankill Road Protestants were 'Bible lovers even if not Bible readers'.[102]

The Orange disturbances each July since 1995 at the Church of Ireland church of Drumcree, and the sectarian violence and deaths which they unleashed, have given rise to much soul-searching among Irish Protestants. Drumcree widened the gulf between southern and northern Protestants, the perceived continued awfulness of these barbaric northerners acting as a further force developing cross-religious southern Irish identity, while further fracturing any common northern one. But it has also occasioned some impressive rethinking about the political Protestantism represented by Orangeism and the narrowness of Irish British identity which it proclaims, or wrapping up the Bible in a Union flag, as Dean Victor Griffin described it in a June 2000 interview with Church of Ireland rector the Revd Earl Storey.[103] The Revd Storey was prompted to review Orangeism's role in Irish Protestantism by what was happening at Drumcree. 'Orangeism makes a theological link between the desire to resist a united Ireland at all costs and the preservation of the Protestant faith',[104] he wrote, which is nonsensical in the twenty-first century, but entirely understandable if you still weave your origin-myths from the religio-politics of the seventeenth.

Anti-popery became a defining principle of British and Irish Protestant identity, a mode of thought and key organizational principle over centuries. In its widespread and popular anti-Catholicism Britain was unique in Europe. It explains why Catholic emancipation in 1829, and the repeal of other Penal Acts against Catholics, were so unpopular with the British public. For centuries Irish Protestants thought they could take this shared identity with Britain for granted. From the late nineteenth century onwards, however, as British anti-Catholicism declined and secularism grew, Irish Protestants were no longer able to count on a common religious bond with the mother country, and were baffled, nervous, and resentful.

Popery was that intangible enemy which allowed generations of Irish Protestants to consider themselves tolerant and reasonable and to live by a code of double standards in everyday social relationships with Catholics. And, as Steve Bruce has pointed out in his seminal study of Paisleyism, conspiracy theory easily overcomes the absence of any proof: 'an absence of evidence of evil Roman Catholic intent poses no problem for anti-Catholicism because one can always posit a secret conspiracy. If there is little modern evidence that the Jesuits . . . are actively engaged in conspiring to subvert Protestantism and democracy, then one simply supposes that they have become more subtle and devious.'[105] The longevity of this perception of Catholicism as persecutory and subversive of true religion is extraordinary. And the belief that they would be made victims should Catholics ever regain power was part of Irish Protestant psyche in the past and continues to be for significant numbers of Protestants in Northern Ireland. Anachronistic as the Orange Order may appear, it survives because there are enough Protestants who still believe this and enough Catholics who still believe Protestants the guilty descendants of those who had wronged them in the past.

4

The Church of Ireland as Establishment

> If a person was a Catholic, it invariably meant he was of old
> Gaelic stock . . . And if he were a Protestant, it also meant that he
> was a foreigner, a persecutor, a privileged person, an enemy.
>
> (Peadar Livingstone, *Monaghan Story*)

One of the reasons for Protestantism's fears of Catholicism as a threatening monolith was its own divisions, divisions reflected in social and economic status as well as theology. Irish-language sources periodically made the distinction between Church and Dissenting Protestants. However, whatever the social class or denomination of Protestants, there is a common thread in Irish-language, Catholic, and later nationalist sources: Protestants were foreign and excessively privileged. This, of course, has been part of Catholic thinking for centuries. Yet it has also been part of internal Protestant tradition, sometimes defensively so, sometimes as part of a belief in the inherent superiority of Protestantism over popery. Such stereotypes are most often associated with the Church of Ireland because of its role as the established state Church until 1871, its long-held position as a virtual department of state, and its members' monopoly of landed property. Indeed, the association of Protestantism with the state was such a given that Home Rule was denounced by the Church of Ireland Primate (1893) as 'a Bill to suppress the Protestant faith'.[1]

Rise and Fall of the State Church

The process by which the Established Church arrived at this position was by no means straightforward. It is not really until the eighteenth century that the state church character of the Church of Ireland was confidently established. Many of the accusations later made against the Church of Ireland could equally have been made against the pre-Reformation Irish Church—Church appointments and property in the hands of noble families (in Gaelic and Anglo-Irish areas alike), Englishmen often occupying top positions. So the early stages of the Reformation did not cause widespread change (except in the suppression of the monasteries in 1539, which were already largely confined to Anglicized areas). The reformed religion took a very long time indeed to settle into its modern character. Crypto-Catholic clergy abounded in Ireland (in England too). They were politically 'loyal'—inasmuch as the Tudor authorities were reluctant to test that loyalty by precipitate imposition of the Reformation. Whatever successive English monarchs' preference for persuasion and tolerance, however, almost from the outset a Cambrensis-like mentality infected the Church and 'civilizing' or Anglicizing the Irish was considered a prerequisite for their conversion. Predictably, given language barriers and the dismissive treatment of the few native Protestant clergy, by the 1630s the Church was largely administered by settler clergy and concentrated in areas of plantation. Failure to make much impact on the Irish gave rise to the belief that the Irish had not been chosen by Christ, and Ireland never experienced a sustained effort at conversion to Protestantism.[2]

Second-generation reforms under Elizabeth I introduced a more identifiable Protestantism and 'New English' officials. More recent settlers, and more firmly Protestant, they were devoid of the semi-tolerant views of their immediate predecessors. Since these new arrivals found the leaders of the Irish Church largely unwilling to implement the new state religion, existing clergy were progressively replaced with English-born Protestants. These tended to be more theologically Protestant, and increasingly so as the Irish Church became the haven for those with Puritan leanings.

Indeed, in the more easygoing atmosphere in Ireland, far removed from the centre, there was a chance that a Presbyterian form of Church structure might have been established. When in 1622 commissioners were sent from England, the prevalence of Presbyterian clergy in the Irish Church was noticed. The Church was then pulled into line with that of England, the Thirty-Nine Articles being imposed in 1634, and 'reliable' English clerics brought over to fill the Irish sees. So began Irish Presbyterianism's dislike and contempt for Anglicanism as an inferior form of Protestantism. So also began a recognizable English tinge to the Church of Ireland, even though it was, in theory, independent of the Church of England until 1801. It was, writes Alan Ford, historian of the Reformation in Ireland,

> a fundamental fact of the Irish reformation—that it was imposed on Ireland from England, and lacked, for a considerable period, Irish theological or doctrinal roots. Repeatedly its leaders and its preachers had to be drawn from England. Repeatedly, in times of crisis, it had to turn to the English church and state for support.[3]

The Cromwellian period (1649–58), with its attack on episcopacy, left the Church in a precarious state and it was not until the restoration of the Stuarts in 1660 that the position of the Church of Ireland as the Established Church was finally secured and large numbers of Dissenting clergy—operating within the Church until then—expelled. The loyalty to monarchy had brought its rewards, and the Church readily accepted the principle of divine monarchy under the Stuarts. This was not easily reconciled with the later deposition of James II, though no clergy resigned, the fears of popery prevailing over such scruples.

By the eighteenth century the link between political loyalty and established religion was formally recognized in the Penal Laws. Catholics and Dissenters were excluded from official life, and the 1704 Test Act made taking communion in the Established Church a prerequisite for any kind of public office—a sort of initiation rite into the official Protestant state. Even after Catholic emancipation, Catholics were debarred (until 1867) from wearing robes of civic office at Catholic church services.[4] By this stage the idea of Established Churches was under attack, even from the London government. In the eighteenth century, however, such association between state and Church was the European norm, 'an integral and indispensable part of the theory and practice of governing', as David Hempton explains.[5] The Church of Ireland 'as by law established' was part of this.

Not only did Church of Ireland members dominate every aspect of state life, but the Church itself acted as a department of state, collecting for its own use the equivalent of local taxes, peopling the magistracy, and mingling religious with state ceremonies. On formal occasions all manner of state officials, from the Lord Lieutenant down, processed to church, visibly demonstrating the oneness of state and Church. All Church of Ireland bishops sat in the Irish parliament before the Union, and half did so in the imperial parliament thereafter, adding to the perennial problem of episcopal absenteeism. Moreover, the episcopal bench was full of Englishmen and political appointees—as many as 50 per cent so appointed before disestablishment in 1871. Lord John Beresford's appointment to the primacy of the Church of Ireland in 1822 was the first of an Irishman in 120 years.[6] All this, of course, can be overplayed. There was considerable internal criticism of the appointment of Englishmen to the Irish Church, often to the most important and lucrative sees and offices, while lower down appointments were usually not only of Irishmen, but of Irishmen from the locality. Moreover, English appointees were frequently more liberal than Irish ones.

Since in Ireland the Established Church represented only 10 per cent of the populace in the eighteenth and 12 per cent in the nineteenth centuries, it was difficult to argue the same kind of cultural identification between the people and the Church as existed in England, and by the second half of the eighteenth century British politicians were doubting the justification of a minority Established Church and of the very concept of Protestant ascendancy. The Penal Laws were progressively repealed from the 1770s, usually at the behest of the London government against a reluctant Irish parliament, which on this issue was much more intolerant than the Irish Protestant population at large. The Established Church was fundamental to maintaining the British state in Ireland, they argued. The connection could not survive without us, much less the Protestant land settlement and the whole system of law and order, argued Richard Woodward, Bishop of Cloyne, in an influential pamphlet of 1787.[7] It was an argument which resurfaced repeatedly in the nineteenth century as Britain inched towards democracy and in Ireland democracy meant opening up the state to Catholics as the majority population. 'The present is the most awful crisis in the history of England', warned the Tory *Dublin University Magazine* in April 1836, in protest against the Irish municipal reform bill. 'The throne, the altar, civil liberty, the social order, are all at stake.'[8] Against criticism by the Protestant gentry, who seemed as reluctant as Catholics and Dissenters to pay tithes, the magazine returned to an oft-repeated argument: the fate of the Church and the landed establishment was bound up in a common colonialism. 'In the story of the Church the landed aristocracy may see their own perils predicted ... *They are a colony in a hostile country, and if not closely and effectually united*—THEY ARE LOST.'[9]

The article was prompted by Whig reforms reducing Protestant ascendancy and Church privileges, in this case reform of the town corporations, the bulk of which (fifty-six out of sixty) were still exclusively Protestant, in spite of the terms of earlier Relief Acts admitting Catholics. As such reforms continued, their claims to being a garrison for England became more strident, as did warnings that their own demise would preface that of the Church of England and their replacement with a popish ascendancy in Ireland. 'They thought themselves, as members of the threatened State Church, to be in danger of losing their privileged position, if not their emoluments', reflected the liberal editor of the *Northern Whig*, Thomas MacKnight, looking back to the eve of disestablishment. 'They felt themselves on the defensive, but even their defence partook of the character of defiance.'[10]

Increasingly, as Irish nationalism became more vigorous, the Church of Ireland pinned its colours firmly to England, to the dismay of the few who thought its members should be leading the nation as they had done in the days of Grattan. 'They have quite forgotten that their grandfathers stood for Irish nationality. They have chosen to call themselves English', lamented the Church of Ireland rector of Westport the Revd James Hannay (George Birmingham). 'They conceived of themselves as an English garrison, and held loyalty to England as their prime duty.'[11] Bishop Alexander often sensed the incongruity of their position and tellingly relates a humorous moment from an otherwise traumatic experience. He had been in the House of Lords on the evening the bill to disestablish the Irish Church went through. As he emerged in a state of shock, he felt 'a kindly touch' on his arm. It was from a Catholic bishop with whom he was acquainted who had been in the gallery. 'I cannot pretend not to be pleased,' he said, 'though personally I am sorry for you and the others.' Then he patted my arm again, and added—'Now, my dear Lord, you see what these English are!'[12]

An Irish Church

In England the Church of England saw itself as the national Church, representing and defending national values. In Ireland, however, the Established Church's claim to be the national Church was deeply resented by other denominations. Just as Catholics scored what D. H. Akenson has called a 'semantic coup' in terming Gaelic the 'Irish' language[13] (and, one might say, in capturing the term 'Catholic' itself after the Reformation), so Protestantism scored a religious coup in assuming the name 'Church of Ireland'. The Church of Ireland jealously guarded its national name, laying claim to affinity with the ancient Church founded by St Patrick. From the time of Archbishop Ussher's influential *A Discourse of the Religion Anciently Professed by the Irish and British* (1622), this was one of the Church's central arguments in combating the accusation that it was a foreign implant.[14] And there has been a recurrent war of words ever since over whether Irish Protestantism or Irish Catholicism could claim to be his true heir. This is why Patrick is one of the few icons which both traditions can celebrate.

The Church of Ireland argued that St Patrick's mission to Christianize Ireland was not ordained by the Pope and Ireland remained apart from papal influence until the twelfth century, when it was introduced by Henry II. Ireland was then plunged into 'papal darkness' until the Reformation set it free and restored its Church to its primitive purity. The real 'Catholic' Church was the Church of Ireland and there was vigorous competition to acquire the oldest church structures to prove as much. As all the churches recovered from the ravages of earlier conflicts, the Church of Ireland clung doggedly to such sites as, once abandoned, they tended to be reoccupied by Catholics.[15] Where Ussher led, scores of writers followed, reproducing his arguments for different times. In the eighteenth century patriotic Protestant antiquarianism frequently took the form of looking at cases where Irish Christianity diverged from Roman practice. Clare O'Halloran has written on how successive Protestant writers handled the conundrum of having to condemn Pope Adrian's 1155 bull *Laudabiliter*, which sanctioned Henry II's conquest of Ireland, without also attacking England, and conversely how Catholic writers strove to condemn the Anglo-Norman invasion without also attacking the papacy.[16] In the nineteenth century, with London Whig governments apparently in league with Daniel O'Connell to unseat the Church from its privileged position, Irish Tory nationalism again emphasized the foreignness of the papacy in splitting Irish Christianity. The effort by the Revd Charles Stanford to illustrate Rome's errors was part of this. The Church of Ireland was the only true national Church, they argued, with a God-given role to lead the nation—which is one of the reasons why disestablishment was so difficult to comprehend.[17]

Such 'national' claims continued to embitter inter-Church relationships into modern times. The Catholic Church in Ireland never became an Established Church, but in independent Ireland after 1921 it was to act very much as if it was, and its resentment of the Church of Ireland's claims was made increasingly explicit. At the 1929 celebrations for the centenary of Catholic emancipation, Thomas Gilmartin, the Catholic Archbishop of Tuam, expressed his hope that 'they would hear no more about the laughable claims of the so-called Church of Ireland to be regarded as the descendant of the ... Church of St Patrick'.[18] The verbal contest climaxed in 1932, the alleged fifteen-hundredth anniversary of Patrick's foundation of the Christian Church in Ireland, the same year in which Catholics were commemorating Patrick as the founder of *their* Church. At the closing conference in Dublin's Mansion House in October, the Church of Ireland primate, Archbishop Charles D'Arcy, repeated their historic claim:

> If we can only learn how things in Ireland came to be as they are, we who belong to what is at once by continuity of succession the ancient Church of Ireland, and yet through historical causes the Church of a minority, shall be able to stand our ground fearlessly and with a sense of mission. The Church of Ireland is the most Irish thing there is in Ireland. Holding its Apostolic ministry in unbroken descent from the Celtic bishops who succeeded St. Patrick... To-day the Church of Ireland turns neither to Windsor nor to Rome...It is an Irish, self-governing organization, as free from intervention ... as the Celtic Church was in the days of Columba. It is well that, even if the main body of the Irish people refuse to be in communion with us they should, from time to time, have plainly set out before them the historical facts concerning the Church which claims to be their own.[19]

It was, said another speaker, the Church brought by Patrick and in succession to Columba, Comgall, Columbanus, part of the universal, the 'Holy Catholic Church'. The Church of Ireland Synod of 1929 had commissioned a new collective history of the Church from Trinity Professor Walter Alison Phillips to be launched at the Mansion House conference and designed to show the Church of Ireland as Patrick's 'legitimate successor'. It is 'a national institution deep-rooted in the past history of Ireland... It is an Irish Church... It has no need to apologize for its existence.'[20] This was an argument reiterated by Dean Victor Griffin in his 1976 pamphlet *Anglican and Irish: What we Believe.*[21] Ironically, it was Protestants' *bête noire* Eamon de Valera who formally recognized the title Church of Ireland in the 1937 Constitution, against the protests of the Catholic primate, Cardinal Joseph MacRory.

In a recent reflective essay on the history of his Church, Richard Clarke, Bishop of Meath, writes:

> It is probably fair to say that until the nineteen-sixties, the self-understanding of the Church of Ireland, north and south, was that it was the only real and legitimate heir of a Celtic and Catholic church that had blossomed in the time of St Patrick. It had recovered this tradition at the time of the Reformation and, although it had been somewhat tarnished by associations with the established national church in England, the Church of Ireland was nevertheless an entirely Irish church, fully entitled to its title,

and the accusations levied at it were 'wicked propaganda' by Roman Catholics and Dissenters. He now considers this 'a grotesque distortion' and points to 'glimmerings of a reluctant willingness' to accept as much at the 1999 General Synod. It began in 1641 to take on 'the mindset of a garrison', not necessarily a garrison for England, but unloved by every other religious denomination and with a defensiveness and paranoia still 'sensed' today.[22]

The reputed foreignness of the Church of Ireland was thus vigorously denied through the centuries, though defensively so, much as Catholics repudiated stereotypes of themselves, in part recognizing elements of accuracy in them. Toby Barnard, who has done more than any scholar to investigate Protestant identity in

Ireland in the seventeenth and eighteenth centuries, concludes that the stereotype of Church of Ireland leaders as Anglophile and promoting English interests, generally holds, at least until the rise of 'patriotism' later in the eighteenth century.[23]

At times too the very names adopted by members of Ireland's Established Church underscored its sometimes ambivalent place in the nation. Unlike Presbyterians, there was considerable variety over the centuries in how Church of Ireland people referred to themselves. The self-identification as 'Protestant' was more common in times when fears of 'popery' or English reformism were high. 'Church of Ireland', 'Church of England', were terms used interchangeably in Ireland in the seventeenth and eighteenth centuries, at least by the higher clergy. 'Anglican' comes into use in the period between the Union and disestablishment, as does 'Church of England', though Bishop Alexander cannot have been alone in recalling his childhood puzzlement at the use of such to describe the Irish Church. 'Of the spiritual entity called the Church of England I had some confused idea even then, because in those simple days of the established Church of Ireland, most of us learned to call ourselves members of the Church of England'— hence his and others' sense of abandonment by England, with disestablishment in 1869 (taking effect in 1871). It was 'a confusion which we have unlearned, some of us with sinking hearts and bitter tears'.[24] Given this long-standing hesitation to call themselves 'Anglican', and preference for the name 'Church of Ireland', the absence of a suitable adjectival religious identity continues to create confusion (at least among non-members of the Church of Ireland). As for the old chestnut of which Church could claim to be truly Irish, it is perhaps time for more humility all round as this also impacts on the desirability of moving away from the exclusive association of Irishness with Catholicism.

A Privileged Church

The idea of an excessively privileged Church and community also threads through Irish-language, Catholic, and Dissenter sources. Presbyterianism's historian the Revd Dr Finlay Holmes called it 'the landlords' church'.[25] In Art MacCooey's poem 'Tagra an dá Theampall' ('The Argument of the Two Churches'), the Protestant Church tries to tempt the Catholic:

> My flock has estates, with land and demesnes,
> All riding in state in their coaches,
> While taxes arrears, and cesses severe
> Upon your Gaedhelian broaches.[26]

This neatly summarized Catholic perceptions of the state Church as a pampered part of the landed elite, far removed from the Irish poor. Indeed even internal critics believed that if the Established Church was less pampered it might have been more effective. The land settlements of the seventeenth century meant that by the eighteenth century 95 per cent of landed property was held largely by Church members, and this dominance remained until the late nineteenth century. Church members dominated the landed classes and the landed classes dominated the Church and every other organ of state. As the implications of the Irish Church Act 1869 were worked out, they were largely concerned with finance and property, £7.6 million being lodged with the new Representative Church Body to replace lost endowments, land, and property. The following year a General Convention of the Church met to sort out the detail of the new disestablished structure. Of its 446 lay members, ninety-five held titles and 365 public office.[27] J. C. Beckett likened the Church's General Synod to the old Irish parliament in the eighteenth century, an assembly of the Anglo-Irish, the same families dominating, much as they had done a century earlier.[28] And since business, the professions, politics, and all manner of public office were recruited from the landed world, there was an economic and structural imbalance between the religious communities, which survived independence into the twentieth century. Even as the rise in Catholic democracy was resulting in significant readjustments in the nineteenth century, the Church of Ireland still dominated public and professional life. In the early 1880s, for example, although just over 12 per cent of the population, church members accounted for 70 per cent of the JPs, 80 per cent of army officers and 60 per cent rank and file, 60 per cent of barristers, and 54 per cent of bankers.[29]

Local studies show how this all worked out on the ground. In Donegal, for example, Church of Ireland landed families who had arrived in the seventeenth century continued to control all aspects of local government until the twentieth century, to the exclusion of Presbyterian and Catholic alike.[30] Private church pews were fought over as symbols of social status, and the clergy very often had family connections with the landed gentry.[31] The Church was still led by old ascendancy families, the Beresfords occupying the Armagh Primacy 1822–85 and acting like the old ascendancy, when it was obvious (at least in England) that if the Church did not reform itself, reform would be forced on it. The Oxford intellectual Richard Whately, Archbishop of Dublin in 1831–63, was extremely critical of the privileged complacency of the Irish Church, of the lavish lifestyles of its bishops, and of Trinity College (where most Church clergy received their training), and his episcopacy was one long battle with the Irish bench.[32]

Whately arrived in Ireland in the middle of the anti-tithe war, which involved widespread refusal to pay tithes and serious violence against those trying to collect them. Tithes were an agricultural tax, impacting particularly on the peasantry because of the exemption of pasture (until 1823). They were hugely resented, since they were levied to pay the clergy of a minority Church and their collection was open to widespread abuse by non-clerical tithe-proctors. They increasingly figured among the grievances of rural protest in the eighteenth and early nineteenth centuries and became one of the main targets for critics of the Church of Ireland's privileged position. Thomas Moore's hugely popular *Memoirs of Captain Rock* (1824) identified state support for the Established Church as one of the factors in Irish discontent and violence, armies of 'valuators, tithe-farmers, and Bishops courts... (and constables)' all geared to maintaining 'the Church... as by law... established in Ireland!'[33] The Tithe Commutation Act 1838 effectively ended anti-tithe violence, but not the central issue of all denominations being taxed to support a minority Established Church.

This was one of the main criticisms in James Godkin's influential *Ireland and her Churches*, published in 1867 at the height of the disestablishment debate. Godkin, from a prosperous Wexford Catholic farming family, converted to Presbyterianism in 1834, and became an evangelical missionary and Congregationalist minister. He was unusual in lacking the anti-popish zeal of other prominent converts, and spent the rest of his life campaigning for Church and land reform, for which he was awarded a pension by Gladstone in 1873. Godkin trawled the census records and costed how much each Church of Ireland member was being subsidized by the state: ranging from £1 6s. 6d. in Dublin, where they accounted for an eighth of the population, to £10 2s. 0d. in Cloyne (Cork), where he calculated that Church clergy received £12,228 from the state for ministering to 1,209 souls.[34] He illustrated how wealth and nobility had launched the clerical career of the Hon. Revd Conyngham Plunket as rector of Kilmoylan in Connacht, with an income of £320 p.a. for a parish which had no church and only four Protestant inhabitants. Vast sums had been granted by the state for the building and refurbishment of Church of Ireland buildings, while nothing was ever given to the Catholic Church 'although the tithe-rent charge is levied off the lands they [Catholics] cultivate'. It was only with disestablishment in 1871 that such state payment was finally resolved. It took much longer—the 1898 Local Government Act—to break landed Protestant monopoly of local government.

The visible wealth of the Church concealed the many poor clergy on the ground—half the curates in Cork city, for instance, earned less than a journeyman carpenter in 1829. In the poorest areas tithes were their only income and they suffered real distress from non-payment during the tithe war of the 1830s.[35] Even so, it was not a Church which readily identified with the poor. Godkin commented wryly on the contrasting charitable donations of the Protestant Guinnesses in Dublin (£120,000 to renovate St Patrick's steeple, overlooking the poorest alleyways of the city) and that of the Peabody fund in housing for the London poor. He also thought the Catholic Church had a better record. 'What she [the Established Church] has done and is doing for religion, charity, and civilization, will, I fear look very small beside what has been done in the same towns by the Roman Catholic priesthood from their own unaided resources.' As he travelled, he noted Catholic churches constantly open and full; rich and poor, upper and lower classes intermingled. Church of Ireland churches, in contrast, were invariably locked, opened briefly for services, and as hastily closed again, while its cathedrals shut out the congregation with iron railings, the clergy and choir occupying the comfortable area within.[36] Other, internal, critics pointed to 'poor Protestants . . . sliding into Romanism, the natural consequence of neglect' by their own clergy and a major factor in the decline of the Church in poorer parts of the country.[37]

Asenath Nicholson, on a personal mission to the Irish poor, made much the same complaint. She found well-heeled 'lofty' pharisees of the Established Church, with the Bible at 'tongue's end', but 'great haters of the low Irish, and quite careful that the Apostle's injunctions should be religiously observed, where servants are required to "be obedient to their masters" '.[38] In Wicklow she found a Protestant family in 'a miserable hut', where the children displayed bibles distributed at Sunday school, but the pastor never visited and the parents could not afford appropriate clothing to go to church. Because of such pastoral neglect, she found poor Protestants knew less about their religion than poor Catholics about theirs, and she was particularly upset at the colonies of converts she visited. Those who ran them put up a good story and provided good dinners when 'the quality' came, but their uncharitableness towards the poor was a 'counterfeit' of 'Bible Christianity':

> I had looked in the cabins of many of the converts in Dingle and Achill, and though their feet were washed cleaner, their stools scoured whiter, and their hearths swept better than in many of the mountain cabins [cleanliness being presumed a Protestant virtue], yet their eightpence a day will never put shoes upon their feet, convert their stools into chairs, or give them any better broom than the mountain heath for sweeping their cabins. It will never give them the palatable, well-spread board around which their masters sit, and which they have earned for them by their scantily-paid toil.[39]

In George Birmingham's novel *The Seething Pot*, Father Fahy is the epitome of the demagogic priest. Yet Sir Gerald, the Protestant hero, came to respect his sympathy for the poor. While recognizing the 'tyranny and greed . . . craft and narrow dogmatism' of the priests, he recalled Father Fahy's care for the poor in the mountains and bogs and did not think it right to free the people from their priests.[40] In contrast, the Church of Ireland rector spends much of his time in the 'Big House' and in gentry company, recognizing that much of his income and well-being depends on the landowner, since 'the interests of Protestantism are bound up with those of the landlords'. His church was built on the edge of the estate.

> It has turned its back deliberately, even ostentatiously, on the town. Within the locked gates that lead to it, the gravel walk is smoothly raked, and the grass on the graves trim and tidy.... Compared to its new and wealthier rival [the new Catholic Church at the other end of the street], it has the prim air of a decayed gentlewoman in the presence of some self-assertive *nouveau riche*.[41]

A church which had so revolved around the landed class was slow to catch up with urban development and its attendant growth of urban poor. Churches such as St Anne's and St George's in Belfast could be built (1776 and 1813) with little or no seating for the poor, and, before the late nineteenth-century rebuilding programme, the notable absence of the less well-off from congregations was often commented upon. Evangelicalism started to change this, though efforts were often blocked by the privileged laity and clergy. When the evangelical revival started to fill the churches, Cork solved the problem posed by private pews by building an entirely new church (1830s), against the protests of the Bishop.[42] The Established Church and the landed gentry occasionally granted relief to the indigent of all communions, notably in the famine conditions of 1740–1. However, this was unusual. Relief usually carried a denominational tag. Given the belief that poverty was synonymous with popery, conversion to Protestantism was often the prerequisite for relief and there was a significant element of proselytism in most charitable institutions. When this continued into the nineteenth century in the now state-funded workhouses (where most inmates were Catholic, but most appointed to oversee them were Protestant), the Catholic Church protested.[43] Sean O'Casey did much to challenge the belief that all Irish Protestants were privileged. Martin Maguire's research on the Protestant poor of Dublin adds further compelling evidence. Yet he too is critical of the treatment of poor Protestants by their Church. There was a strong moralizing tone, differentiating the deserving from the undeserving, and in the early twentieth century, when the Protestant middle class moved out to the suburbs and the wealthier wards, the divorce between those providing charity and those in receipt of it became even more noticeable.[44]

Thus, Lily O'Shea's Protestant family was unusual in the Dublin tenements of the 1930s. Both the Catholic charity St Vincent de Paul and the Protestant Church afforded much-needed practical relief. Lily remembered the smell of soap, the 'posh' accents, the upright stance of the Protestant charity visitors (just the same class aspects as those in Catholic perceptions of Protestants), the way the Boys' Brigade left the Christmas hamper and could not get away fast enough, the fact that they had to go out to the more well-to-do areas to fetch the clothes parcels from the people donating them, the abruptness of the Protestant clergyman when her mother died.[45] The bulk of Protestants who were not privileged, therefore, can be overlooked and they were far more likely to suffer attacks by Catholics and reverse discrimination than their wealthier co-religionists.[46] But even they often shared a common sense of superiority. 'Protestants . . . were on top because they were better,' Jack White described this self-belief in his 1975 study, 'and they were better because they were Protestants.'[47]

The term 'Protestant ascendancy' is often used in a narrow sense by historians to mean the monopoly by propertied Protestants of Irish political life in the eighteenth century. However, in popular imagination (Protestant and Catholic alike) it denotes Irish Protestant privilege and dominance and it was not confined to the Protestant elites. All manner of minor offices could be held by Protestant artisans and others. They too shared in a sense of privileged status, and the sight of the Protestant state treating Catholics equally or of Catholics prospering was a source of friction throughout the centuries. A belief in their partnership with the state made every class of Protestant custodian of the Penal Laws. This is why disestablishment was such a shock. Until then the Church of Ireland and its members considered themselves part of the governing structure, but from the 1830s the London government progressively whittled back its powers and attendant privileges. Between 1830 and 1867 it was the subject of a number of reforming commissions and lost most of its political power as a result, culminating with its disestablishment in 1871. The Church of Ireland was poorly led on the eve of its disestablishment. Its churchmen 'thundered' from something of a position of imperious isolation against the British parliament. Not for the first, or the last, time, they pointed out that they, the loyal, were being treated like rebels.[48] In 1905 Bishop Alexander reflected back to the pre-disestablishment Church: 'Young people were brought up to believe that the relation between Church and State could not be broken without a lowered moral atmosphere, as well as peril to Protestantism.' His wife, the popular hymn-writer Cecil Frances Alexander, conveys the despair felt by many Church members at disestablishment's rupture of this relationship in a hymn sung in Derry Cathedral and other churches on 1 January 1871, when the new slimmed-down Church came into being:

> Look down, Lord of Heaven, on our desolation!
> Fallen, fallen, fallen is now our Country's crown,
> Dimly dawns the New Year on a churchless nation,
> Ammon and Amalek tread our borders down.[49]

A century later, in the worst decade of the Northern Ireland Troubles and another time when Protestant fears of extinction were to the fore, J. C. Beckett, himself a prominent member of the Church of Ireland and a much-admired historian, was reflecting on disestablishment in much the same terms, as an 'omen' of things to come, 'the first clear and unmistakable step towards the British government's abandonment of the Anglo-Irish'.[50] Bishop Clarke, writing in 1999, believed that the Church came close to 'disintegration' at the time of disestablishment and that its relations with the Church of England have never recovered.[51] Internal critics had often stated that the Church of Ireland was damaged by being an arm of state and it was now launched on a journey of spiritual renewal. Unfortunately for inter-faith relations, this went in a profoundly evangelical direction.

The Church of Ireland as Evangelical

Although a less privileged Church emerged after disestablishment, it also had the perverse effect of making the Church of Ireland more intolerant. Landed Protestants were motivated by older concepts of patronage and prestige and tended to be more liberal than urban Protestants. O'Connell, himself a landed gentleman, knew this and valued the Whig landed vote. But the power of the landed gentry had gone by the time of disestablishment. Thereafter the laity acquired more influence, and that laity was far more anti-Catholic than most of the clergy. Catholic clergy in rural areas testified to good relations with their Church of Ireland counterparts when evangelicalism did not sour them. Bishop Alexander cited Canon Sheehan's popular novel *My New Curate* (1900) as one of his favourite books, and remembered many of his fellow clergy speaking disapprovingly of the extremes.[52] The Revd Thomas Rolleston was 'a fierce Protestant' who loved 'public controversy' and delighted in challenging the Catholic priests of his neighbourhood. Alexander recalled a market day in Coleraine, and his clergyman father in friendly conversation with the priest of an adjacent parish. Rolleston approached, taunted the priest with 'his usual formula', and challenged him to a discussion in the Town Hall to 'examine the questions at issue between our churches'. ' "Oh! Mr Rolleston, sure you might leave me alone," said the quiet old man, and referring to one of his inquisitor's favourite examples of the venality of the Papacy, he added: "Don't we all know that Dr Borgia [Pope Alexander VI] was not an exemplary prelate?" '[53]

'Brash and aggressive' and engined by cliques of evangelical clergy with followings of 'some few minor gentry, small town shop-keepers and city merchants and their wives and daughters', so Ian d'Alton described religious developments in Cork in 1812–44. The evangelical revival was not for the upper classes.[54] Bishop Alexander was a great admirer of John Henry Newman and the Oxford Movement. This was a movement within the Church of England to restore some of the Catholic ritual lost at the Reformation— hence the term 'ritualism' often attached to it. It was also a reaction against the Erastianism of the Established Church, sparked off by the state's abolition of a number of Irish bishoprics in 1833. Some of its leaders, notably Newman himself, ultimately converted to Roman Catholicism. Indeed Alexander, when a student at Oxford, almost followed Newman's example. He had supported Archbishop Whately in many of his contests with the more anti-papist clergy, and preached tolerance as Bishop of

Derry (1867–96) in anniversary sermons of the siege of 1690. Unsurprisingly, he was considered not quite kosher and rarely invited to preach.[55] Given the strength of anti-popery in Irish Protestantism, this 'Romeward trend' in Anglicanism occasioned many battles, and further strengthened what David Hempton calls the 'hotter sort of Protestantism'.[56]

Much as Swift's Jack had divested himself of popish showiness, so evangelicalism now set about removing vestiges of popery from the Church of Ireland, including the term 'priest', lighted candles, crosses, incense, processions, the names of saints—apart from feast days—and a host of other practices deemed to have been taken from the 'Romish' ritual at the time of the Reformation. In the 1840s the Revd William McIlwaine, the evangelical rector of St George's in Belfast, waged an ultimately successful campaign against his own bishop, the Englishman Richard Mant, Bishop of Down and Connor. Stained-glass windows might be 'very well in by-gone days of Romish and earlier superstition, but not today when people could find the truth for themselves in the Bible'.[57] Bishop Alexander recalled the horror expressed by a parishioner in Garvagh (County Derry) at his curate's following of the Oxford Movement and eventual conversion to Rome. Pointing to furniture used by the apostate, he commented: ' "yonder big drawer was found full of false gods—and of all the antics that went on in thon room—!" with an awful sense which could find no grammatical conclusion'.[58] Thus did the Church of Ireland remove even further from the Church of England, which seemed to be moving in the other direction. The impact of the Oxford Movement on church building and decoration was particularly problematic. There were violent protests against excessive ornamentation in various parts of Ireland. The windows of Down Cathedral depicting the Apostles and Virgin Mary were smashed and eventually removed. Protests raged over the introduction of crosses in Dublin and in much of Ulster, prompting a novel solution from one donor's family: since gable crosses seemed most controversial, designing circular, wheel-like ones might trick those with 'hot heads and bad eyes [to] ... take it for a chimney'.[59]

A Minority Church

The Church of Ireland, then, was powerful and privileged, but very much a minority and, like all privileged minorities, apt to see conspiracies all around. At 10 per cent of the population in the eighteenth century and 12 per cent in the nineteenth, its minority status outside the towns was accentuated by the sparse and scattered nature of its parishioners. Government enquiries in the nineteenth century revealed just how isolated and scattered Church of Ireland members actually were, clergymen having to travel great distances between congregations. An 1835 return revealed a significant number of parochial benefices with no, or tiny numbers of, parishioners, and Godkin in the 1860s pointed to sparse congregations rattling about in its churches. In the diocese of Cork and Ross they were only 3 per cent of the population, 2 per cent in that of Cloyne, and all but 'abandoned' in Connacht, where Archbishop Trench's visit (1820s–1830s) to carry out confirmation in the parish of Killenummery was said to have been the first in ninety years.[60] By 1871 census data show an Anglican population of less than 4 per cent in much of the west and southwest, with only parts of Ulster (particularly Armagh and Fermanagh) and the Dublin area showing 20 per cent or more.[61] There were periodic worries about levels of Protestant emigration, and talk of being outbred by Catholics and of possible extinction, and during one of these scares the *Dublin University Magazine* blamed the enfranchisement of the Catholics in 1793 for Protestant emigration. Until then, it was claimed, Protestants could count on preferential treatment and lower rents, because they were expected to vote according to the landlord's wishes. Thereafter, it was argued, they had no political advantage in the competition for leases and Catholics were thought to be willing to pay higher rents.[62]

But, as ever, the leaders of Protestant society tended to exaggerate the threat. Clergy and churches were not generally attacked, except briefly during the tithe war of the 1830s. No, the real problem was a sense of isolation, of standing apart from the general populace. And while Toby Barnard finds his eighteenth-century rural Protestants 'relaxed', his case histories depict vividly this sense of isolation. Nicholas Peacock, a County Limerick agent and tithe farmer, told of Sundays in the 1740s when his church remained unopened or the clergyman did not appear (this being a parish with no resident clergyman) and of evenings alone while his servants socialized in the largely Catholic popular gatherings of the locality.[63] 'Until it shall please God in his good time to dispel in some degree this almost impenetrable cloud of superstition and idolatry with which this country is enveloped', wrote the Revd Samuel Riall to Archbishop Agar in February 1809, he thought it would be foolish to build churches in parishes with only two or three Protestants, 'then finding ourselves on the outside with perhaps 200 or 300 people laughing at us'.[64]

Although most members of the Church of Ireland would have been small farmers and urban working-class, its public face was as privileged as the legend implies. D. H. Akenson suggests that the Church

> and the Anglo-Irish ascendancy which was its prime constituency, were both headed for defeat. From the mid-nineteenth century they were being beaten from their privileged positions by the rising

Catholic majority, with its long memory of insult and repression. The narrow-mindedness, suspicion, and ethnic snobbery of the Anglo-Irish and of their churchmen prevented their making any of the ecclesiastical and economic adjustments and concessions that might have won [them] ... more acceptable accommodations in the new Ireland that was emerging.[65]

5

The 'Outlanders' of Ulster

A North land apart like a Queen on a throne
That's Ulster, our birthland, the place we call home.

(The Orange Cross: The Voice of the Loyalist Political
Prisoners, no. 50, 1974[1])

Arthur Clery thought the southern Protestants capable of absorption into 'Irishness'. Look north, however, and there you would find the 'unabsorbable' 'outlanders'.[2] 'To pass Goraghwood[3] is like crossing the highest ridge of the Alps. You leave behind you the kindly people of the South, and come upon the cold and harsh-tongued members of another nation.' He envisaged shedding east Ulster north of a line drawn from Newry to Derry, 'our' boundary, shorn of 'a disaffected body of turbulent and bigoted aliens', then being made to coincide with 'our people'.[4] Such nervousness about the North long pre-dated partition in 1920 and has not been confined to one creed. Wolfe Tone found mutual incomprehension between southern Catholic and northern Presbyterian reformers in the 1790s. Yeats, far from being dismayed at partition, declared that when 'surly disagreeable neighbours shut the door, it is better to turn the key in it before they change their mind'.[5] Northern identity came to be associated with a particular brand of Protestantism; even northern Catholics were thought to have been infected.

Reflections on Why Ulster Protestants Seem Strange

Ulster then was seen to have contained a people with a peculiar accent, a blunt manner, a philistine outlook on life, an intransigent frame of mind, and, in the case of the religion which came to be most associated with it (Presbyterianism),[6] a tendency to lace everyday speech with scriptural references. And even though William Carleton's Protestants span a whole spectrum, his Presbyterians are generally unsympathetic figures. The unsavoury attorney Solomon McSlime in *Valentine McClutchy* sings metrical psalms, gives religious tracts to the hungry, and tells evicted tenants that 'God loveth whom he chastiseth', and that he and the Orange yeomanry were simply God's instruments.[7]

Many later commentators came to see Ian Paisley (at least the pre-2007 one) as the lowest common denominator of Ulster Protestantism, and in particular of Presbyterianism, much to the dismay of mainstream Presbyterians, who insisted on Paisley's lack of Presbyterian background to distance themselves from his extremes. They argue that Ian Paisley was raised a Baptist and his Church structure has little of the democracy of Presbyterianism. However, Paisley's mother was a Scottish Covenanter and he was partly trained at the Reformed Presbyterian Church's Theological Hall in Belfast. His father's Ravenhill Evangelical Mission Church was itself a breakaway from the Ravenhill Presbyterian Church, and the establishment of Free Presbyterianism was assisted by five Presbyterian elders, who—in good Presbyterian tradition—had split from their own Church. Free Presbyterianism also subscribes to the Westminster Confession, its references to the Pope as Antichrist appearing repeatedly in Dr Paisley's statements. Accusations of consorting with popery have been made against ecumenism, O'Neillism, the European Economic Community, the

Presbyterian Church in Ireland, the World Council of Churches, and the Anglo-Irish Agreement, among others.[8] 'There is no difference between Europe today and Europe in Reformation times', he told the European Parliament in 1988 at the time of a visit by the Pope. 'The Hapsburgs are still lusting after Protestant blood. They are still the same as they were in the days of Luther.'[9] Squeamishness apart, the Revd Ian Paisley serves a real need in Ulster Protestantism, allowing many Protestants—who share his dislike of Rome—to appear moderate. He also represents the underpinning fundamentalist Protestantism of Unionist identity. His participation in politics, as Steve Bruce has argued, is attributable entirely to the perceived need to defend Protestantism, his political career beginning in 1946 with an attack on ecumenism.[10] Paisley speaks for a fundamentalist Calvinism and anti-Catholicism which lies at the heart of Presbyterian identity. Surprise at the inexorable rise of his party, the Democratic Unionist Party (DUP), is misplaced.

The reverse of such stereotypes is Presbyterians' self-image as an honest, industrious people whose pursuit of truth has exposed them to persecution in the past. Indeed, while all the traits of anti-popery identified in Chapter 3 can be found in Presbyterianism, their sense of victimhood also perceived the Church of Ireland, the landed classes, and various governments as among the victimizers, and their 'loyalty' has had a peculiarly covenanting and conditional aspect about it. Indeed, there is even a rebel element in their origin-myth, though not referred to as such and fundamentally different from Catholic rebel traditions. It is firmly associated with the Dissenting tradition (vigilance against and resistance to excessive authority, whatever its origin), and its revolutionary incarnation in the United Irishmen raises the questions, where did the Dissenting tradition disappear to in the Stormont years and, how, despite disclaimers, did it find a home in Orangeism?

Presbyterianism's historic contempt for other religious groups stems from an even stricter reading of biblical revelation than that of other Protestants. Their seventeenth-century forebears believed themselves to be a covenanted people with whom a contract was made with God to fulfil his will—a will laid out in strict rules in the different texts of the Bible, most notably in the Old Testament. In return, they and their descendants would be a favoured people, given a specific land, which would prosper if all the conditions were honoured. This is why, argues the historian and biblical scholar D. H. Akenson, such covenanted peoples have a very precise, legalistic turn of mind and an acute sense of place.[11] They were not given to generosity towards anything or anyone who might compromise what they believed God had asked of them, for the Bible indicated adverse consequences. Nor should they jeopardize the purity of the chosen people by marrying outside it. Indeed, at one point or other in their history, the Irish Presbyterians have spanned the whole gamut from militant rebelliousness to militant loyalism and all shades in between. This is because, unlike the hierarchical systems of both Catholicism and Anglicanism, authority in Presbyterianism lay at local level. Local groupings often split from overarching national or regional structures, hence the bewildering array of Presbyterian splinter groups: New Lights, Old Lights, Seceders, Burghers, Anti-Burghers, Covenanters or Reformed Presbyterians, Unitarians, and latterly the Free Presbyterians of the Revd Ian Paisley.

Presbyterians are extremely proud of their Scottish origins and inheritance—though here too there is a certain elitism which usually fails to recognize that the Ulster–Scottish connection long pre-dated the Reformation. They regard Ulster as their particular homeland, for it is where their ancestors came from Scotland, often to escape persecution. Some had come as part of the Ulster plantation, to lands confiscated from the Gaelic chiefs. Others were part of the most successful private settlement of lowland Scots in Antrim and Down. In their disputes with England in the early seventeenth century, John Milton accused the Presbyterians of ingratitude since they had been invited into Ulster by the English Crown: 'a generation of highland thieves... neighbourly admitted by the courtesy of England to hold possessions in our Province... have proved ungrateful and treacherous guests'.[12] Presbyterians have been happy to accept this origin-myth of their forebears as a 'Scotch colony' and 'planters', even though the bulk of Presbyterians came long after the Ulster plantation. Even so, the strong identification with the Ulster plantation is fundamental to the Presbyterian self-image of a hard-working people bringing a rough and uncultivated land to civility.[13] Patrick Adair, one of the first Ulster Presbyterian ministers to be ordained, likened it to the people of Israel being settled in Canaan amidst threatening and idolatrous Canaanites. By their removal, God had 'made way for others who professed the gospel'.[14] The barbarism of the natives became one of those myths underpinning Ulster Protestant identity. 'Owing to the vicinity of Scotland, and the enterprising character of its people', commented Godkin in his 1867 *Ireland and her Churches*, 'industry, order, and peace' were brought to the province, 'disturbed only by the marauding incursions of the natives, who issued from their fastnesses in the woods.' Ulster became 'the model province of Ireland' because of 'the religious and moral culture brought to bear... by the Presbyterian Church'. He added—in line with his perception of the Anglified and pampered Church of Ireland—claims by a seventeenth-century settler that the less 'tenderly bred' English came in fewer numbers, finding the harsh terrain and climate 'unwholesome to English bodies'.[15]

Just as the covenant with God had rewarded their godliness with survival and prosperity, so their civilizing mission in Ulster was deemed to have established a contract with the London government, a contract which was regularly invoked to remind London of their precarious situation in a sea of hostile natives. 'When the Ulster settlements were made,' wrote Thomas MacKnight, reflecting in the 1890s on the letters to his paper, the *Northern Whig*, over the past twenty-five years, 'there was an implied compact that they who crossed the Irish Sea on what was believed to be a great colonizing and civilizing mission should not in themselves, nor in their descendants, be abandoned to those who regarded them as intruders, and as enemies.' The nationalist press spoke of them as the 'Scotch Colony', and there was a belief abroad that 'lots have been cast by Nationalists for the future proprietorship of houses and lands now possessed by Protestants'. This was a repetition of arguments used against the repeal of the Penal Laws in the eighteenth century, another example of stock images continuing through the centuries, though nationalist 'memory' of who owned what before the confiscations was real enough.[16]

And finally these Presbyterians were highly political, believing that the governing order should reflect the religious. This idea was behind the various covenants in sixteenth- and seventeenth-century Scotland, achieving a Presbyterian structure in Church and state, and guarding against a feared return of Catholicism. They also have a firm sense of history. A pamphlet produced by the Presbyterian General Assembly in 1993 for use in Sunday schools (and largely written by the Revd Dr Finlay Holmes, one-time Moderator and an admired historian) is dominated by an explanation of its historical origins and development. Descriptions of its populist organization, of congregations choosing their own minister and other representatives upward to Presbytery and

General Assembly, are sourced in biblical quotations. Presbyterians believed that theirs was the only truly biblical Church structure and they denounced the Established Church 'for going so near the papists in their former worship and government in the church'.[17] The pamphlet then explains its origins in the Reformation and the teachings of Calvin, 'the Father of Presbyterianism', how it was brought to Ulster from Scotland, its disputes with the Established Church, the Covenants of 1638 and 1643, the various persecutions, their involvement in the American Revolution, the United Irishmen, and the 1798 rebellion—its historical background then truncated in the nineteenth century, not without reason for the tradition of dissent was already in retreat.[18]

Presbyterians as Dissenters

Ulster Presbyterianism's first presbytery was established by the chaplains and elders who accompanied General Monro's Scottish army, sent in 1642 to suppress the rising of the Ulster Catholics. It took its theology from John Calvin (via John Knox)—a particularly pared-down and dour form of Christianity, organized around strict Old Testament social and religious codes, its predestinarianism defining who was saved and who was not. It was, in Akenson's words, 'a perfect tribal religion' for the Ulster Scots in their new promised land.[19] Calvin set the model for this religion of the word in his writings, which told biblical stories to illustrate how a chosen people should organize their lives. Bible-reading has been fundamental to Presbyterianism, sales underwriting the early book trade in Ireland and ensuring greater literacy levels than in other denominations. Calvinism also defined godly political structures in the state and implemented them in the city state of Geneva. These were reconfigured in the Scottish context, helping to overthrow its Catholic monarch and secure a signed covenant with the new monarch (James VI, and future James I), and two further covenants in 1638 and 1643. The latter was the famous Solemn League and Covenant, seeking to establish Presbyterianism also in Ireland and England. Those subscribing to the Covenant pledged themselves to maintain the reformed religion, to extirpate 'Popery and prelacy (that is Church government by Archbishops and Bishops)...superstition, heresy, schism, profaneness'.[20] At Westminster it was accepted by a joint assembly of English and Scottish religious leaders. Then commissioners were sent out to administer it through England, Ireland, and Scotland. In Ulster it was brought by an armed guard and administered to the troops of Monro's Scottish army and to the settlers. The settlers were told 'that their miseries had come from those sorts of people who were there sworn against, though specially from the Papists'.[21] The Westminster Assembly also produced Presbyterianism's central doctrinal statement: the Westminster Confession of Faith.

There had been strong resistance to a Presbyterian religious settlement for England, and the hierarchical structure inherited from the Roman Church was retained in the state Church, when Presbyterianism tolerated no intermediary between God and Man. Moreover, although Presbyterians sometimes considered the monarch God's temporal representative on earth, the idea of the monarch as head of an Established Church was denounced as unscriptural and a sinful confusion of Christ's kingdom with the kingdoms of this world. For much of its history Irish Presbyterianism had a quietist approach to the state. But a strict interpretation of the Solemn League and Covenant was held by its more fundamental branches, the Covenanters or Reformed Presbyterians. They emerged in Scotland in mid-seventeenth century and when the establishment in Church and state was restored after the 1660s under Charles II, they denounced such interference by the civil power in God's Church, stretching the concept of Antichrist as defined in the Westminster Confession to include such establishments.

The idea of Presbyterians as loyal and law-abiding, then, is a modern myth. In the seventeenth, eighteenth, and intermittently in the nineteenth centuries Presbyterians were proud to be called Dissenters. If you believed that you had the only true key to God's kingdom on earth, then you were naturally contemptuous of Church and state structures which did not subscribe to this. This attitude was well recognized by others, and they were often called 'levellers' and 'republicans' by Anglican statesmen. The Dissenting tradition had its heyday in the eighteenth century, particularly the last decades, when contemporary thinking in the Western world was in tune with (indeed was partly created by) their belief in the possibility of reordering society. We tend to see Presbyterians in the eighteenth century through the prism of those 'New Light', enlightened middle-class Belfast thinkers who refused to subscribe to the Westminster Confession and whose descendants went on to found the Society of United Irishmen and participate in the 1798 rebellion.

However, Catholics considered them the most anti-papist of all Protestants, and we must never lose sight of their fear and dislike of Rome. The radicalism of the 1780s and 1790s was the product of a time when the papacy was weak, the Irish Catholic hierarchy unusually compliant, and Gallicanism riding high among middle-class Catholics. In the rarefied atmosphere of eighteenth-century Belfast, with Catholics few on the ground and local landed magnates particularly unpopular, Presbyterianism's radical tendencies came to the fore. Wolfe Tone, in extolling the Presbyterians as true and enlightened republicans, did not fully understand them, mistaking their dislike for the landed class and government for ecumenical liberalism. So while there is continuing Presbyterian pride in a radical past, this is often accompanied by the traditional imperiousness towards Catholics and the claim—still heard today—that they might have suc-ceeded in the 1798 rebellion in Ulster had the Catholics not proved so unreliable.[22]

There was quite a gulf between these rational urbanites and their rural, often poorer and more fundamentalist brethren. Both Covenanter and Seceder ministers attracted huge audiences to their open-air sermons, their tents and refreshments belying the modern image of dour Presbyterians. Disparagingly called 'moun-tain ministers', they supplied an emotional need before the arrival of Methodism, and in a religious culture where the community was lord, some congregations left the coldness of formal Presbyterian-ism and set up with these more fundamentalist and populist Calvinist ministers. Indeed, it was a call in 1745 from Presbyterians in Lisburn and Lylehill in County Antrim which brought from Scotland another breakaway grouping in the strict covenanting tradition, the Seceders. Predictably, they became concentrated in areas where large numbers of Catholics favoured the spread of Protestant fundamentalism, particularly in south Armagh, Monaghan, and west Down.[23] John Wesley was more critical of Seceders than of any other denomination. He had already dec-lared predestination 'a dangerous mistake . . . subversive of the very foundation of Christian experience'.[24] When he visited County Armagh in 1767, he thought Portadown 'a place not troubled with any kind of religion', but on hearing that the Seceders had settled nearby he had harsh words:

> I was not glad to hear that some of the Seceders had settled in these parts also. Those of them who have yet fallen in my way are more

uncharitable than the Papists themselves. I never yet met a Papist who avowed the principle of murdering heretics: but a Seceding Minister being asked, 'Would not you, if it was in your power, cut the throats of all the Methodists?' replied directly, 'Why, did not Samuel hew Agag in pieces before the Lord?' I have not yet met a Papist in this kingdom, who would tell me to my face, all but themselves must be damned. But I have met Seceders enough who make no scruple to affirm, none but themselves could be saved. And this is a natural consequence of their doctrine...That we are saved by faith alone.[25]

At this stage there was little love lost between Presbyterians and Methodists. The late nineteenth-century historian of Presbyterianism the Revd W. T. Latimer considered Methodism a form of 'religious communism' which he thought unlikely to attract Presbyterians from a 'religion founded on principle to one founded on feeling'.[26]

The Presbyterian United Irishmen had operated in largely Protestant milieux at a time when they considered popery had lost its threat. But the reaction to the O'Connellite linkage of Catholicism and Irishness by even the United Irishmen's venerated veteran Dr William Drennan, a friend of Catholic emancipation, showed that Presbyterian radicalism could only flourish when there was no Catholic threat, and weakened on its reappearance.[27] It was anti-popery ultimately which underpinned the eventual 'absorption' of Presbyterians into a wider British culture.[28] Even former United Irishmen in the early nineteenth century accepted the Union with England as necessary, though without enthusiasm. Indeed this lack of enthusiasm about England and its role in Ireland can be detected in Presbyterianism in every age, though the wistful belief by generations of Catholic nationalists that Presbyterians might yet be recalled to their radical past misunderstands the basis for their Unionism. To the radical

Presbyterian recoil from the events of 1798 was added the extraordinarily rapid industrial development of north-east Ulster,
assisted by the expansion of markets through the British empire.
Look to 'the masted grove within our harbour', Henry Cooke
challenged O'Connell, 'our mighty warehouses teaming with the
wealth of every climate—our giant manufactories lifting themselves on every side', products of the Union with Britain. 'Look at
Belfast, and be a repealer [of the Union], if you can.'[29]

Even so, the older mistrust of English politicians and Anglican
churchmen remained. Although the creation in 1840 of the General Assembly of the Presbyterian Church in Ireland through the
reunion of orthodox and seceding branches is seen as a major
milestone in Presbyterian history, there was considerable dissatisfaction with its main architect, Henry Cooke's, cosying up to the
Established Church in his pursuit of a common Protestant alliance.
Godkin, in his *Ireland and her Churches* (1867), dismissed Cooke's
proclaimed 'marriage' between the two as not amounting to
much, since Presbyterian ministers were still ignored and Cooke
himself would not be invited to preach in 'the meanest parish
church'.[30] In a huge outpouring of print, another generation of
Presbyterians was reminded of the unscriptural nature of the
Established Church, headed by monarchs who had betrayed the
covenant and by 'pampered' and 'haughty' churchmen 'wallowing
in indolent luxuriousness' on the back of forced contributions.[31]
Cooke's association with some of the most hated figures of the
landed establishment caused outrage among Presbyterians. The
County Down landed magnates, the Londonderry (Stewart) family, in particular was reviled for having betrayed a Dissenting past
and converted from Presbyterianism to Anglicanism to advance
their political careers. They were criticized for having hounded the
United Irishmen in the 1790s, shown scant sympathy to the poor

during the Famine, and been unsympathetic when Presbyterian issues came up in parliament—all of which ensured a long afterlife for the Presbyterian radical the Revd James Porter's *Billy Bluff and Squire Firebrand*.

This was a hugely popular satire, first printed in 1796 in the United Irish paper the *Northern Star* and still being reprinted in 1868. It satirized the stupidity and intolerance of the landed ascendancy in the person of Lord Mountnumble (Londonderry), and Presbyterians believed that Porter's hanging in front of his own home in 1798 was a vindictive act of revenge. Unsurprisingly, his grandson the Revd A. P. Goudy of Strabane was a particularly powerful critic of the landed elite. In the second half of the nineteenth century the tenant-right campaign witnessed an unusual coalition of Presbyterians and Catholics against the landlord interest. Dr James McKnight, editor of the Presbyterian *Banner of Ulster* and the *Londonderry Standard*, developed an argument which accorded well with Presbyterians' self-image: those who had received the grants of land under the Ulster plantation were not owners but trustees, the tenants having made the land valuable by their improvements. There were some flashes of cross-community support, and the nationalist newspaper *The Nation* mused wistfully that this signalled another coming together of the different religious traditions. But it was never difficult for the landlords or the government to play upon sectarian tensions, and Presbyterians drew back at the sight of Catholic priests appearing on tenant-right platforms.[32]

Even so, the Church of Ireland received no Presbyterian support at the time of its disestablishment in 1869–71, even if its own state grant, the *regium donum*, was abolished at the same time.[33] Paid intermittently to Presbyterian clergy from 1672 onwards, it was considered by some Presbyterians to be a government attempt at state control (particularly since it was subject to annual parliamentary renewal) and was rejected as such by the Covenanters. And as if all this was not enough, the Established Church had even hijacked the central part of the Protestant story of siege, delivery, and sacrifice: the siege and relief of Derry in 1689. In George Walker's classic account, for which he was fêted throughout Britain, the Presbyterians were all but excluded, even though they had been to the fore in welcoming William and in the decision to defend Derry. As Ian McBride has shown in his analysis of siege of Derry mythology, Presbyterian resentment and counter-claims against Walker continued for over two centuries, even after twentieth-century Unionism was presenting the image of a united Protestant front.[34]

The Presbyterian as Victim

In contemporary Northern Ireland there has been something of a competition for the moral heights of victimhood, and most definitely a sense among Presbyterians that Catholics have rather exaggerated their sufferings, particularly in the centrality afforded the Penal Laws. Indeed, in that perennial tendency of papist-watching, it was those areas where Catholics did not suffer, but Presbyterians did, that most infuriated. And just as Catholic stories of persecution come from a short period early in the eighteenth century, when the Penal Laws were actually enforced, the same period provides stories of Presbyterian ministers compelled to hold services in secret.[35] Presbyterians never really had a landed class, the tiny landed element being eroded by the same principle that had caused a similar decline of Catholic landowners: if you wanted status and power, you had to be Anglican. Landlords have a bad name in Presbyterian and Catholic folk traditions alike.[36]

Presbyterians were feared by successive governments and actively persecuted in the seventeenth century. In an age when the state religion denominated loyal subjects, Presbyterians were politically suspect and subject to various disabilities. Once Protestant victory was secured in 1690, the High Church party, rendered nervous by the huge influx of Presbyterians from Scotland, turned on their erstwhile allies, excluding them from public office and reviving restrictions on Presbyterian marriages, funerals, and schools. 'I was content every man should have liberty of going to heaven,' commented the Lord Chancellor Richard Cox, 'but I desired nobody might have liberty of coming into government but those who would conform to it.'[37]

The Test Act of 1704—whereby Communion under the rites of the Established Church was required for civil and military office— was viewed by Presbyterians as another sign of Anglican ingratitude. Presbyterians protested 'at being joined with your Majesty's Capital Enemies, the Irish Papists', and 'being included in an Act to Prevent the further growth of Popery', along with those same papists that they had fought against.[38] It also effectively expelled Presbyterians from local government, with particular consequences in their strongholds of Belfast and Derry. Ironically, the ordination of Catholic priests was recognized under the Penal Laws, while that of Presbyterian ministers was not, and until 1738 their marriages were considered illegal.[39] Presbyterians were also excluded from Dublin University (until 1793) and the English universities until 1871, their dependence on the universities in Scotland further consolidating historic links. With such restrictions and oaths of loyalty demanded to an establishment in Church and state which they found blasphemous, Presbyterians' sense of persecuted purity received frequent fortification and also became part of their story of emigration to the New World.[40]

The result was a distaste and distrust for central government which has continued in various forms to the present.

In Ulster Presbyterianism, however, there is not the same dwelling on persecution under the Penal Laws as in Catholic traditions. Some might say this is because the levels of persecution of the two faiths bore no comparison. Certainly, Presbyterians never faced quite the same loss of status as Catholics. Undoubtedly the most educated and literate portion of Ireland's population, they came to dominate the wealthy middle class and the skilled trades, the association of Presbyterianism with economic prosperity becoming part of the campaign against Home Rule at the turn of the nineteenth–twentieth centuries. So, unlike Catholics, who had been pushed down the social scale by penal legislation, this happened less to Presbyterians, even if, in their Ulster heartland, public office and landownership was still dominated by Anglicans.[41]

Presbyterian origin-myths of heroic suffering and redemption tend to focus on the seventeenth rather than the eighteenth century. For much of the seventeenth century Presbyterian ministers had operated within the Established Church, for which they were later chastised by Irish Presbyterianism's first historian, J. S. Reid. They had temporized and were forgotten. Those who had not and were persecuted were remembered. One such was the Revd Robert Blair, who, having resigned his post at Glasgow University rather than accept King James's imposition of bishops on the Scottish Church, had been invited into Ulster by the Presbyterian Sir James Hamilton. Summoned in 1626 by the Church of Ireland Bishop of Down and Connor, Robert Echlin, and suspecting he would 'lay snares for us', Blair prepared 'a discourse' for the occasion. Having meditated upon 2 Corinthians 4: 1, he argued that 'Christ our Lord had instituted no bishops, but presbyters or ministers' and it was merely custom and human laws which had given them their power.[42] Another classic history of Irish Presbyterianism by W. D. Latimer (1893) tells its story through a series of persecutions, Blair figuring prominently in that of the 1630s. Suspended from his ministry on a number of occasions, he and other Presbyterian ministers tried to sail for New England on the ill-fated *Eagle's Wing*, only to be forced back by storms. They eventually took refuge in Scotland.[43] The importance of the religious conflict of the seventeenth century was to determine attitudes for centuries to come, not least in displays of a touchy sense of persecuted purity among Presbyterians.

Geographical proximity meant that Scotland and Ulster had a shared culture. This was particularly true of north-east Ulster and south-west Scotland, barely an hour away by sea and the stronghold of the Covenanters. They could and did escape from persecution in Scotland to Ulster, figuring particularly in the waves of those arriving in the last decades of the seventeenth century—an important factor in making Ulster a predominantly Protestant province by the early eighteenth century. In the popular histories of Irish Presbyterianism it is the persecution of these 'ultra-Presbyterians' in Scotland which figures prominently in the victim reading, and which is integrated into the story of Ulster Presbyterianism. Much as in Catholic stories of persecution, there are accounts of torture, barbarous executions, exile, and religious services in the open fields as lookouts watched for soldiers and persecutors.[44] The requirement to subscribe to the Covenant and to consider ungodly those who did not was, as Ian McBride shows, 'quietly dropped by chastened Presbyterians with various degrees of relief', and from 1672 state payment was accepted by most clergy; but not by the Covenanters and it was their refusal to swear allegiance to an uncovenanted king which led to further

persecution. The Church of Ireland complained of 'Scotch presbyters who ramble up and down to debauch the people in their
religion and loyalty', and episcopal courts levied fines on their
followers.[45] Such clergy endured real hardship. Even in the nineteenth century Bishop Alexander recalled one such minister suspended by the Ulster Synod for opposing the *regium donum*, his
family going hungry and ill-clothed in consequence. These were,
he commented, 'the industrious, but somewhat "dour" and repub-
lican-looking men—the Yankees of the North—with a tinge of
Scotchism in feeling, in appearance, in personal peculiarities, in
religion—who with all their want of the picturesque and romantic,
are the glory of Ulster'.[46]

The Scottishness of Ulster's Presbyterians was and has continued to be an important part of their heritage. Travellers in the
nineteenth century already noted how they and Catholics pronounced place names differently. Gamble thought the cultural
differences with the rest of Ireland so great that the short trip
between Drogheda and Monaghan was like falling asleep in
London and waking up in Edinburgh. In Tyrone he asked a
Presbyterian man about an Irish-sounding place name. He
answered: 'I canna spake Erish . . . I neither love it nor the breed
that spakes it.' 'Are you not an Irishman?' asked Gamble. 'I'm
nane', he responded. 'I, and aw my generation, ha gone to Meeting this fowr hundred years.'[47]

This self-image of Presbyterians as a persecuted people and the
Church of Ireland as past persecutor survived into the twentieth
century, defying efforts at Protestant ecumenism. In the 1930s
discussions on Protestant unity collapsed over continuing doubts
about the validity of Presbyterian ordination and sacraments,
while in the 1940s a heated pamphlet exchange occurred over
who persecuted whom in the past. Once again it focused on the

seventeenth century and on events in Scotland, the Bishop of Down and Dromore, the Rt Revd W. S. Kerr, citing the intolerance inherent in the Covenants, and the Presbyterian ministers the Revd R. L. Marshall and the Revd J. E. Davey retorting that if there was any intolerance on the Presbyterian side, it was at least based on religious principle, whereas that of the Anglicans was based on state power, class, and a sense of superiority.[48] There was some recognition by Bishop Kerr of past persecution of Catholics, though he charged the Presbyterians with more responsibility than the Anglicans. The Presbyterian response treated such accusations with contempt: any intolerance towards Catholics was simply a response to the intolerance of Rome, which 'could stage a massacre of St. Bartholomew's Day, a Spanish Armada, or a Scullabogue'. But Protestant intolerance towards other Protestants was another matter, and the Church of Ireland was thought to be particularly unfair in the case of marriages, 'where a new kind of Anglican *Ne Temere* seems to have been envisaged'.

Restrictions on Presbyterian marriages were a very sore issue with Presbyterians. Presbyterian marriages were illegal until 1738 and Church of Ireland courts periodically levied fines, forced offending couples to confess to fornication, and declared their children illegitimate. But the 1738 Act only legalized marriages between Presbyterians, not mixed marriages conducted by a Presbyterian minister. In the 1840s the whole issue caused a furore when a declaration of their illegality by the Armagh ecclesiastical court gave a convicted bigamist the excuse he needed, and, what was more, his claim was upheld (or rather not resolved) by the House of Lords. Ironically, the only voice arguing the Presbyterian case in parliament was that of Daniel O'Connell, so dominated was it by Anglican landowners.[49] There must have been many such cases in the past, for all Churches disliked inter-faith marriages and it is hard not to sympathize with the hapless couples who simply emigrated or avoided religious services altogether.[50]

'Narrower bounds'—Northern Ireland

There is, then, some confusion in Presbyterian tradition about relations with the state and it required a significant decline in their 'Dissenting' tradition to permit the emergence of the 'pan-Protestant' traditions of Unionism. Political and religious developments already outlined go a long way to explaining this. In essence it had come about because the sheer numbers game meant that Catholic democracy would translate into Catholic dominance and become a new ascendancy, without Britain as the buffer. 'We are now on the brink of great changes', wrote Latimer, concluding his 1891 *History.* 'Year by year there is an increasing tendency for the rulers of Ireland to become a Roman Catholic democracy rather than an Episcopal aristocracy.'[51] Surviving liberal values among some middle-class Protestants were swamped when the 1884 Reform Act (granting male household suffrage) gave thousands of lower-class Protestants and Catholics the vote for the first time. Catholics also now had a powerful nationalist party to vote for. The result was that in the 1885 general election the Liberal Party, which had commanded cross-denominational support until then, was extinguished, and Ulster's future pattern of sectarian voting was established: Catholics voting for Nationalists, Protestants for Unionists. The introduction of Gladstone's Home Rule Bill in 1886 set the scene for violent sectarian riots in Belfast, and the Presbyterian Church's General Assembly issued a statement declaring that 'a separate parliament for Ireland ... would ... lead to the ascendancy of one class and creed in matters pertaining to religion, education and civil administration'.[52] Although

Presbyterianism had been divided in its attitudes to the Orange Order, that year too marked the full acceptance of the Order as a partner in defence of Protestantism, disestablishment and the various land bills having removed the barriers to a common Protestant identity.

In the years before partition there was a heightening of religious tensions. Signs of the resurgence of popery seemed all around. A number of works arguing as much were best-sellers, while a series of Catholic Church pronouncements were distinctly hostile towards Protestants.[53] Foremost among these was the papal *Ne Temere* decree of 1908, which declared mixed marriages of Catholics and Protestants invalid unless witnessed by a priest. It also effectively meant that the priest would require children to be brought up as Catholics, although this was not explicitly part of the decree. One case attained particular notoriety. This was the 1911 McCann case in Belfast. Alexander McCann, a Catholic, was said to have been influenced by his priest to leave his Presbyterian wife, Agnes, taking their two children with him. The case caused a furore, occasioning mass protest meetings in Belfast and elsewhere and a debate in parliament. It was denounced as a new example of popery's persecutory tendencies and so it entered Protestant understanding thereafter, particularly in the North. It seems that the marriage was already in trouble and some, not least the Chief Secretary, Augustine Birrell, accused the Unionists of exaggerating the case as part of their opposition to Home Rule.[54] Even so, Mrs McCann's minister, the future Presbyterian Moderator and noted evangelical the Revd William Corkey, slotted the case into Presbyterianism's story of persecution.

To understand our position, argued Corkey, it is necessary to go into the past, and he told of how their ancestors came to Ulster after fleeing 'fierce struggles on behalf of civil and religious liberty. The story of the bitter experiences endured under the Church of Rome has been handed down from generation to generation. There is scarcely a home in Ulster that cannot tell the story of how some member suffered for the Truth of God.' His own family had been victims of the brutal persecution of the Covenanters in the seventeenth century. 'Stories are still told in many houses of those who suffered in the cruel massacre of 1641, when 20,000 Protestants in Ulster were put to death. You cannot blot the history of the past out of the memory of the Evangelical Christians of Ulster... We feel that it is not right or just to put us under the yoke that was too heavy for our fathers.' Rome taught that salvation came through her mediation; she did not allow liberty of conscience and required total obedience to 'the foul "*Ne Temere*" Decree [which] was launched against innocent Protestants in Ireland'. This is why a Protestant minority could never receive justice or fair play from a Roman Catholic majority.[55]

Ne Temere also figured in the Presbyterian Church's 1912 declaration against Home Rule, which reminded the government of the trust that they claimed to have been established between Britain and the Ulster Presbyterians in the seventeenth century. 'Remember that we Presbyterians are now in Ireland because three centuries ago our forefathers were "planted" in Ulster by the English Government in order that, by their loyalty and industry they might secure the peace and prosperity of our province and promote the mutual welfare of both countries', and they called on their fellow citizens in the United Kingdom to fulfil their side of that trust.[56] 'Our fathers found Ulster a wilderness, and by hard work and integrity they have made it one of the most flourishing centres of industry... We cannot surrender our heritage of civil and religious liberty.' Once again they saw themselves as the last line of defence against Rome.

> If the Church of Rome can bend and break the Ulster Protestants,
> depend upon it England's day of trial is coming. We feel that we
> have been placed in the providence of God in the front rank in this
> great struggle to maintain our religious freedom against the efforts
> of the Church of Rome to overthrow the work of the Reformation
> in these lands.

It was Presbyterianism's Solemn League and Covenant which became the model for Unionist refusal to accept Britain's declaration of Home Rule for Ireland. It had been suggested by Thomas Sinclair, a Presbyterian elder, and the signing of the Ulster Covenant was preceded by services in which the religious basis for their political opposition was made clear. The former Moderator the Revd William McKean, flanked by Sir Edward Carson and the Lord Mayor of Belfast, identified the Unionist plight with the sufferings of the reformed religion in the past and above all with the fight against popery. 'The Irish question is at bottom a war against Protestantism; it is an attempt to establish a Roman Catholic ascendancy in Ireland.'[57] On Ulster Day (28 September) 1912 Protestant churches were open for members to sign the Solemn League and Covenant, and over 218,000 did so, almost the whole adult male Protestant population. Besides the title of this historic document, the wording could have come from any number of declarations in Presbyterian history. Proclaiming Home Rule as 'subversive of our civil and religious freedom' and perilous to the empire, it evoked the trials of their ancestors which God had brought them through, and pledged the use of 'all means'—they were already arming—to defeat this 'present conspiracy'. In fact, in a parliamentary democracy this was proposing treason,[58] once again exposing the contradiction at the heart of this exclusive arrogation of 'loyalty' to Protestants.

Why did the term 'Dissenter' fade in the twentieth century? The short answer is that with the creation of the Northern Ireland state,

Presbyterianism became part of the establishment, its politics one and the same as ruling Unionism, its theological college hosting the new Northern Ireland parliament until 1932. Safe in their Protestant state, they became complacent, and the manifestations of popery south of the border were the constant excuse for doing nothing about problems in their own backyard. In his 1942 tercentenary sermon the Revd R. L. Marshall recalled past persecution. But they had now safely arrived in their chosen land and were 'at ease in Zion'.[59]

In Anne Crone's 1949 novel *Bridie Steen*, set in Fermanagh border country, the kindly, though at times fanatically Protestant, Jerem had narrowed his entire vision after partition. When the Free State was created,

> Jerem could show his contempt for it in no stronger way than by completely ignoring it. From its creation the Ireland that lay girdled in blue mountains a few miles beyond the lough...no longer existed for him. He had turned his back upon it. In the old halcyon days, when the remotest postman on the wildest craggy mountainside was a servant of His Majesty, he had not infrequently ridden towards those same blue mountains... 'for a bit of a spree'. Now it was not only increasing age which caused such places to know him no more. When directly questioned on the subject, he always answered that he 'had never put a foot across the Border and never would.' He had completely adjusted his vision to narrower bounds.[60]

In his impressive analysis Patrick Mitchel sees Presbyterians as sharing 'unionism's cocooned complacency' and wonders why there was 'no theological reflection from a Church with a radical heritage'.[61] Much of the history of Ulster Protestants after 1920 was taken up with protecting the purity of their Zion, politics and religion becoming indistinguishable. Elections were fought on one issue, keeping Northern Ireland within the Union, old anti-popery given a contemporary spin by successive Unionist politicians. It is perhaps difficult to see genuine religious principle behind the sectarian arrogance and lack of a sense of justice of political Protestantism in the Stormont years. And yet it was entirely consistent with the Calvinism outlined above, the contractarian myth assuming Catholics would be enemies.[62] Given London's preference for a non-partitioned island, and the dangers of the Protestant vote fragmenting, the continuation of the Union was very precarious.[63] Sectarian politics united Unionism. It needed the old enemy, and the old enemy frequently provided the justification.

The volatile atmosphere around the time of partition gave new meaning to Protestant mythology of the unchanging papist threat. With the dreaded Home Rule a reality, due to come into effect when the First World War ended in 1918, Protestant paramilitarism prepared to resist, while Catholic paramilitaries had taken the rest of Ireland down the road of full independence. The sectarian violence of these years cast a long shadow over the northern state, which came into existence in 1920. Attacks on Protestants and members of the security forces in the South brought retaliation against Catholics in the North. Between 1920 and 1922 sectarian conflict resulted in 557 deaths (303 Catholics, 172 Protestants, 82 members of the police and army).[64]

Civil war in the South (1922–3) gave Unionists some breathing space. But it also increased nervousness, since the anti-Treatyites were effectively denying the northern state's right to exist. Given the continuing uncertainty and violence, the Unionist government set about securing its new state, abolishing proportional representation in local elections and redrawing the internal boundaries, which halved the number of councils in nationalist areas. This was so against the Government of Ireland Act that

Britain at first withheld consent and also queried the absence of any Catholic names among the twenty-four magistrates about to be appointed.[65] But with Unionist premier James Craig threatening resignation, Britain gave in, setting a precedent for non-interference in Northern Ireland's domestic issues when its role as the sovereign power and signatory of the Government of Ireland Act required it to do so.[66] Numbers in the new, exclusively Protestant, police reserve force (the B Specials) were ramped up to 48,000 (encompassing over half the Protestant male population in vulnerable areas like County Fermanagh), real incidents of their involvement in sectarian attacks giving rise to the long-lasting Catholic belief that policing in general was biased against them.

And nowhere (except among a few intellectuals) was unbiased information available. Dennis Kennedy tracked the frosty relations between the two new Irish states through the Protestant press (including the popular Presbyterian newspaper *The Witness*). Real incidences of killings of southern Protestants were intertwined with frequent references to another 1641 and other past massacres of Protestants. Little wonder that Protestants felt besieged. There was no recognition that most of the police murdered in the South were Catholic, or that families with southern accents in hot spots like Fermanagh were as likely to have been families of Catholic Royal Irish Constabulary (RIC) officers based there, as Protestant refugees from the South, as was claimed. Indeed the British army officer commanding in Belfast complained to Craig of such one-sided reporting, when loyalists were just as responsible for the violence as the IRA. Even so, there was enough happening to sustain claims that once again Protestants were being assailed, and the old sectarian stereotypes underpinned Protestant beliefs that all Catholics were responsible.

Unsurprisingly, the Catholic Church was portrayed as being behind the conspiracy. Had it not shown that its ultimate aim was to destroy the empire by organizing anti-conscription campaigns during the First World War in Canada and Australia, as well as Ireland? Once again the Roman Church was conspiring against British liberty as it had done in the seventeenth century. 'What is going on in Ireland is part of the anti-British campaign inspired, organized and directed by the Catholic Church', claimed the *Belfast News Letter* on 1 November 1921. Had its Irish side not shown its true colours by attending the beatification in Rome of Archbishop Oliver Plunkett, 'an Irish rebel', and visiting the graves of the Gaelic chiefs? Unionist MPs, particularly from the border areas and Orange working-class parts of Belfast, then cited the newspapers' one-sided reports as evidence. 'We know this is a religious question', Robert Lynn, the Unionist MP for the fiercely Orange Shankill area and editor of the *Northern Whig*, told the Northern Ireland parliament in November 1921. 'There are two peoples in Ireland, one industrious, law-abiding and God-fearing, and the other slothful, murderous and disloyal.'[67] The Catholic Church taught rebellion in its schools, argued the Revd William Corkey at the Presbyterian General Assembly in June 1920. He had already written about this in *The Witness* and in a number of pamphlets two years previously. Why was there so much 'disloyalty' in Ireland, he had asked, and then referred to the kind of popular history readers used in Catholic schools (examined in Chapters 6 and 7), where 'the irreconcilable rebels are spoken of as the Irish and their cause is praised as the cause of Ireland'.[68] At the end of 1925 the Boundary Commission—whose delays in deciding the territory of the two states had stoked the violence— was wound up, and finally left the border as it was. The *Northern Whig* likened it to the deliverance of Derry 200 years earlier, and

6 December was declared a day of thanksgiving by the Protestant Churches.[69]

Given the anti-papist underpinnings of reformed Protestantism, we should not be surprised at their reinvigoration and their pervasiveness in Northern Ireland. Nor was there much of a thaw until the 1960s, only for the Troubles to re-enforce them in a way not experienced since the 1920s. Catholics were thought inferior in every way. They bred like rabbits and lived in squalor; they were devious but slavish in mind all at once, such stereotypes masking a real fear of being outbred by Catholics and voted into the southern state. Catholics were work-shy and preferred to live on state benefit, given out like alms by 'our' Protestant state. The arrival of the welfare state in the late 1940s became another stick with which to beat Catholics, as was every educational concession. Southern poverty was pointed to as the product of popery, and working-class Protestants living near and working in the big industrial concerns, usually sited in their areas, had their communal self-perceptions reinforced as an industrious and reliable people, looked after by their politicians, prospering in their state.[70] In 1963 the Ulster poet and one-time Presbyterian minister of Loughall, in Armagh, W. R. Rodgers described this age-old Protestant wariness of popery:

> I am Ulster, my people are an abrupt people
> Who like the spiky consonants in speech
> And think the soft ones cissy
>
> .   .   .   .
>
> Anything that gives or takes attack,
> Like Micks, Tagues, tinkers' gets, Vatican.
> An angular people, brusque and Protestant,
> For whom the word is still a fighting word,
> Who bristle into reticence at the sound
> Of the round gift of the gab in Southern mouths . . . [71]

The 'Mickeys' are the unseen ghoul of Robert Harbinson's autobiography, always hovering somewhere on the other side of the railway track, childhood fears almost invariably invoking some popish rationale. Harbinson (Bryans) grew up in poor Protestant Belfast in the 1930s and 1940s. It was a narrow world defined by loyal murals, Orange popular culture, evangelical meetings, and severe warnings about popish wiles. He recalled his childhood war evacuation to Fermanagh. Eire's neutrality in the war was seen as another sign of popish treachery, much as the Easter rising of 1916 was deemed a stab in the back to Ulster's sons, shortly to be massacred at the Somme. On the train to Fermanagh a rumour spread that they were about to cross the border.

> None of us believed it. A train-load of us Protestant children being taken across the border into the Free State to be massacred? Things had not quite come to that, even if all the German spies that ever existed were hiding down in Dublin.... Where, I asked, were the battlemented walls, the moats and the vast palings with cruel iron spikes which must separate the dirty Free State from our clean and righteous Ulster?

It could not be. Nevertheless, 'just in case we should be in the danger zone, we determined to show the rascally Fenians the stoutness of our Orange hearts, and sang "Dolly's Brae" '.[72]

The young Robert was to have his prejudices seriously challenged in Fermanagh, and his autobiography is one of the best examples of the North's sectarian humour, appreciated by northerners of all religions, misunderstood and disliked by everyone else. His first billet in a Church of Ireland rectory introduced him to posh Protestantism and a Church with its headquarters in the South. The rector's wife spoke approvingly of Dublin and disapprovingly of Belfast. 'I had never heard anyone make such disparaging remarks about our Protestant capital', a much superior city to 'dirty Dublin'. 'Could this woman be a bit of a Papish' after all? She bore no resemblance to the Church of Ireland he knew through his Orange rector, affectionately known as 'Ould Willie', who watched over his working-class flock in Belfast.[73] A trip to Enniskillen—another beacon in the Protestant story of siege and redemption, celebrated alongside Aughrim and the Boyne in Orange songs—brought another shock. There indeed was the Protestant Church, full of regimental flags and military memorials to Protestant 'victories and sacrifices' befitting such an important 'Protestant town'. And there opposite was a Catholic one, bold as could be, and those passing crossing themselves with not one Orangeman trying to stop them. What would King Billy have said about 'such a canker at the rose's heart'?

Ann Crone's novel *Bridie Steen* is a much bleaker depiction of the worst consequences of such religious stereotyping. Bridie is naturally good and innocent, thinking well of everyone, but is ultimately destroyed by a tug-of-war between the faiths. She is the child of a mixed-religion, mixed-class marriage, and, having been rejected by her father's rich, 'nonconformist' family, is raised by an aunt and uncle, poor Catholic tenant farmers. The Catholic aunt is overtly devout, but also spiteful, bigoted, and ungenerous. Bridie is sent into service with a Protestant lady, where she befriends the handyman, Jerem. Everything about her new home and how life is ordered speaks Protestant orderliness, cleanliness, and regulation. Jerem is an ex-soldier who fought in India and in the First World War. He is 'the most ardent Protestant', who declaims against English politicians, yet 'Ardently, stubbornly, passionately, all his life through, he had looked towards the British flag,' and would have followed it to the ends of the earth.

He would paint with indescribable vividness the plight of the Irish Protestant encircled by foes; his long struggle for the preservation of religious liberty; the treachery, and bigotry of the Irish Catholic, whipped to fury by the clandestine teachings of the priests and by every kind of Jesuitical plot of which the unsuspecting Protestant mind had no conception; the perils which still lay before the defenders of the Protestant cause so long as Rome plotted and stretched out her blood-stained fingers to stifle the breath of free men, which plotting and stretching-out would endure till the crack of doom.

And he 'enriched his dogma with an inexhaustible fund of illustrations' from personal experience and history. The threat posed to Protestant Ulster by Home Rule was part of this story. He recalled the fear of the 'lurking gunman', the smuggled guns, the patrolling of the roads against possible attack from the south or west in 'those heated days of panic and exaltation when the North in her extremity saw herself cast off by Britain', and 'steeled herself to die in the cause'. Then Jerem would burst out laughing at his own pomposity and apologize to Bridie. But he thought 'the law of Catholics and Protestants was stronger than the law of fathers and sons or brothers and sisters'. His anger at the grandmother's rejection of Bridie is religiously determined: 'she has left that unfortunate child to be reared in ignorance and fear like a sheep, terrified by every sort of Popish mummery, and with nothing before her but crazy superstition and the rule of the priests . . . she has left a child of God in the hands of the devil'.

Once reconciled, Bridie observes her grandmother's religion: she is shocked at her supercilious treatment of the minister (for his was a position corresponding to that of the priest). Her grandmother laughs, attributing Bridie's reaction to Catholics being priest-ridden and bamboozled: 'We Protestants judge for ourselves and act accordingly.'[74] Yet for her and those before her, Protestantism is part of her life. 'Without it you were not free. Without it you cast yourself loose from the eternal order of substantial, respectable, honest things. Without it you joined the meaningless hordes of those poor benighted who gazed at plaster-saints, kept public houses, and flocked to huge, rowdy dances on Sunday evenings.' Her son, by marrying a Catholic, has 'sold his birthright', and she begins a sustained campaign to win her granddaughter from her popery, targeting with particular viciousness her rosary beads. Bridie is shown the family Bible and the ancestral names written on the first page. She has never seen a Bible at close quarters. It is a symbol of Protestantism, 'a bogey book which spelled doom and destruction to Catholics...Her father was inside that queer book...she alone was outside it, with nobody of her own kind to support her loneliness', in a house where the one retainer greets her with hostile mutterings about 'the other'.

Such stereotypes were relatively easy to maintain, given the highly segregated nature of Northern Ireland's society, its religious demography little changed since the seventeenth century. However, they were just as strong in mixed areas—often against the evidence—surviving in a remarkably unchanged fashion over the centuries. In the best study into communal relations in Northern Ireland (*Prejudice and Tolerance in Ulster*), Rosemary Harris looked at a rural border area in the 1950s and 1960s. The very nature of farming communities require neighbourliness and cooperation and Harris found it in abundance. But almost everyone thought in religious stereotypes, even poorer Protestant farmers applying them to Catholic farmers, their neighbours, and subscribing to all the stereotypes about Catholic inferiority. Generally, while there was outdoor sociability, there was little social visiting. Catholics socialized around the Catholic Church, Protestants around the Orange halls. There were informal systems in place to prevent Catholic or Protestant land from being bought by the other side, and mixed marriages were regarded as almost criminal. Since group in-talk was so infused with such stereotypes, how could you ever relax with one of 'the other' marrying into the family? And above all else, these poor Protestants feared the Catholic Church. Priests kept their people poor and in ignorance and that is what Protestants would be sold into if ever united with the priest-ridden South. This was why even neighbours might prove treacherous, and real examples from the past would be invoked to support their arguments, some of them trivial, even farcical—hence the primacy of symbols in communities otherwise similar.[75]

How had such stereotypes survived for so long? The simple answer is that they were passed on, literally at your mother's knee, segregation and new threats giving them contemporary relevance. Partition had perpetuated Catholic inequality and Protestant insecurity. This is why they have been so enduring, particularly among non-churchgoing Protestants. The history of Northern Ireland is, of course, far more than the sum total of such attitudes, and because of them the widespread politeness and restraint were rarely cynical. However, that history also concentrated the mutually antagonistic attitudes described in this book and explains why the Troubles flared up so suddenly and why they continued for so long. There was widespread ambivalence. Violence was condemned, but you partly understood why it was happening.

Should the Protestant Churches have been doing something to improve communal relations? On the whole they shared the same ideas as the community from which they came and which they served. The Church of Ireland, with its wider constituency and recruitment pool, did try. However, as Robert Harbinson's recollection testifies, some of its non-home-grown clergy, ill-attuned to the North's sectarian social codes, could seem like unwelcome cuckoos. The Church's relations with the Orange Order were a constant embarrassment to its southern members (not least because many of its clergy in the North were members). Northern clergy had to be very careful not to upset their people by any hints of Romish trends. Despite the amendment in 1964 of the canon forbidding crosses to be placed behind the altar, Archbishop James McCann felt obliged to continue the prohibition. The embarrassing 'Ripon affair' of 1967—when an invitation to the Anglican Bishop of Ripon to talk in Belfast about contacts between Canterbury and Rome had to be withdrawn because of violent protests—made all too clear the continuing sensitivities. In 1973 Richard Hanson, the scholarly Bishop of Clogher, was forced out by a storm of protest (much of it from his own select vestry) at his criticism of the Orange Order. It was, notes Daithí Ó Corráin, the shortest tenure of any Church of Ireland bishop in the twentieth century, Hanson writing sorrowfully to his friend Archbishop George Otto Simms of Armagh: 'had I had to endure another summer or so of Orange parades and Orange flags on the Churches in [the] Clogher diocese I would have had a nervous breakdown'.[76] His replacement was a member of the Orange Order. The moral: no Church in Northern Ireland could afford to ignore the opinions of its laity, however objectionable. This was particularly true of the Presbyterian Church. With all but 13,000 of its 336,300 membership living in the North by the end of the twentieth century—half of which lived within a fifteen-mile radius of Belfast—the Presbyterian Church in Ireland was more northern than all the other Churches, its populism ensuring an uncritical alliance with Orangeism. The strength of lay support helps explain the Church's ambivalence towards Orangeism.

The thaw began in the 1950s–1960s, helped by a change of leadership in the Catholic hierarchy, the reforms of the second

Vatican Council, and, ironically, the arrival of Paisleyite Free Presbyterianism—its strident protests outside the Presbyterian Assembly pointing up the distasteful side of extreme anti-popery. The result has been an ongoing debate about past intolerance and regular meetings with Catholic clergy. In a letter to Pope John Paul II on the occasion of his 1979 visit to Ireland, senior Presbyterian clergy sought to explain why they so feared Catholicism. The tone was respectful, even admiring, though there was also a sense of disappointment that his heavy programme with 'your own people' did not allow time to discuss with them ways of achieving

> the mutual understanding which we both desire. There is much which we would wish to say to you as we expect you too would wish to say to us. There are questions on our differing understanding of the Gospel and the Church of Jesus Christ, of God's Son as the one Mediator of Salvation and the place of the Virgin Mary in the Christian faith... There is also the tragic situation of this island where our communities as well as our Churches are seen to be divided, or even in confrontation. The causes of our Irish conflicts may be political rather than religious: but there is a religious factor or dimension as well as a religious label to our differences and even to our violence.

While they recognized that the majority of people living in Ireland were Roman Catholic, in Northern Ireland Protestants were a majority and many 'feel threatened not only by the political ambitions prevailing in the Roman Catholic community but also by the activities of the Church, in the life of the nation or the life of the family'. They had been participating in a large number of ventures, joint prayer, and study groups to bring about reconciliation. Sadly, however, they thought these were going nowhere.[77]

The Presbyterian Church's strong evangelical wing, ever vigilant for signs of softness on popery, was suspicious of inter-Church cooperation, and it was obliged to withdraw from the World

Council of Churches in 1980. In 1999 its Assembly voted by almost two to one against a new inter-Church body, denouncing any move which threatened 'compromising Calvin' by associating with 'those who detract from the centrality of Christ and the glory of the Gospel of His grace'. Moderates were deterred from protesting by the knowledge that they would have to face many in their congregations who did not consider Catholicism a Christian faith.[78] As Maria Power has shown in her recent analysis, Church cooperation has gone backwards since the early days of the Troubles. But there has been significant progress at the level of practical Christianity, once divorced from the theological gulf. 'We cannot opt out of society', the Methodist leader Dr Eric Gallagher wrote in 1983. The Churches needed to do more than just preach the Gospel. They had to become active 'agents of reconciliation'—an area in which he led by example throughout the Troubles.[79] Eric Gallagher thought that when the history of the Churches' response to the Troubles came to be written, it would be seen as an honourable and positive one. And so it has been. The sad thing is that they have finally engaged with each other at a time when fewer people are listening to them and have retained old attitudes, very largely created by religion in the days before Christian charity and forgiveness meant something.

6

'Our Darkest Days': Religious Persecution and Catholic Identity

We possess a vast capital of strong faith inherited from the ages of persecution.

(Father P. Corcoran, 1958[1])

Catholics responded to Protestant perceptions outlined in previous chapters with resentment, sometimes expressed in violence (though far less than Protestant mythology has claimed), sometimes in constitutional campaigns to win back what they had lost, and, most of all, in the development of a counter-culture espousing the very traits disliked by Protestants. And since it was their religion for which they were penalized, this became the most important aspect of their identity. The idea of a suffering, persecuted Catholic Church has been a core theme of modern Irish nationalism. Eamonn McCann, describing his upbringing in nationalist Derry in the 1950s, recalled how he was told of the redcoats murdering penal day priests, of the English offering food during the Famine if Catholics would 'turn'; but 'through it all the people stayed faithful'. 'An essential part of the Irish freedom for which patriots had fought through the centuries was, we understood, the freedom to be Catholic.' There were daily reminders of the threat from red communism. The plight of Cardinal Mindszenty (the Hungarian prelate imprisoned by the Communists) was known to every Catholic schoolchild in the 1950s. 'That, one gathered, was what communism was about. The church was persecuted everywhere. The fact that it had survived was proof positive of its divine mission.'[2] 'To be a Catholic is still a political thing', commented the Sinn Féin leader, Gerry Adams, in 1992; 'the Church was part of the people's struggle'. This shared sense of suffering is the main reason why anticlericalism did not become open in Ireland until recently. The sense that Catholics were still being perse-cuted in Northern Ireland postponed (or at least muted) Irish criticism of the Catholic Church until after the 1994 ceasefires, when the Fr Brendan Smyth affair opened the paedophilia scandal.

At the turn of the nineteenth–twentieth centuries some Catholic priests started to write novels to meet the needs of Catholic Ireland's new sense of respectability. In came the figure of the Soggarth Aroon—literally the dear priest, a model of virtue and a guide of his people. Part of that new identity as seen by one of the foremost proponents of such priestly fiction, Canon Joseph Guinan, was the memory of 'the long dark centuries of persecu-tion'. The soaring spires of the new churches and cathedrals he contrasted triumphantly with the 'dear' thatched mass-houses under the 'barbarous penal code'.[3]

As noted earlier, the implementation of the Protestant Refor-mation in Ireland was very protracted, and it was not at all inevitable that Ireland would turn out to be a largely Catholic country. The medieval Irish Church was by no means wedded to the kind of institutional Catholicism prevalent elsewhere, and resistance to Church reforms in the thirteenth and fourteenth centuries had seen both a revival of pagan practices and an organizational division between Gaelic and Anglicized areas. The great monasteries were confined to the Anglicized areas, so that the Henrician Reformation's suppression of the monasteries made little impact on Gaelic areas, where an older, more informal type of monasticism prevailed. A less institutionalized form of Catholicism was totally enmeshed with the Gaelic order. It was endowed by and recruited from its leading families, and lands donated in earlier centuries were passed down in hereditary succession to the same clerical families, who often also supplied the learned classes. In later dispossessions these were particularly badly affected, and it is no accident that they came disproportionately to supply vocations to the Counter-Reformation clergy, or that their colleges on the Continent should be responsible for creating the idea of an organic link between Catholicism and Irishness.

The Penal Laws in Irish Imagination

The image of ivy-clad ruins of abbeys and churches is prevalent in the poetry, song, and writings of Irish nationalism, part and parcel of a glorious past which the teacher was instructed, in the Christian Brothers' *Irish History Reader*, to convey to the pupils.[4] Irish Catholics in the past have generally believed that the older Church of Ireland buildings were stolen from them. As a child in the 1940s and 1950s, Robin Bury (whose father was Dean of Cloyne in Cork) wondered why Catholics crossed themselves when passing the twelfth-century Church of Ireland cathedral. Then one day he was confronted at the gate by the parish priest, who told him it was stolen property and he had no right to be there.[5]

In the nineteenth century, as the modern national story was taking shape, 'the penal days' of Thomas Davis's much-quoted poem of that name came to symbolize the suffering nation.

> Oh! Weep those days, the penal days,
> When Ireland hopelessly complained.
> Oh! Weep those days, the penal days,
> When godless persecution reigned;
> When year by year,
> For serf and peer,
> Fresh cruelties were made by law,
> And filled with hate,
> Our senate sate
> To weld anew each fetter's flaw.
> Oh! Weep those days, those penal days—
> Their memory still on Ireland weighs.
>
> They bribed the flock, they bribed the son,
> To sell the priest and rob the sire;
> Their dogs were taught alike to run
> Upon the scent of wolf and friar.
> Among the poor,
> Or on the moor,
> Were hid the pious and the true—
> While traitor knave,
> And recreant slave,
> Had riches, rank, and retinue;
> And, exiled in those penal days,
> Our banners over Europe blaze.[6]

This was further condensed later in the nineteenth century in a number of reading books specifically produced for Catholic schoolchildren—an antidote to the British-inspired reading material used in the National schools. Most included Davis's 'Penal Days', though shorn of its final conciliatory verse, declaring such times long gone, and in the case of the Christian Brothers' influential *Irish History*

Reader, there were some changes toughening the message. The prototype popular Irish history A. M. Sullivan's *Story of Ireland* (1867) sees no need to explain the Penal Laws, except through a series of shock-horror pronouncements. 'It was now there fell upon Ireland that night of deepest horror—that agony the most awful, the most prolonged, of any recorded on the blotted page of human suffering.'[7] Mrs Stephen Gwynn's hugely popular *Stories from Irish History* (1904) was a masterpiece of compression. Of the Penal Laws she wrote:

> This is such a sad chapter that I shall make it a short one. It is the story of wrong and cruelty and persecution . . . All the articles of the treaty [of Limerick[8]] were broken. Laws were made against the Catholics. No Catholic could sit in Parliament, nor be a lawyer, a doctor, or a soldier. No Catholic might teach in a school . . . All bishops and monks were banished, and Mass could not be said except by a very few priests who had been registered by government, and when they died the government hoped that there would be no more priests at all, as no bishops would be allowed to ordain them. But in spite of danger, the priests continued to risk their lives among their people, ministering the sacraments on hill-sides and in secret glens; for there was a price on the head of every priest . . .
> Unhappy Ireland lay in weakness and despair.[9]

These little books are very easy to read, mixing verse, adventure tales, and simple pictures. They were extraordinarily successful—Sullivan's quickly selling 50,000 and going through many editions—and decisively established for the opinion formers of the Irish cultural revival that streamlined history of Ireland as that of the suffering Catholic nation. The people's suffering had been subsumed into that of the Church.

Though hardly impartial, nevertheless some of the criticisms of these children's books by the Belfast evangelical minister the Revd William Corkey, mentioned earlier, are well founded. They do present Protestantism as the outcome of Henry VIII's adultery and greed and suggest that any bloodshed in the past, including that of 1641, was alone shed by the English and the Protestants. They also identify the Catholic Church throughout as part of the people's struggle and identity. Corkey pays particular attention to their treatment of the Penal Laws: 'When sedition-mongers wish to stir up rebellion and hatred against the British connection they always rehearse in detail the Penal Laws, and at the same time take great care not to hint at any reason as to why these laws were introduced.' He lists them and agrees that they sound severe. But, he argues, they were the result of rebellion, they were not as harsh as similar laws against Protestants in Catholic countries, and they were largely inoperative. 'Irish children are led to believe that these laws were enacted by the English Parliament out of pure cruelty and malice against the unoffending Roman Catholics.' Corkey singles out from these books the most emotive image of their account of the Penal Laws: the priest's blood being shed at the mass-rock. 'We have not found the history which gives a record of these murders', yet such accounts serve to strengthen 'the antagonism of Irish Roman Catholics against Protestant England'.[10]

From the earliest days of the Reformation, Protestant and Catholic polemicists alike were compiling vivid martyrologies.[11] In Catholic ones there is a pervasive folklore of priests being killed at the mass-rocks, page after page in a popular devotional work of 1919 taking the reader around the country, identifying mass-rocks and suggesting massacre at each:

Picture to yourself the tragedy enacted there . . . See the start of the terror . . . Hear the last absolution of the priest, the gasping moans of the dying. Mark the inrush of the persecutors . . . the flash of the musket, the priest lying across the stone . . . an imperishable monument, telling of Ireland's sorrow and of Ireland's glory! For thou, O holy Rock of the Mass, art the Calvary of Ireland![12]

So pervasive was the mass-rock in the image of past persecution that Pope John Paul II spoke of it during his 1979 visit to Ireland, and it was one of the first images to appear in republican areas of Belfast as the supposedly less threatening cultural wall murals began to replace militaristic ones after the ceasefires of the 1990s. It shows the priest at the mass-rock in the snow with the military closing in, and is undoubtedly a depiction of the same scene in William Carleton's *Willy Reilly and his Dear Colleen Bawn* (1855), the most popular novel of the nineteenth century.

Based in Monaghan, it is set in the early years of the eighteenth century when the laws against priests *were* being enforced. It tells the story of an apparently doomed romance between a member of an old Catholic Gaelic family (Willy Reilly) and a beautiful Protestant heiress, and along the way has vivid portrayals of fugitive bishops, hunted priests, and wronged Gaels. The villains include the ascendancy politician using the Penal Laws for personal gain, the nasty priest-catcher Captain Smellpriest, and the turncoat Gael betraying the hero. The heroes include sympathetic Protestants who dislike the Penal Laws and hold Catholic property in trust. It is a Victorian melodrama with a happy ending and all the villains meet their just ends. Whether or not this tradition of murder at the mass-rock was already in existence, Carleton's writings are a good example of fiction interacting with popular folklore.[13] Sullivan's *Story of Ireland* also has the priest at the mass-rock as the representative image of penal times: and 'in instances not a few ... the blood of the murdered priest wetted the altar stone'.[14]

However, although there are strong traditions of a priest being killed at a mass-rock in Donegal, the folklore is largely unproven, some executions of priests which did happen in earlier centuries being subsumed into the story of penal times. The main reason for the prevalence of mass-rocks was poverty rather than persecution: the people simply could not afford to build mass-houses, and the Presbyterians (at least until the economic take-off in the latter decades of the eighteenth century) were also having difficulty financing the construction of meeting houses. This was particularly the case in Ulster. Carleton recalled of his south Ulster childhood that 'there was nothing in existence for the Catholics for the worship of God except the mere altar, covered with a little open roof to protect the priest from rain', and such mass-rocks figure prominently in his stories.[15] From as early as the 1720s, however, mass-houses began to replace the open-air structures and were frequently built on land donated by Protestant landlords.[16]

Part of the Catholic Church revival of the late nineteenth century was the suppression of rowdy religious festivals and the promotion of church-regulated ones. Foremost among those preserved were the religious processions to local mass-rocks. This was the priest and the community as one against the alien oppressor, Church and nation's suffering one and the same. In the twentieth century after independence, major events such as the 1929 centenary of Catholic Emancipation or the 1932 Eucharistic Congress saw the streets of towns in the Free State taken over for weeks on end by Catholic religious services and celebrations. The speeches and reports in the nationalist press during the 1929 centenary celebrations told of the particular spirituality and endurance of Irish Catholicism: 'nowhere was the attack so severe and prolonged as in Ireland' and the Irish should be proud 'that their race was deemed worthy to suffer with Christ'. Newspaper headlines told of 'The Darkest Days of Irish History: Laws that Failed to Crush the Ancient Faith', 'Days of Terror', 'What Ireland Suffered for the Faith. The Days of Tyranny', Ireland having endured 'Centuries of Blood and Tears' in 'The Struggle for the Faith' now a 'World Example Today'.

A formal series of lectures delivered at the Mansion House in Dawson Street, Dublin, and relayed by speakers to huge crowds outside, were again dominated by themes of the Penal Laws and the association of Catholicism with Irishness. The message was that 'the ultimate purpose of the Penal Laws was to destroy the life of the Irish nation in its entirety'. But 'the Irish people have survived and once again have power to shape the destinies of this nation'. Significantly, the climax of the 1929 commemoration— high mass in Phoenix Park—used the sacred vessels of Bishop Oliver Plunkett, executed in 1681, and Cardinal Paul Cullen, the cleric most credited with shaping the modern Catholic Church. The 'Church suffering' was now 'the Church triumphant', and in these years it became fashionable to proclaim the success of the Catholic nation by associating the most unlikely things with the persecution of the past. Nor was the opportunity missed to remind Protestants that they were held responsible. The partition of Ireland had shown that the 'methods' used by the descendants of 'the minority who fashioned so skilfully the unjust laws of oppression . . . have never changed', the Dominican priest the Revd A. M. Crofts told the Mansion House gathering. The Bishop of Ardagh (where he remained until 1966), the Revd Dr James Joseph Mac-Namee, claimed that Irish Catholics had resisted every material inducement 'to abandon their fathers' faith and embrace that of its pampered rival on the high road to worldly wealth and prosperity'. He made the by now ritual reference to the good Protestants of the past, Grattan, Burke, and Tone, distinguishing them from the 'odious ascendancy', and he hoped one day Protestants would be restored to 'Christ's true Church'.[17]

Through suffering and endurance Irish Catholicism was portrayed as having attained a special purity. 'Surely then, it is a miracle of the Providence of God,' states the Christian Brothers'

1. Martyn Turner, 'Bloody Zero Tolerance'. Cartoon, *Irish Times*, 15 March 1997. Reproduced in Martyn Turner, *Brace Yourself, Bridge It! A Guide to Irish Political Relationships 1996–1998* (Belfast, 1998).

"*Oh dear, not the **Irish** Christians again!*"

2. 'Oh dear, not the *Irish* Christians again!' Cartoon, *Punch*, 12 January 1977.

3. Cú Chullainn, republican memorial, City Cemetery, Brandywell, Derry.

4. Republican mural of Robert Emmet defaced by ultra-Protestant graffiti, Ardoyne, Belfast.

5. 'Irish Out'. Loyalist mural, Rathcoole, Newtownabbey, just outside Belfast.

THE NEW PAPAL NUNCIO.

Balfour, who has got on a suit which is kept in the Castle for Chief Secretaries to wear on certain occasions, to Erin -
"Ha! Ha! See what I have got over from Rome. Now, I think you will give me up that paper?"
Erin.—**NEVER** !!! That document in your hand was obtained by fraud and misrepresentation, and has therefore no moral force."
Balfour,—"Ho!! Ho!! Then you mean to split with Rome?"
Erin.—**"NEVER**!!! I have always been a faithful child of the Church. and will ever remain so, but I mean to manage my own
domestic affairs, as everyone else does."

6. Balfour posing as papal nuncio. Cartoon, *Weekly Freeman,*
5 May 1888.

7. 'One faith, one crown'. Loyalist mural, Oak Street, off Donegall Pass, Belfast.

8. Orange banner (Magheragall Lodge) commemorating the Oxford martyrs Latimer and Ridley.

9. 'The Irish Massacre of 1641'. Engraving, *Foxe's Book of Martyrs* (1785 edition).

10. 'The persecution of the Protestant people by the Church of Rome 1600. The ethnic cleansing still goes on today'. Loyalist mural, Hopewell Crescent, Shankill Rd., Belfast.

11. 'Mick manufacturing the orphans'. Cartoon, *The Shamrock*, 23 February 1867.

12. 'The Covenanters'. Engraving, J. A. Wylie, *A History of Protestantism* (1878).

13. Loyalist stereotypes of Catholics. Cartoons, *The Orange Cross*, nos. 18, Dec. 1972, 30, July 1973, and 44, Jan. 1974.

14. 'The Mass Rock'. Republican mural, Ardoyne, north Belfast.

15. 'The Rescue: An Episode from the Penal Days'. Engraving, *Weekly Freeman*, 17 March 1906.

16. Mass being said on O'Connell Bridge during the Centenary of Catholic Emancipation 1929, *Irish Independent Eucharistic Congress Souvenir Number*, June 1932.

17. 'The Flight of the Earls'. Republican mural, Ardoyne, north Belfast.

" *And, were Magee alive to-day . . . he might truly exclaim as he beheld the golden column of priest-money rearing its shameless yellow crest, &c.*" (p. 148).

18. 'Priests and People'. Frontispiece to Michael J. F. McCarthy's *Priests and People in Ireland* (1902).

19. Belfast celebrations for the Eucharistic Congress, 1932.

20. Battle trophies, St Nicholas's Cathedral, Galway, 1932. *The Genius of Father Browne*, ed. E. E. O'Donnell SJ (1991).

Irish History Reader, 'that after a hundred years of this unexampled persecution, the Irish people should have retained their faith as pure and inviolate as they received it from St. Patrick.'[18] In contrast to 'pagan England' Catholics were told, 'we kept the faith'—as I was reminded recently by an Irish-born academic in the United States, who thought in the paper I had just delivered that 'I had let the Protestants off too lightly', after 'what they had done to us'. The Penal Laws thus became the prime symbol of past suffering, underpinning an entire national culture of religious conformity, complacency, and resistance to criticism.[19]

The Penal Laws in Reality

The Penal Laws were passed between 1695 and 1756, with the most severe in a short period of political tension when the Protestant succession in England seemed anything but secure. Since James II's reign had shown that Protestants might experience a complete reversal of fortune if Catholics once again gained political power, the Penal Laws were designed to ensure this would not happen. Several times in the seventeenth century it had almost gone the other way, and a sense of insecurity about land title made the Irish parliament—dominated by Protestant landowners—far more anti-Catholic than the Protestant population at large. And since landed property was the key to political power in the early modern world, this was the main focus of the laws.

Under the Penal Laws, Catholics were prevented from purchasing land or acquiring leases longer than thirty-one years; Protestant heiresses lost their claim on marrying a Catholic; Catholic estates had to be divided among the male heirs, unless the eldest turned Protestant, in which case he became sole owner, even during the lifetime of the father; Catholics could not act as guardians to minors; a Protestant 'discoverer' could acquire the Catholic's share in any transaction if he could prove any infringement of the 'Popery Laws'. Indeed, such was the continuing fears of Catholics in power that the late eighteenth-century Acts relaxing the Penal Laws retained restrictions on Catholics acquiring property in parliamentary boroughs. Faced with the loss of their land, many remaining Catholic landowners conformed to the Established Church. So the idea that all Catholics chose poverty to retain the faith is false. Honoria McManus, wife of Oliver O'Hara of Bally-mena, County Antrim, raised her sons as Protestants, explaining that if she did not do so, 'she might as well make tailors or shoemakers of them as their prospects in life would be destroyed'.[20] After 1693 Catholics were effectively debarred from sitting in Parliament by the requirement of oaths against the Pope's deposing power and transubstantiation. But qualified Catholics could continue to sit in Parliament if they took oaths of allegiance and abjuration (renouncing the Stuart succession to the throne), until that right too was removed in 1728.[21] Other measures debarred them from local government, from the higher levels of the legal profession, and from Ireland's only university, Trinity College Dublin.

The kind of collusive trusts which figured in Carleton's *Willy Reilly* did exist. But since nearly a century passed before the laws affecting property were repealed, the descendants of the neigh-bourly Protestant who had held the land in trust—as the Magen-nises of County Down would discover—were not always willing to hand it back. A strong Catholic farmer class of 'middlemen', or prosperous tenant farmers, emerged outside Ulster. But the political system continued to privilege land*ownership*. A tiny handful of Catholic landowners (largely of English stock) remained. However, the top tier of Irish Catholic society was gone, giving substance to the belief that Catholics were an inferior breed. There was no real alternative to leadership by the clergy. And the lower-middle-class ethos of independent Ireland was the long-term consequence. In Ulster—which lost a Catholic elite much earlier and more completely than any other province—the situation was much worse and the ground has never been made up.

It was their impact on the Catholic Church and religious practice, however, which, as noted above, came to symbolize the Penal Laws, rather disguising the area in which they did most damage. For the first few decades of the eighteenth century the open practice of Catholicism was very difficult. Statutes banishing certain categories of clergy, including bishops, threatened its future, and there were some very nasty priest-catchers around, including the Spanish ex-priest John Garzia. But, contrary to the legend, there was no British government policy to outlaw Catholicism. The wording of legislation passed by an Irish parliament full of landowners, many of whose titles rested on confiscation, and the parliamentary records of their passage, were the basis for the histories of the nineteenth century. The most accomplished and admired by Catholic writers of such histories was that by the liberal Unionist W. E. H. Lecky, his Protestantism serving to emphasize further the bleakness of the Penal era, when a Protestant willing to admit as much was rare at that time.

Yet in the hierarchical society of eighteenth-century Europe, there was intense dislike by the Protestant governing elite for jumped-up Protestants (or Catholics for that matter) trying to pull down their social superiors. Those Catholics deemed 'gentry' (including the bishops) were tolerated provided they did not cause trouble. This, argues Ian McBride, was 'the unspoken bargain of the Penal Laws [which] required deference and subordination in return for de facto toleration'.[22] Church of Ireland bishops were often critical of the legislation, as was John Wesley, despite his anti-popery and experience of regular attacks by hostile Catholic crowds. 'Nor is it any wonder that those who are born Papists generally live and die such,' he wrote in his journal for August 1747, 'when the Protestants can find no better ways to convert them than Penal Laws and Acts of Parliament.'[23] There were parts of the country where the Penal Laws *were* utilized by a particularly bigoted element in Protestant society, notably in Munster. But the murdered-priest-at-the-mass-rock image which has come par excellence to represent the penal era has little basis in fact (at least as far as we know to date), though the prevalence of mass-rocks throughout the country made them places of local pilgrimage and sustained the folklore of the priest and people preserving the faith against persecution.[24]

After the upheavals of previous centuries, the wanton iconoclasm of the first stages of the Reformation, and the wars and destruction of the seventeenth century, all Churches, even the Church of Ireland, were in poor shape. In Gaelic areas in particular (where Catholic practices had not been Church-based) the lack of places of worship was particularly acute. Even so the eighteenth century saw the Catholic Church grow in strength, free from the kind of state interference which happened in Catholic European states (and indeed with the Church of Ireland itself). This traditionally hierarchical Church was quite different from that of the peasant one in later Catholic historiography, and its leaders spent much of the eighteenth century arguing its support for monarchical government, against the kind of anti-popery noted earlier, which claimed that Catholics could never be loyal to a Protestant regime. In fact they could, notwithstanding widespread popular Jacobitism, and there was considerable irritation with the papacy, which made it difficult to devise an adequate oath of loyalty. In continental Europe, where the Catholic Church was part and parcel of *ancien régime* elites, it was caught up in their collapse after the French Revolution. This did not happen in the Irish Catholic Church, one of the reasons for its growth thereafter as a popular institution.

We still know very little about the operation of the Penal Laws on the ground, and most historians—including myself—have argued that they were not as fierce in their application as the legend would suggest. Religious persecution was common throughout early modern Europe. Religion and statehood were inseparable, and those who did not conform to the state religion were deemed disloyal. After an initial period of persecution Catholic priests were generally left alone. When Methodists protested in Cork in 1749 at receiving less protection under 'a Protestant Government' than if they had been priests saying mass, the Mayor replied: 'The Priests are tolerated, but you are not.'[25] The few notorious cases of Catholics being executed usually involved issues other than religion. The primacy of the mass-rock–persecuted religion aspect of the Penal Laws in the national story has distracted from their real significance. For they *were* successful in their main aim: ensuring that political power and the landed property on which it was based remained Protestant.

It was not until the 1880s that Catholics returned fully to politics, after the 1884 Reform Act. In the penal era much Catholic talent and wealth had to go abroad—later identified by Protestant reformers as a real drain on the country—or into business and trade, where some became extremely wealthy. It was this wealthy Catholic middle class which sought to have that position recognized by some kind of return to political participation. This was the source of the campaign for Catholic emancipation, starting in the middle of the eighteenth century but not succeeding until 1829.

By excluding the rich Catholic from parliament, the pro-emancipist MP for Tyrone George Knox argued in 1793, you will simply cause him to ally with the needy and disaffected. We will admit him eventually, he predicted. 'But we shall withhold that admission so long, that at length we shall give without generosity what will be received without gratitude.'[26]

This was prophetic. Some, thwarted of reform, went on to become United Irish leaders. Others, under Daniel O'Connell, a leader who loathed the United Irishmen and their resort to violence, organized a vast Catholic campaign, threatening popular revolt and so scaring the life out of Protestant Ireland that, in Sean Connolly's words, emancipation was 'taken' in 1829 rather than 'given'.[27] Knox's statement also pinpointed a very important aspect of modern Catholic identity: it frequently transcended class. But this was not inevitable. In the eighteenth century the elite of Catholic society were of their class; the idea of a Catholic democracy was in the future. Catholic magnates like lords Gormanstown, Fingal, Trimleston, and Kenmare and the Catholic hierarchy disliked radical tendencies in the Catholic middle class. These in turn sought admission to the privileges attending membership of parliament, only to be dismayed when the 1793 Catholic Relief Act extended the vote to the Catholic forty-shilling freeholder (expected to vote according to the dictates of the landlord) but still excluded *them*. It remained a Protestant parliament until its dissolution with the Union in 1800, and Catholics were still excluded from the united parliament in London until 1829. Initially there was some resistance by the Church to O'Connell's transformation of the Catholic Association into a mass movement. Very quickly, however, the growing sectarian climate of the early nineteenth century and the real advantages perceived in raising funds for Catholic issues brought the clergy into O'Connell's campaign, and with that, the image of priest and people together in their struggle became a reality.

Given the strength of Protestant beliefs outlined earlier, however, it should not surprise that there was more than insecurity of land titles underlying the Penal Laws. There was, too, a belief in the superiority of Protestantism and Protestants' natural right to rule, which found its most strident expression in the further definition of 'Protestant ascendancy' at the time of the Catholic campaign in the 1790s. A concerted attack by the landlord-dominated Grand Juries assumed the general inferiority and disloyalty of Catholics, and chastised them for their ingratitude and lack of submissiveness. God had given victory to Protestant liberty over Popish tyranny a century before, they argued, and this was why there was an ascendancy of Protestants: 'A Protestant King of Ireland, A Protestant Parliament, A Protestant hierarchy, Protestant elections and Government, Benches of Justice and Army through all their branches Protestant, and the system supported by a connection with the Protestant realm of Britain.' So the key to understanding the Penal Laws is this: if Catholics were submissive, they were tolerated, and the few causes célèbres when they suffered usually involved 'insolence' and refusal to accept such a role, or, as Tone argued at the time, a Protestant ascendancy compelled even the wealthy Catholic to live 'in a state of inferiority to every little Protestant Squire'.[28]

As the Penal Laws were progressively repealed, a reluctant ascendancy tightened up the application of those remaining. Even after it became legal for Catholics to carry arms (1793), loyalists were claiming that attacks on Catholic homes in search of weapons were simply an enforcement of the Penal Laws. The municipal corporations—exclusively Protestant until the 1790s, and technically open to Catholics after the 1793 Catholic Relief

Act—became one of the battlegrounds. Previously moneyed Catholics had been happy to integrate with Protestants when they could, and in 1799 the Cork city authorities had made the Catholic Bishop of Cork, Dr Francis Moylan, a freeman of the city. But increasingly in the early nineteenth century Protestants resented signs of Catholics prospering and being allowed into those clubs and associations once the preserve of Protestants. Bishop Moylan's successor, John Murphy, was not accorded the same dignity.[29] Despite the now considerable wealth of some Catholics, exclusion from parliament made them ineligible for a range of offices which MPs could hold. They also had no official local consequence because of their continuing exclusion from the local offices which gave them such, and from the largely Protestant Yeomanry, which by 1810 accounted for 80,000 men, some 70 per cent being drawn from areas of largest Protestant concentration, notably Ulster and Leinster.[30]

Timing is everything, and from the late eighteenth century sectarian divisions were increasingly visible, even liberal Protestants who had supported the Catholic cause being frowned upon by the newly powerful Catholic emancipation movement. The radicals had actively courted every level of Catholic in the 1790s, and Catholics were given a taste of potential empowerment through sheer numbers. The vast popular power of the Catholic Church became clear in O'Connell's marshalling of its organizational network in the 1820s campaign. Why, asks the historian Jacqueline Hill, did the British government not establish some formal relationship with the Catholic Church, much as it had done in Canada in 1774, as a counter to the disloyalty of its Protestant colonists in the rest of North America? The point was also made by Godkin in 1867 when there was intense criticism of the established status of the minority Church of Ireland.

> Religion is too powerful an element in Ireland, and the Roman
> Catholic priesthood are too ambitious and sensitive ever to rest
> satisfied with the government which ignores their Church as a
> church; which holds diplomatic communion with the Sultan and
> outlaws the Pope; which endows with wealth and privilege the
> clergy of a small section of the community, and leaves the clergy
> of the majority to subsist upon the precarious...supplies of the
> voluntary system, requiring for its successful working the constant
> application of sectarian and factious stimulants, with the violent
> exaggeration of religious differences.[31]

The Irish Catholic hierarchy had been favourably disposed
towards the state in the late eighteenth century. But the occasion
passed, and the stridency of political Protestantism's resistance to
emancipation made the Catholic Church very resistant to state
interference from early in the next century.

Though the penal era was officially over with the grant of Catholic
Emancipation in 1829, and although this Act made Britain one of
the most religiously liberal states in Europe, the Penal Laws were far
from being a thing of the past. As with previous Catholic Relief
Acts, that of 1829 came burdened with new and old restrictions.
There was even a successful vote in parliament requiring O'Connell
to take the old Oath of Supremacy (since he had been elected before
the Emancipation Act), and he had to seek re-election.[32] Catholics
were barred from certain named offices, including the Irish Lord
Lieutenancy and offices in Dublin University and public schools.
Significantly, the language contains all the old obsessions about
popery. To hold any public office or sit in parliament, Catholics
were required to take a new oath—accepting the Protestant succession, the Established Church, and the existing property settlement,
and denying the temporal and deposing power of the Pope—all of
which continued to suggest that Catholics were potentially disloyal.

Public religious services and the use of ecclesiastical titles were forbidden, as was recruitment to the male religious orders. In fact, this was unenforceable and unnecessary, for the orders had never recovered from the papal bans of the late eighteenth century.[33] Examples of other Penal Laws remaining and being enforced included: the 1697 Act banishing ecclesiastics and regulars, old clauses continuing to be invoked up to 1865; the ban (until 1870) on Catholic clergy conducting mixed marriages, resulting in six convictions between 1820 and 1832;[34] the requirement of oaths of allegiance and abjuration and a declaration against transubstanti-ation for Catholics entering Trinity College Dublin (nor could they become scholars until 1854, or fellows until 1873);[35] and the con-tinued reluctance to appoint Catholics to municipal office (one of the concessions in the 1793 Act). As a result, fifty-six out of the sixty corporations were still exclusively Protestant by 1836, which meant that local patronage was also denied them. Prior to the Local Government (Ireland) Act of 1898, local government had been dominated by the Protestant elite for over two centuries.

There were, then, quite sufficient grounds for Catholics to be resentful, even if the image of the persecuted Church is exagger-ated. In a series of writings in the early 1800s, William Parnell, Charles Stewart Parnell's grandfather, referred to the many dis-abilities against Catholics which remained. 'As long as the Cath-olics are treated as a subservient sect,' argued Parnell, 'the recollection of former injuries will have almost as great an effect as the suffering for actual grievances . . . grievances ought never to be removed by halves' for it highlights those remaining, which then become 'insults'.[36] Although good-neighbourliness prevailed between the religious communities at local level, there were com-munal stories of insults and bad treatment handed down the generations, which were not spoken of in mixed religious company. Even one of the most publicly successful of Irish Catholics, Thomas Moore, carried the scars and resentments.

In Carleton's novel, Squire Folliard, the Colleen Bawn's father, is good-hearted, but weak-willed and impressionable. His speech is peppered with anti-popish statements and he is ready to believe the worst of Catholics, even though he employs and treats well a largely Catholic workforce. Eighteenth- and nineteenth-century travel accounts have many similar stories from real life, though, as a bemused Arthur Young commented, those making such statements were often one and the same as those who assisted in the building of mass-houses.[37] 'The popishers have only got liberty to clatter their beads in public,' Mrs Smellpriest tells her priest-catcher husband in *Willy Reilly*, 'but not to marry a Popisher to a Protestanter.' Carleton was here clearly echoing the 1796 United Irish satire *Billy Bluff and Squire Firebrand*, which remained phenomenally popular in the nineteenth century. 'O what a happy world we had,' sputters the bigoted Squire Firebrand, when 'Catholics thought nothing but just getting leave to live.' The use of the term 'Catholic' was new. 'Papist' and 'popery' would have been the norm and they remain terms of insult in modern Ulster. In Art MacCooey's *c.*1770 bilingual poem 'Tagra an dá Theampall' ('The Argument of the Two Churches') the English-speaking Protestant Church taunts the ruined Irish-speaking Catholic one:

> You silly old dame, I would have you forsake
> your ignorant papist notions,
> for all your sliocht Gael [seed] are declining away
> from popery's vain devotion.

Under the Penal Laws the process of converting (conforming) to the established religion was demeaning and one is left with the impression that those who converted were not made welcome.

The potential convert was required to recant 'the errors of Rome' publicly, before the Church of Ireland clergyman and congregation at Sunday service. The convert's name appeared in the press; large, often hostile crowds would gather, and the press was full of incidents of insults and physical attacks. Land conformism is not disparaged in the Irish-language poetry of the eighteenth century, though poets and priests conforming are.[38] But such was the later distaste of Catholics converting to Protestantism that the Irish Manuscript Commission in the 1970s was very reluctant to publish the so-called 'Convert Rolls' from the eighteenth century.[39]

The Loss of the Land

Far more important than religious penalization, then, was the destruction of the top tier of Catholic society in the seventeenth century and the political, social, and economic consequences which flowed from that. The Penal Laws completed the virtual destruction of a Catholic landowning class which had begun the previous century. A 1921 French novel set in 1858 in Salt Lake City has Pastor Gwinett assessing the marital value of an Irish Catholic widow. What about the castle in Kildare, he asks. The term 'castle', she responds, is something of an exaggeration. It is rather a large property, a wing of which has been burnt down by Cromwell's soldiers and which has never been rebuilt, 'as much from lack of funds as from a desire to maintain the hate and the memory'. At this the pastor marvels: 'That country does have a singular way of managing property.'[40] Anyone familiar with rural society in Ireland will recognize this frame of mind, local resentments about dispossession stretching back many centuries.

English plantations of new landowners and settlers happened after most of the conflicts in the sixteenth and seventeenth centuries.

They particularly affected Munster and Ulster, with smaller ventures in north Wexford, Laois, Offaly, Leitrim, and Longford. The belief that the Catholic population was generally dispossessed by English and Scottish Protestants was a widely held one, and in the land purchase schemes of the late nineteenth–early twentieth centuries, not a few Irish Catholics considered that they were simply buying back land that was rightfully theirs in the first place. The terms 'settler' or 'planter' and 'native Irish', when referring to Protestants and Catholics respectively, can still be heard in Ireland today. This belief lies behind the attacks on Protestant property in successive IRA campaigns and fed into a deep sense of insecurity in Protestant psyche. This thirst of the landless bequeathed impossible expectations to the new Irish state after 1921, and when in 1940 the Minister for Industry and Commerce, Sean MacEntee, criticized this as the cause of the stagnation of Irish farming, he found himself denounced as 'an upholder of British imperialism'.[41]

A remarkable feature of the Irish landscape is the prevalence of tiny fields. Far from being a leftover from Gaelic times, however, this is something very modern, the creation of a peasant proprietorship from British land legislation prior to independence. It is also a symptom of that fiercely proprietary instinct of the small farmer, often based on folk history of ancestral dispossession. This needs some explanation, because in the vast majority of cases their ancestors were not actually dispossessed. Gaelic society was highly elitist and had a large unfree element. Technically the only lands actually owned were those of the particular clan of the Gaelic lord, his officials, soldiers, and learned men, including the ecclesiastics. However, 'kinlands' as distinct from 'individual' lands were subject to wider considerations. There were also a significant number of declining clans who claimed similar rights and a long-standing identification of certain families with certain territories. It was not quite the same as ownership, but certainly created a base for the later belief in widespread dispossession.

What actually happened was this: in the last part of the Gaelic era, society had turned increasingly militaristic as overlords increased their territory and power and made agreements with Tudor monarchs. These effectively turned them into feudal lords over lands to which they would have had no right under the Gaelic system. When they resisted the monarch, their lands were declared forfeit. Hence, when later Protestant propagandists claimed that Catholics had lost their lands because of treason, they were technically correct, at least in terms of the Gaelic overlords. Quite a number of Gaelic families threatened by such aggrandizement welcomed the downfall of the overlords and benefited from the secure title which English common law gave them. The clans of Cavan, bordering the Anglicized Pale for instance, had long learnt to manipulate English laws. As the details of the Ulster plantation were being worked out on the ground, they employed a Pale lawyer to argue that they held their lands in freehold, which their chiefs had no rights to forfeit.[42]

They were, however, soon exposed to Protestant adventurers attuned to working a money economy. They found themselves hostage to mortgages, and their lands became forfeit when they could not pay. In their loss, sharp practice was also a factor. Catholic Anglo-Normans–Old English also lost land, while Gaelic Old Irish who became Protestant retained theirs and were often just as exploitative as the newcomers. Hence it is somewhat inaccurate to identify the dispossessed with the Gael, even though to do so with Catholics is valid enough.

Ireland was underpopulated in the sixteenth and seventeenth centuries, and it was probably inevitable that settlers would have come from Britain, regardless of the religious and political upheavals. Indeed some Catholic lords were already importing British settlers, even without enforced plantations.[43] There were land confiscations after every upheaval in the sixteenth and seventeenth centuries, and in most of these Catholics were on the losing side. This, combined with land conformism to the established religion under the eighteenth-century Penal Laws, had reduced the profitable land in Catholic ownership from 90 per cent at the beginning of the seventeenth century to 5 per cent by 1778 and none in Ulster, where the last significant Catholic landowner conformed in the 1720s. It has been estimated that by the end of the seventeenth century Ireland was owned by around 5,000 families, almost exclusively members of the Established Church.[44] These comprised the Protestant 'nation' described earlier, and at a time when landed property was the base of power, they did not see the ambiguity of their position in governing a largely Catholic populace. The Catholics had rebelled; Protestants as loyal were entitled to the benefits.[45] In Ulster the change was particularly dramatic; the flight and subsequent outlawry of the main Gaelic lords in 1607 permitted James I's government to declare six counties confiscate, and a scheme whereby English and Scottish Protestant settlers were 'planted' was implemented.

This is a very simplified version of what happened in the Ulster plantation, and at the outset 'loyal' Catholics were not removed, though often resettled in different areas. But it provided the basis for the transformation of the religious demography of the province, which by 1732 had become, and was to remain, the most Protestant in the country. Before the plantation had settled down, Ireland was caught up in the religious wars of seventeenth-century Europe. Huge numbers died in warfare, plague, and famine (an estimated 112,000 of English and 504,000 of Irish extraction in a population of just over 2 million). Cromwell's massacres in Drogheda and Wexford, his expulsion of Catholic priests, and his ultimate solution for the Irish problem—sending all Catholic rebels west of the Shannon, thereby liberating a further 50 per cent of Irish land for Protestant settlement—came to symbolize the reality of English policy in Ireland, even if his policies did not work out on the ground. Lloyd George was exasperated in 1921 when the Irish delegates kept interrupting the treaty negotiations with reminders of Cromwell.[46] Indeed the British Dominions Secretary, Malcolm MacDonald, traced improving relations with de Valera by the fact that in their four-hour talk in 1936 he had not mentioned Oliver Cromwell once.[47]

However much we historians might show that a powerful layer of Catholics remained after such confiscations, or that the majority of people in Europe would have been leaseholders rather than outright owners of property, this does not change the stark reality that by the eighteenth century property, like power, was Protestant and the implications and resentments remain, even today.[48] There is not one Catholic landowner in the Clogher valley, an SDLP councillor told the gathering at the 2004 Carleton Summer School—a statement which Protestants in the audience accepted as accurate. 'Plantation was a monstrous crime against the Irish people!' exclaimed another nationalist representative at an Opsahl Commission public hearing in 1993, and he likened Unionist attitudes to the rest of Ireland to the siege-like requirements that the seventeenth-century planters build defensive walls and fortifications.[49]

Catholic Ireland still mourns the loss of its Gaelic aristocracy and Catholic landed class, a trend surely unusual in modern democracies. Behind the romanticization is the sense of a loss of status and the perpetuation of the new economic reality of low status and lack of power. There can be no doubting the sense of resentment and the belief that the loss of status then permitted those who took the land to treat Catholics as an inferior breed.

In Carleton's work most Protestants do not like the Penal Laws and the Catholics are largely law-abiding. But the opportunity which the laws provided for petty persecutors was real enough and there would have been more incidents in Ulster than elsewhere. Dervla Murphy, in what is still the most perceptive account of the issues underpinning the Northern Ireland Troubles, *A Place Apart* (1978), tells of an evening in a republican west Belfast shebeen:

> a man of about fifty, poorly dressed...began to air all the old obsessions...'I could tell you where the land that was ours is, away below in the Co. Down—and rich planters gettin' fatter on it every day and talkin' all the time about the lazy Taigs who wouldn't work for a livin' but go drinkin' on the dole!'...It was... impossible to unhook Gerry from the past; he seemed to need his grievance, to have built his whole personality around it...so much resentment—generations of resentment, forming the very marrow of his soul.

In this chapter I have been looking largely at Catholics' sense of victimhood, where it came from, and how it developed into a specifically Catholic reading of history in which the Catholic is always the underdog and present grievances are sustained by the memory of past ones. 'Even in the darkest days, the hopes of our ancestors were sustained by their strong spiritual values. As we look back today on that long chapter of religious and political oppression...we feel a deep humility...a quiet pride in their stubborn dignity. This would not have been possible without the Church.' So claimed the Irish Minister for Foreign Affairs, Peter Barry, in 1985.[50] The Penal Laws lie at the heart of Ireland's national origin-myth, shorthand for that kind of reductive reading which portrayed Ireland as the 'most distressful country' in the world, persecuted and penalized by a foreign Protestant power for the faith, but steadfastly clinging to it. This produced a national spiritual catharsis whereby the assumed sufferings of our ancestors gave a unique and superior quality to Irish Catholicism. Persecution had made the Irish 'the most prayerful, spiritual-minded and religiously inclined people on the face of God's fair and beautiful earth'.[51] In the 'ourselves alone' reading it could also become an excuse for doing nothing. Hubert Butler noted this when he attended the League of Nations 1939 conference on the plight of the German Jews. All the nations attending were guilty of doing nothing, but he was particularly upset by Ireland's representatives, who explained such inaction with the comment 'Didn't we suffer like this in the Penal Days and nobody came to our help.' It was hardly a valid analogy.[52]

Marcus Tanner, in his excellent book *Ireland's Holy Wars*, tells a representative story. It was the summer of 1691 in the west of Ireland. Catholics—once again in the ascendant under James II—were attempting to overturn the land and religious settlement of the past century, which had seen Protestantism triumph. The Catholic priest in Kilmurry, County Clare, was exacting his revenge on the ousted Protestant rector. Not that the Protestant minister feared for his life. The murderous sectarianism of the recent Northern Ireland Troubles, of the 1641 Ulster rising, or of the 1798 rebellion have not been the main feature of Ireland's 'Holy Wars', even if propagandists on all sides have sought to depict them as such. No, the priest was rather determined to turn the tables on the rector, exacting tithes and demanding deference much as the other had done and was soon to do again after the victory of William of Orange. It is a story encapsulating what the author returns to time and time again:

The representatives of the two great religious communities of Ireland are shown as bodies that lack charity towards each other. There is intimacy here, but no affection, or even respect...The gloating priest of Kilmurry was replaced [after William's victory] by the triumphalist vicar. Ireland returned to the familiar regime of victorious but nervous Protestants taking a high hand over bitter, humiliated Catholics.[53]

7

The Poor are Always with us; the Poor are Always Catholic

I noticed in the political Irishmen a strain of continuous apology for their existence and a desire . . . to prove that they might stand unabashed before the great English, if the latter had not treated Ireland so scurvily. This got on my nerves, for I saw no necessity for this 'God-help-us' spirit.

(D. P. Moran, *The Leader*, 8 Sept. 1900[1])

Independent Ireland's predominantly Catholic culture was frequently blamed for its economic underdevelopment before the 'Celtic Tiger' of the 1990s. Certainly there is some justice in the argument that a national narrative based on victimhood and persecution scarcely encourages renewal or self-criticism. Protestant identity had its own narrative of victimhood, but with one major difference: it did not see poverty as a key element. Quite the contrary, those who were poor were still led to believe that they were better-off than Catholics. The Queen's University academic Edith Devlin, recalling her poor Protestant upbringing in 1930s Dublin, tells of her Ulster father's contempt for Catholics. He instilled in his children the image of Catholics as the unthinking herd taught by their Church to accept adversity as the will of God and therefore disinclined to do anything about it. 'We might all be

poor but the difference between them and us was t...
slaves and we were not.'[2]

The Stereotype of the Slavish Catholic

This belief—that Roman Catholicism shackled the mind, inducing lack of spirit, indolence, and poverty—can be found at almost every level of Irish Protestant society in every century since the Reformation. It was a long-held belief by the Church of Ireland that it was the upholder of everything deemed good in the British constitution (the law, moderation between extremes, devotion to monarchy, polite culture). This belief in a 'natural' right to lead sometimes involved a desire to make Catholics more 'respectable', 'polite', 'decent' like themselves, rather than engaging with them as they were. The popular eighteenth-century rhyme 'St Patrick was a gentleman; he came from decent people' identified the national saint with social values which were Protestant.[3] George Miller, Wolfe Tone's old college friend, Trinity College fellow, and now ultra-conservative Church of Ireland clergyman, argued in his *Lectures on the Philosophy of Modern History* (1816–28) that the Penal Laws, by securing the Protestant interest, had been necessary for Ireland to enjoy its current prosperity.[4] This was a variation on that recurrent argument made by Church of Ireland clergy in the eighteenth century: papists might establish their religion by bringing back the Stuarts, but they would lose their civil liberties and properties under an arbitrary government.[5]

The self-declared intellectual elitism of Presbyterianism made such beliefs particularly pervasive in Ulster, and it found plenty of examples to feed its prejudice since Ulster's Catholics were the poorest in Ireland, their loss of a landed elite more complete than elsewhere. Even William Drennan—United Irishman and supporter of Catholic emancipation—gave voice to such attitudes. He spoke of Catholics' 'milk and water spirit'; even their gentry retain 'the brogue in the face' and 'smack...of the bog-trotter'.[6] In the eighteenth century surviving Catholic gentry identified more with the Protestant gentry than with the Catholic poor, and if they still had wealth they were reluctantly accepted by Protestant society. But in general the terms: 'Catholic noble' or 'Protestant pauper' were oxymorons, the latter category, as Toby Barnard has shown in his studies of early modern Ireland, tending to be merged with 'abstract popery'.[7]

Evangelicalism was encouraged (though not universally so) by some landed Protestants as a means of bringing civilization to 'poor wicked Ireland', as Selina, Countess of Huntingdon, referred to it.[8] Examples of genuine Protestant philanthropy can be found in every age and are often overlooked. Even so, the instinctive belief in the superiority of Protestant social values is evident even in the most apparently benevolent and liberal of Protestant commentators, from Henry Grattan and Wolfe Tone through to Terence O'Neill. With such condescension went the expectation of deference. It was resentment at such expectations—and even more so at their own social leaders' acceptance of such—which sent many middle-class Catholics into the United Irishmen in the 1790s. This is a frequent theme in George Birmingham's writings. In *The Seething Pot* Lady Clonfert is introducing embroidery to the local girls:

> I hope by degrees to teach them habits of industry and self-reliance...
> At present they are deplorably indolent; and as for the state of the
> houses, they are simply shocking. I wish I could import some Eng-
> lishwomen for a few months just to show them what cleanness
> means...Do you know...I was trying to explain to a woman the
> other day that she ought *sometimes* to wash her children's faces, and

what do you think she said to me? 'Saving your ladyship's presence, so long as they are clean enough to be healthy and dirty enough to be happy, and don't be cutting and burning themselves, I'll rest content.'[9]

It was, of course, the stereotype of what the English and the Protestants were expected to think about the Catholic Irish and is presented as such by Birmingham—the hero of the book thinking that Lady Clonfert was speaking as if quoting something she had read, her daughter and husband mocking her for her views. As the Revd James Owen Hannay (Birmingham) was to discover, however, any kind of social observation by a Protestant could all too easily be read as patronizing. The parish priest of Westport thought Hannay's writings had depicted him as 'less than a gentleman' and mounted a bitter and successful campaign against him. Hannay had not been sufficiently alive to the acute sensitivities involved in the apparent Protestant condescension of which he was accused. And this Belfast man who had spent all his career in parishes in the South was denounced in the *Mayo News* as 'a superior kind of gentleman' with 'his electroplated English accent and his bitter sectarian bitterness'.[10]

This resentment at being seen as inferior has infused Catholic consciousness for centuries. It was a major factor in the riots at the Abbey Theatre in the early 1900s against 'Protestant' playwrights such as Yeats and Synge. Moran likened the Abbey to 'some prayer meeting of the foreign element in Ireland'. This was 'England's faithful garrison' presenting plays about 'papishgoms' and stammering peasants and never about their own.[11] James Joyce was one of those students at the Catholic University College Dublin who devoured Moran's writings; and while he was out of sympathy with the Catholic cultural nationalism of the day, he too commented acidly on the Protestant monopoly on respectability, wealth, and status. In his writings Protestants are 'quality'; they speak with English accents and talk down to Catholics, even if their economic superiors. In *A Portrait of the Artist as a Young Man*, Stephen tells a flower-seller in Grafton Street that he has no money and moves on quickly to spare himself the indignity of a Trinity student or an English tourist purchasing the bouquet. This 'moment of discouraged poverty' becomes one of real bitterness. Joyce was far more critical of Irish Catholics. However, he remained a cultural Catholic in his attitudes towards Protestants.[12]

Lower-class Protestants shared their betters' contempt for Catholics and expected, and usually received, special treatment from their social superiors. Ascendancy politicians, the Orange Order, and later Unionists were able to play on this perceived cross-class special relationship at times of constitutional crisis. Indeed, much of the bitterness behind loyalist activities today in Northern Ireland is a perception of Catholics prospering while they are not.[13] This sense of cross-class Protestant cohesion against a common enemy also lay behind the Orange Order and the attacks on civil rights marchers in the lead-up to the recent Troubles. The sight of so many Catholic university students on civil rights marches in late 1960s Northern Ireland (when progress through education was not a part of working-class Protestant thinking), or the 1990s rise of a new consumerist Catholic middle class, were profoundly unsettling to this mindset.

The Counter Stereotype: The Virtuous Catholic Poor

In contrast, Catholic culture often privileged the poor and was just as critical of upwardly mobile Catholics. However, this was quite a late development, and the process whereby this informed the culture of a nation has been inadequately researched. There is a good understanding of the coexistence of lower-middle-class snobbery with a culture of the virtuous poor in modern Irish Catholicism. In the late eighteenth century, however, such snobbery was on quite a different level. This was a time—the Penal Laws notwithstanding—that the Catholic hierarchy still sought to enter the establishment and taught loyalty to the state. Eighteenth-century Catholic bishops' wills show a sense of being part of the social elite.[14] The pastorals issued by the Catholic bishops during the 1798 rebellion take a class line: 'the poor will still be poor, under every form of government', so the French Revolution's notions of equality were quite unrealistic and dangerous. 'How can there be cultivation, where there are no tillers? And where shall you find tillers, if all become gentlemen? Rank and property must go hand in hand.' Inequality, in other words, was part of the natural order.[15]

By the later nineteenth century such deference had gone and the social realities of a largely poor community were being represented as virtuous. In some priestly writings of the turn of the nineteenth–twentieth centuries, there is a belief not only that Catholicism is a religion of the poor, but that social progress and education might endanger its essential characteristics and 'might make them less docile to the teachings of the church, and possibly less vivid and simple their wonderful faith'.[16] Canon Sheehan takes it for granted that all landlords were Protestants, which was far from being the case. 'Our religion you must know is the religion of the kitchen, the poorhouse', he writes in his 1911 *The Intellectuals*, and he laments the current 'scramble for land and respectability' (pursuant to the Land Acts) as leading to degeneracy, where poverty had bred 'patience and resignation'. In words which prefigure similar criticisms of the effects of the 1990s 'Celtic Tiger' on the Irish national character, he writes:

> So long as there was a Cromwellian landlord to be fought and
> conquered, there remained before the eyes of the people some
> image of the country. Now the fight is over; they are sinking
> down into the abject and awful condition of the French peasant,
> who doesn't care for king or country; and only asks: Who is going to
> reduce the rates?[17]

Such sanctification of poverty and endurance would feed into
independent Ireland's inadequate welfare policies and its reluctance to interfere with Catholic charities. This is witheringly
exposed in Frank McCourt's *Angela's Ashes* (2001), and there is
additional anecdotal evidence to uphold his picture of the shame
the Catholic poor felt at receiving charity from the better-off who
organized Catholic charities.[18]

In fact, the idea of the downtrodden Irish Catholic had some
basis in reality, and its elevation to national symbol was part of the
same process whereby traits long denounced by the English or
the Protestants or both were presented as peculiarly noble. Thus,
the celebration of peasant culture and the association of Catholicism with Irishness became part of the Gaelic revival (and through
it the ethos of the Irish state). It was, as Roy Foster has commented,
'the logical response to generations of English and Anglo-Irish
condescension towards "priest-ridden", "backward" Ireland'.[19]
That condescension had a lengthy lineage. The extremely negative
views of the Irish in the works of the twelfth-century Giraldus
Cambrensis, justifying the conquest of Ireland, inspired a trend
in English writings about Ireland and equally provoked Irish
rebuttals in the form of the island of saints and scholars counter-
myth. This is pre-eminently and most influentially expounded in
Geoffrey Keating's 1634 *History of Ireland*: 'Every one of the new
Galls [the English] who writes on Ireland writes . . . in imitation of
Cambrensis . . . who is the bull of the herd for them writing the

false history of Ireland.'[20] Although often quite complimentary, Giraldus' message was that their love of freedom has made the Irish libertine, lazy, and deceitful. It starts at birth when, contrary to practice in England, nature is left to take its course and Irish infants are not swaddled, nor frequent hot water used to lengthen their limbs, raise their noses, or press down their faces. They preferred wandering, 'primitive', pastoral ways, which he thought made them lazy and lacking in ambition, and all of this was reflected in their 'barbarous' loose dress and long hair. The Irish, he concludes, were 'a filthy people, wallowing in vice'.[21]

This created the standard English stereotype of the Irish which after the Reformation was affixed to Irish Catholics, not least by Edmund Spenser. Indeed, although the Elizabethan period witnessed a more modern and sceptical writing of history generally, Tudor writers on Ireland were prepared to believe just about anything about Ireland's barbarity, so influential had been Cambrensis.[22] Spenser set the agenda in arguing that the Irish were inherently barbarous and it was England's historic mission to establish civility and true religion through conquest. Spenser also put forward an argument which would be used to justify future penalization: 'the evil which is of itself evil will never become good'. He continued Giraldus Cambrensis' attack on Irish people's very manner of living, in 'boolies' (temporary abodes), their thick hair and mantles, their lurking in glens and fastnesses, their homes 'rather swine-styes than houses . . . a beastly manner of life . . . living together with his beast in one house'.[23] The very shape of the landscape, with its prevalent bogland and forests, was attributed to national indolence, and draining, clearing, taming, and building became part of the Protestant civilizing mission to Ireland. The Cork Protestant exile in London Richard Cox, writing in the 1680s, claimed that the inferiority of the Irish was illustrated in their failure to build in brick and stone, their religion and depressed culture having accustomed them to dwell in 'cabins which are worse than hogstyes', and he hoped that enforced changes in building would lead the Irish to become 'neat and clean'. In this view buildings represented the perceived superiority of Protestant or English culture, and in modern times were viewed as alien by the Irish state and 'left to vanish unlamented'.[24] The quite substantial buildings which did exist in early modern Ireland were attributed to the Anglo-Normans, and acquiring them became a particular aim of the Church of Ireland, their loss adding a further grievance to Irish Catholic culture.

The nineteenth-century evangelical tradition of open-air preaching was particularly important in convincing the working-class Protestant that the prosperity of Ulster was conditional on its Protestantism and increasingly on its attachment to Britain and its empire. Underpinning this was the long-standing Protestant world-view in which Protestantism equalled prosperity and popery meant poverty. The influential Presbyterian cleric Henry Cooke said as much in 1836:

> Our Scottish forefathers were planted in the wildest and most barren portions of our lands...the most rude and lawless of the Provinces. Scottish industry has drained its bogs and cultivated its barren wastes, has filled its ports with shipping, substituted towns and cities for its hovels and clachans and given peace and good order to a land of confusion and blood.[25]

'If you set up a Parliament on College Green,' the Liberal Unionist MP T. W. Russell warned in 1912, 'the wealth, education, property and prosperity of Ulster will be handed over to a Parliament which will be elected by peasants dominated by priests, and they again will be dominated by the Roman Catholic Church.'[26] Home Rule would bring economic ruin, a belief apparently substantiated by the poor performance of the Irish economy after independence.[27]

The idea that one was economically stunted if Catholic and correspondingly advantaged if Protestant has had an extraordinary innings and was perpetuated via Macaulay's massively influential *History of England* (1849–61), still quoted by some Ulster Unionists. Macaulay combined popular Protestantism with the idea of an Anglo-Saxon race to argue that Ulster Protestants were superior to the 'aboriginal Roman Catholic Irish, who are considerably inferior in civilization'. Hence, the flourishing industry of Ulster was due to its British character.[28] Of course, the association of Protestantism and success was to find its chief guru in Max Weber and his invention of the idea of the 'Protestant ethic', whereby he traced modern capitalism to Calvinism. However, Irish Protestant self-perceptions of superiority scarcely needed further endorsement.

The authoritarianism and complacency of the twentieth-century Irish Catholic Church is indisputable. But to attribute the lower socio-economic status of Catholics vis-à-vis Protestants to religious culture is, argues D. H. Akenson, 'a confusion of association and causation'. In a detailed statistical analysis of the Irish around the world he systematically demolishes the idea of Catholic economic backwardness and instead shows how several centuries of being kept out of political and economic power has meant a lot of catching up has been necessary. In a devastating analysis he both demolishes the Weber–Protestant ethic industry in academic writing, as well as the counter-tendency in Irish American writing in particular to endorse the Catholic victim-reading of the past.[29]

References in some nationalist literature to the success of the 'Wild Geese' (Irish Catholic exiles on the Continent) make a similar point:

> While traitor knave,
>   And recreant slave,
> Had riches, rank, and retinue;
> And, exiled in those penal days,
> Our banners over Europe blaze.
>
> A stranger held the land and tower
> Of many a noble fugitive;
> No Popish lord had lordly power,
> The peasant scarce had leave to live;
> Above his head
> A ruined shed,
> No tenure but a tyrant's will—
> Forbid to plead,
> Forbid to read,
> Disarmed, disfranchised, imbecile—
> What wonder if our step betrays
> The freedman, born in penal days?
>
> (Thomas Davis, 'The Penal Days'[30])

The enduring Protestant stereotype of the Irish Catholic as inferior finds many outlets: from the claim that William of Orange had saved Ireland from popery and wooden shoes (the sabots associated with French peasants), to Unionist propaganda in 1912, which depicted nationalist Belfast as Microbe Street, its sub-tenants emptying chamber-pots from garrets into infested streets below, to Protestant loyalists protesting at the 1998 opening of a branch of a southern Irish chain store in Portadown by throwing maggots over the merchandise.[31] The sight of Catholics prospering is profoundly unsettling to this frame of mind. 'Jumped-up taigs' was how a Portadown businesswoman described a Catholic couple whom she found eating in an 'expensive' Armagh restaurant in 1999, flaunting their prosperity and 'dripping with Jacques Vert and gold jewellery'.[32] Cleanliness, too, has been associated with Protestantism, a point paraded literally by the proselytizing Charter schools of the eighteenth century in the form of scrubbed and industrious child converts from Catholicism. Susan McKay—researching her book *Northern Protestants: An Unsettled People* (2000)—attended a DUP meeting in Tyrone, where the audience laughed and clapped at one speaker who compared Catholics to the greedy pig in the muck, taking family allowances and government grants and always demanding more. Don't ever accuse the Irish of being dirty, Canon Sheehan's parish priest muses when his new curate, recently returned from Manchester, criticizes Mrs Darcy's cleaning of the chapel—particularly if you are citing English ways as your point of reference.[33]

The lower economic and social status of the majority of Catholics in past centuries is indisputable, the loss of their gentry and land prompting even Archbishop Rinnucini, the mid-seventeenth century Counter-Reformation papal nuncio, to dismiss Irish Catholicism as a religion of cabins. Later censuses showed Catholics disproportionately in the lower social sectors.[34] Of course, it also showed that most Protestants were there too.[35] However, whereas before the nineteenth century it tended to be richer Catholics who converted to Protestantism, in the lower social sectors the traffic tended to be in the opposite direction, deepening the stereotype that Catholicism and poverty went together. Protestants tended to have better and larger farms, and continued to do so even after independence. The closure of the Continental seminaries during the French Revolution created the image (not only among Protestants) of the more lowly, less educated priest, 'hungry clodpoles' going to Maynooth, in the words of the populist anti-papist preacher the Revd Hugh Hanna in 1886. Hanna's statue in Belfast—provocatively erected in a position dominating an interface which witnessed recurrent sectarian clashes—was one of the early casualties of the recent Troubles, blown up in 1970.

Hanna and his like repeated another well-worn insult: that Catholicism was a slavish religion. 'Contrast the Protestant and Romish physiognomy,' one of the most incendiary of evangelical preachers of the nineteenth century, the Revd Thomas Drew, told his audience in July 1857, 'and say where you will find such depressed, saddened, drooping-looking men, as the poor, oppressed, mentally aggrieved Romanist.'[36] The parliamentary commission investigating the sectarian riots of that summer laid particular blame on Drew for promoting 'a feeling of dominancy and insult', reminding one party of 'the triumph of their ancestors over those of the other...of Protestant superiority over their Roman Catholic neighbours'.[37] It was in the later nineteenth century that claims to be able to tell one's religion from appearance began to be made, and a 'stooped carriage' came to be one of the many stereotypical traits by which Catholics were identified. In the 1912 Home Rule debates, one MP argued that if you went to any fair in Ireland you could not tell a Protestant from a Catholic. From the opposite benches came the retort of the member for North Armagh: 'I could.'[38]

Perhaps it is little wonder, then, that two images from the penal era should surface repeatedly in Catholic folklore as symbols of Protestant dominance. The first is of 'hewers of wood and drawers of water'. It is a disgrace, the schoolteacher tells the class in *Angela's Ashes*, that clever boys still have to 'hew wood and draw water'.[39] This biblical phrase (Joshua 9: 21)—often cited as proof that the Penal Laws were designed to enslave the Irish Catholic—was in fact used by the Church of Ireland Archbishop William King in the early eighteenth century as a chastisement to fellow Protestants for making such little effort to reach out to Catholics by providing an Irish-speaking ministry.[40]

The other is 'ascendancy': the Orangemen parade through our areas to maintain 'an ascendancy over us', a complaint made by

Belfast nationalists in the 1990s, can be replicated back through the ages.[41] 'Protestant ascendancy' was a term coined by the most anti-Catholic group of Irish politicians—many in government—at the end of the eighteenth century. The usage and their detailed explanations were widely publicized at the time, particularly by the United Irishmen, to show just how prejudiced and corrupt was the existing system. It then came to be used as shorthand for the penal era and explains the continued contempt for the culture of that period, which saw the destruction of parts of Georgian Dublin in the 1970s and still informs Irish cultural policies more than is generally recognized.

Given such insults, it has been difficult for Catholics to understand the fears and insecurities which lay behind them. In the reductionism of folklore, Catholics were poor because Protestants were rich. The Irish-language poetry is full of social resentment as well as an insistence that Catholics who converted to Protestantism did so for materialistic reasons. An eighteenth-century poem, still being sung in Donegal two centuries later, says as much:

> O Manus dear, is the news true,
> which I heard yesterday in the neighbourhood,
> that you recently abandoned God's church,
> and the mighty Pope of Rome,
> and that you were reading your *recantation*
> in the Protestant church on Sunday?
> [To which Manus replies]
> Even if they go to God's paradise
> it's certain I'll be with them,
> my shining sword hanging by my side,
> and my lease in my pocket.[42]

In Art MacCooey's *c.*1770 bilingual poem 'Tagra an dá Theampall', the English-speaking Protestant temple taunts the ruined

Irish-speaking Catholic Church, associating her popery with her ruin and poverty:

> In spite of your beads my English shall reign,
>   whilst Irish grows daily odious;
> England and Wales have riches in heaps
>   to flourish away most glorious;
> my flock has estates, with lands and demesnes
>   all riding in state [in] their coaches,
> while taxes, arrears, and cesses severe
>   upon your Gaedhelian broaches.

And in his 'Adeir Clann Liútair' ('Luther's Children Say'):

> The children of Luther who are in court and in coaches say
>   that I would have a vote in their own religion
> cheap land and accurate guns
>   and my hat adorned with a cross-cockade;
>
> .   .   .   .
>
> and wouldn't it be better for me to sign up with them
>   than to be a waster in the Gaelic style?

This resentment is particularly noticeable in early to mid-nineteenth-century poems, which reflect reactions to the proselytizing campaign of the evangelicals, largely directed at poorer Catholics.

> Do you hear me O children of the Gaels, look out for yourselves,
> and don't give yourselves for earthly wealth . . .
>   . . . sorrowful is your journey,
> turning away from the holy clergy;
> turning your faces . . . towards the foreigners because of wealth . . .
> The one who does will be forever in torment,
> and no succour from the son of God will he receive,
> when the foreigners are torturing them in hell, receiving their wages,
> the Gaels will be in eternal happiness.[43]

It is not difficult to find examples of such resentfulness, even among successful Catholics. Thomas Moore never forgot his early experiences as one of the first Catholic students permitted to enter Trinity College Dublin after the 1793 Catholic Relief Act. There is a resentment in his writings which suggests a lingering Catholic inferiority complex and, almost certainly, memories of taunts about not quite fitting in at this former bastion of Protestant privilege. As late as 1821 he records, with some bitterness, Trinity's reluctance to acknowledge his fame.[44] He was, as W. J. McCormack comments, 'that most discontented of types, the recently liberated man who has just grasped how thoroughly his past has been enslaved'.[45] Many of Moore's works—not just his *Melodies*—call for remembrance of past oppression.

In *An Irish Gentleman in Search of a Religion* (1833), Moore poses as a 21-year-old student at Trinity College who, on the morrow of the grant of Catholic emancipation in 1829, decides that he now has the freedom to turn Protestant. Penalization has bound him in honour to Catholicism, and such has been the concentration on pursuing the right to actually practise it that he has never really thought about the faith itself. 'And though, had adversity still frowned on our faith, I would have clung to it to the last, and died fighting for Transubstantiation and the Pope with the best, I was not sorry to be saved the doubtful glory of such martyrdom.'[46] He has listened to and read so many Protestant pamphlets and sermons (not least by the college preacher) damning popery as the 'Great Harlot', 'the Mother of the fornications and abominations of the earth', 'damnable idolatry' encouraging 'imposture, perjury, assassination', that 'though myself one of them, I could not help regarding [the Roman Catholics] as a race of obsolete and obstinate religionists, robbed of every thing but (what was, perhaps, least worth preserving) their Creed, and justifying the charge brought against them of being unfit for freedom, by having been so long and so unresistingly submitted to be slaves'. As for the Protestants, he had never had any other perception of them but as 'a set of gentlemanlike heretics, somewhat scanty in creed, but in all things else rich and prosperous, and governing Ireland, according to their will and pleasure, by right of some certain Thirty-nine Articles'. But as part of his newly perceived freedom he straightens up from his Catholic stoop and paces with already 'something of the Ascendancy strut'.

He is encouraged in his conversion to Protestantism by an older Protestant widow offering him marriage and riches. But as he tries to educate himself into his new religion, he discovers that the reformers were guided by lust and materialism, even the recent Second Reformation (a 'saintly farce' and 'last effort of Protestant Ascendancy') had Catholics converting simply from hunger, and he admits—having finally concluded that primitive Christianity was the same as Catholicism—that it had been 'the flesh-pots of Ballymadragget' which had been the main attraction in converting. It is a pretty startling attack by such a public figure; it oozes resentment and is subtitled 'To the PEOPLE of IRELAND this defence of the ANCIENT NATIONAL FAITH'.

Moore's point about Catholics lacking the freedom to criticize their culture when it was under attack is telling. There was a long tradition of patronizing your own, and the long-delayed rise of a Catholic middle class in Ireland was built on servicing Catholic institutions. 'They have the virtue of a persecuted sect', wrote William Drennan in 1791, complaining that Catholics only used Catholic doctors (his own profession) 'to be closely attached to each other', their group identity as Catholics overriding all others.[47] The downside of all this was a sense of claustrophobia and imprisonment, which intensified after 1921 with the emergence of two confessional states north and south, the confessionalism of the one allowing the other to stifle internal criticism.

You had no choice. At its best there was a support network provided by separate Catholic social and welfare bodies, at its worst was the name-calling, ostracism, and murders of those who transgressed the unspoken rules. Accusations of 'selling out' have littered Irish history from the twelfth-century King of Leinster, Dermot MacMurrough, blamed for first introducing the English (nicknamed Dermot-na-Gall, Dermot of the foreigner, according to the Christian Brothers' *Irish History Reader*[48]). The lexicon of insults for Catholics who do not subscribe to the identikit has ranged from 'Castle Catholic' to the most sinister, 'informer', the IRA's and every other militant nationalist grouping's favourite excuse for murder.

'Ireland in the New Century'

Much as ends of centuries generally produce reappraisals of a country's past and future, so Ireland witnessed considerable debate about its future at the turn of the nineteenth–twentieth centuries. Contrary to Unionist belief, the Catholic Irish, including the clergy, largely saw their future as within the British empire, and there was considerable debate about the nature of the Catholicism which would construct that future. In a series of scorching books and lectures (1901–4) Michael J. F. McCarthy, a Catholic barrister from Cork, denounced the power of the Catholic Church in Ireland. A major theme, backed by detailed statistics, was how the huge increase of churches, convents, and other Catholic institutions was funded by exploitation of the Catholic poor. These were particularly popular in Ulster, where he conducted a series of lecture tours, for he constantly claimed an industriousness, cleanliness, and independence of mind in the North which he attributed to its Protestantism. There was certainly enough here to convince his Unionist readers and listeners that Home Rule would indeed mean Rome Rule.[49]

Most famously and brilliantly, the Liberal Unionist MP and founder of the Co-operative movement in Ireland, Horace Plunkett, developed a similar critique. But unlike McCarthy, there is a sense of walking on eggshells in his *Ireland in the New Century* (1904) and he constantly refers to past persecution as the reason why the Irish were as they were and why they were led by their clergy. He also criticized Protestant bigotry in general and accused northern Unionists of distorting the validity of their industrial prowess case against Home Rule by wrapping it up in religion and politics.

But the main theme of the book was a criticism of the sentimentality and unpractical nature of Irish Catholic culture, which he thought held Ireland back from prosperity. 'Roman Catholicism strikes an outsider as being in some of its tendencies, non-economic, if not actually anti-economic... The reliance of that religion on authority, its repression of individuality', impeded 'initiative and self-reliance'; and in a people lacking in education, gave rise to 'a kind of fatalism' and 'resignation' in which listlessness and apathy were presented as virtuous.[50] Individualism, he argued, produced improvement, in contrast to Catholic inattention to comfort.

While Plunkett really did take action to improve the self-reliance of the Irish peasantry (and had significant Catholic clerical support in doing so), some of his criticisms sounded very Protestant. Since the Catholic Church has had control over Catholic education, he argued, it must bear much of the responsibility for such backwardness. And what of those 'extravagant' churches being built from the proceeds of the poor or the unproductive nature of a celibate culture promoted within and without the Church. 'In many parishes the Sunday cyclist will observe the strange phenomenon of a normally light-hearted peasantry marshalled in male and female groups along the road, eyeing one another in dull wonderment across the forbidden space.' Thus had Ireland attained a 'chastity' unique in the world 'by grafting upon secular life a quasi-monasticism', but in the process promoting emigration by removing the 'innocent joy from the social side of home life'.[51] He, like George Birmingham, also pointed to the way low-paid or unpaid clerics and religious undermined local initiative.

Plunkett stirred up a hornet's nest, for his economic arguments were clouded by often indiscreet statements on the nature of Catholicism. It was as another Protestant put-down of Catholics that *Ireland in the New Century* was viewed, the fullest critique being that by Mgr Michael O'Riordan, *Catholicity and Progress in Ireland* (1906). Some aspects of O'Riordan's argument—particularly the preoccupations of a celibate cleric with female chastity—sound ludicrous to modern ears. But on the whole this work deserves more credit than is usually accorded it when opposed to Plunkett's fast-paced and very influential work, particularly since it provided a very full account of Irish Catholic identity, specifically in the way it had developed in response to Protestant criticisms. Plunkett expressed surprise that his one chapter on the influence of religion had provoked a treatise, for that is what O'Riordan's 510-page work was, most counter-arguments backed up with extensive quotations and statistics, more often than not deliberately taken from Protestant sources.

Plunkett's criticism of the expense involved in building huge churches and adorning them with imported artwork O'Riordan attributes to a Protestant utilitarian 'measuring of Catholic religion by Protestant ideas'.[52] And whereas Protestantism was a kind of pared-down religion, their churches little more than places for preaching, Catholics believed in 'the Real Presence' of Christ and in surrounding the tabernacle with appropriate beauty.

Catholics also believed in the veneration and intercession of saints and adorned their churches accordingly. If Protestant utilitarianism had been the model of old, there would have been no Westminster, Salisbury, or York cathedrals and no property for Protestants to steal. 'When Protestantism arose it rejected all the Catholic doctrines . . . and laid hold of all the Catholic churches . . . What is troubling them here in Ireland is, not that our churches are too expensively built, but that we have any churches at all . . . they will never forgive us for having survived' despite all efforts to penalize or proselytize. He equates this criticism with that of another 'philanthropic economist', Judas, who chastised Mary's use of ointment on the dead Christ, 'the Divine Founder of the Catholic Church', claiming as did Protestants that the money would have been better spent on the poor.

He then presents what is a classic picture of the 'Church suffering', the 'Church triumphant', which anyone educated in Catholic schools in the twentieth century will recognize. When a new generation of Catholics emerged, they 'cast off the winding bands from their limbs, and began to walk erect in the presence of their oppressors'. They began to build those churches which

> 'shock the economic sense' of our neighbours, not because they paralyze Catholic industry or consume Catholic money, but because they vindicate the indestructibility of the Irish Catholic faith and patriotism . . . Those new churches are the expression of Irish Catholic faith to-day; the ruins of our old churches stand in their desolation, the memorials of Protestant injustice, the neglected relics of their shame. . . . If we had not been robbed of the old ones, we would not have had to 'shock their economic sense' by spending money on new ones . . . [53]

O'Riordan's historical arguments were, on the whole, well made and his mistakes were those already made by Lecky (his hugely influential five-volume *Ireland in the Eighteenth Century* having recently appeared), from whom he took most of his material on the Penal Laws, the restrictions on Irish trade and manufacture, and past land confiscations. O'Riordan cited many examples of the privileges of the Church of Ireland and how it took money from poor Catholics in the form of tithes and other taxes and then wondered why they were poor. Alerted by Lecky, he singled out for particular criticism what he considered the arrogance of a Church of Ireland cleric, the Bishop of Cloyne and noted eight-eenth-century philosopher George Berkeley, for remarks in his 1749 pamphlet *A Word to the Wise*. This was addressed to the Roman Catholic clergy of Ireland and asked them to use their influence to encourage industry in their flocks.[54] But it seemed to voice peculiarly Protestant prejudices, associating 'Sloth, Dirt and Beggary' with the 'native' Irish and pointing to examples of indus-try among the poor of Protestant countries like Holland and England. In the sensitive times of the early twentieth century it was seen by O'Riordan as unusually prejudiced and offensive.

In fact Berkeley had had a very good record caring for the poor of his diocese and he went to some pains to show that he did not share the belief of those who 'suspect your religion to be the cause of that notorious idleness, which prevails so generally among the natives of this island, as if the Roman Catholic faith was inconsist-ent with an honest Diligence'. His call actually echoed efforts by the Catholic Church all over Europe to restrict the number of holy days and the excesses and idleness perceived by the Enlightenment to accompany them, and his pamphlet was read from the altars by Catholic priests.[55] Even so, given the stripped-down readings of the penal era outlined earlier, O'Riordan looked only for the insults and found them; and he responded with that same prickly social resentment which characterized most Catholic responses to

Protestant criticisms, rather weakening his argument by a petulant attack on this pampered Protestant bishop's cultivation of straw-berries and myrtle hedges on his estate as hardly giving poor papists a good example of industry.[56]

Berkeley's pamphlet was part of that early modern Protestant crusade for a 'reformation of manners' which was fundamental to the proselytizing activities of the Charter schools (established 1734) and is here translated into making the Catholic poor more 'useful' and 'industrious'. If you want to talk about waste, comments O'Riordan, look rather to your own house, to the money spent on such proselytizing, or the vast amounts spent on bibles and 'the Pharisaical conceit of spreading the Word amongst the Irish, the Spanish, the Italians . . . and amongst every people and tribe under heaven, except yourselves' (by which he means the English).[57]

Plunkett had made a classic Protestant case for a link between individualism and material progress. O'Riordan responded with an argument similar to today's worries about the new shopping mall Irish culture: human progress does not consist alone in material or industrial progress, and he pointed to the miserable condition of England's urban poor, as revealed in parliamentary reports. In his heightened defensive mode, what he did not pick up and present as a virtue was the greater sense of community among Catholics, which Plunkett thought a deterrent to economic pro-gress. The Irishman's inattention to comfort and orderliness in home and environment he attributed to a mindset

> still dominated . . . by the associations and common interests of the primitive clan . . . the Irish peasant scarcely seems to have a home in the sense in which an Englishman understands the word . . . he does not endeavour to improve or to adorn it . . . What the Irishman is really attached to . . . is not a home but a social order. The pleasant amenities, the courtesies, the leisureliness, the associations of

religion, and the familiar faces of the neighbours, whose ways and minds are like his and very unlike those of any other people.

But he drew the negative conclusion that this is why Irish emigrants found adjustment to industrial economies so difficult.

O'Riordan's response was typical of that Irish Catholic mode of expression, which appeared triumphal, but which revealed its sensitivity to Protestant or English criticisms by concentrating on their rebuttal rather than shifting the focus elsewhere. This sensitivity was reflected in denying not only Protestants (considered as Protestants rather than Irishmen) the right to criticize, but Catholics too. Virtues emphasized are those which Plunkett had seen as the problem: the social envy of those who succeed, the presentation of sufferings and the ability to endure them a Catholic monopoly. 'For character is proved in passivity as well as ... activity ... It is by suffering and loss rather than by activity and gain that character is chiefly tested.'

And, finally, we can already see the Catholic Church's obsession with sexuality in twentieth-century Ireland in O'Riordan's devotion of an entire chapter to Plunkett's observations on the 'chastity' of young mass-goers. Ireland was proud of the chaste reputation of its womanhood, argued O'Riordan, and he contrasted this to the perceived promiscuity of Protestant countries, notably Protestant Ulster: 'witness the statistics of illegitimacy; of what is known in New England as "fashionable murders"; of marital infidelities which overwhelm the divorce courts of those countries; of sexual unnaturalness which threatens to depopulate them'. Indeed he quotes approvingly sources which suggest Protestant promiscuity, a particularly slanted reading of illegitimacy statistics apparently proving an equivalence with Orangeism.[58]

He took particular exception to Plunkett's 'Sunday cyclists', portraying them as effete upper-class, taking 'afternoon tea' and playing golf and presuming to criticize a Catholic peasantry of whom they knew nothing, and he devoted an inordinate amount of space to address the accusation that the priests stopped traditional dancing at the crossroads. Why was he so exercised by this, even to the point of conducting his own survey among the country people? Possibly it was because killjoyism was a stereotype normally applied to Protestants. Indeed he intimated as much.[59]

Killjoy Ireland

Whatever O'Riordan's historical explanation of why Irish Catholicism had become a peasant religion, the Catholic ethos bequeathed to the new state after 1921 did partly explain its economic underperformance.[60] In this Canon Sheehan has been seen as 'a kind of mascot for Catholic Ireland'.[61] His world was that of the rural poor, where things happened slowly, if at all. Innovation was deemed a foreign import and ultimately defeated. Suffering and endurance could attain their own levels of spirituality and there was a particular purity in poverty. Sheehan and other similar writers had taken their cue for the most popular of all Catholic fiction of Victorian Ireland: Charles Kickham's *Knocknagow, or, The Homes of Tipperary*, published in 1873 but still being reprinted a century later. The author's Fenianism should have excluded it from Church backing, and yet it was the most popular book in the parish libraries of the late nineteenth century, uniting all Catholic classes in a common history of suffering, allowing even the gombeen men—local traders who exploited the poor—and the Catholic landlords who evicted tenants to associate themselves with the peasantry in their victimhood. Thus could the national story of suffering disguise division.[62]

These new puritanical patriots were Joyce's main target. They censored anything which sinned against their view of Irishness, and approved inferior Irish products and literature (the 'Paltryattic Puetrie' of *Finnegans Wake*), while rejecting the great English classics. They ostentatiously signed their names in Irish and proclaimed the moral purity of real (peasant) Ireland. He savaged such literature in a 1902 review of the verse of William Rooney (friend of Arthur Griffith and proprietor of the *United Irishman* newspaper). Anything like quality disappears, he argues, 'when patriotism has laid hold of the writer'. Week after week this 'weary succession of verses... speaking of redemption and revenge' appeared in newspapers and was recited at patriotic societies. 'Religion and all that is allied thereto can manifestly persuade men to great evil, and by writing these verses... Mr Rooney has been persuaded to great evil. And yet he might have written well if he had not suffered from one of those big words which make us so unhappy.'[63] The famous Cyclops scene in *Ulysses* has the Citizen speak in cultural–nationalist clichés. The Narrator describes a dismal musical evening of the Gaelic League:

> there was a fellow with a Ballyhooly blue ribbon badge spiffing out of him in Irish and a lot of colleen bawns going about with temperance beverages and selling medals and oranges and lemonade and a few old dry buns, gob, flahoolagh entertainment... Ireland sober, is Ireland free. And then an old fellow starts blowing into his bagpipes and all the gougers shuffling their feet to the tune the old cow died of.

The event would be overseen by the priests to ensure that nothing vaguely sexual could occur.

Other critics also noted the humourlessness of the new nationalism and the puritanism of the priests, who were so central to it. They denounced young females from the pulpits for attending Gaelic League classes to meet boys, insisted on separating the sexes at meetings, and tried to ban meetings taking place after dark.[64]

After the founding of Sinn Féin in 1905, it was only a matter of time before the younger militants took over the Gaelic League. Hannay was expelled in 1914 and Hyde resigned the following year, since the League by now was dominated by the militants who would organize the 1916 Easter rising as a first blow for independence. The Gaelic revivalists had become the new 'sourfaces', and they were about to take over Ireland.

The revolutionary generation of young men who ran Ireland after 1921, and dominated political life until the 1960s, perpetuated the anti-modernist, sentimental, and fatalistic Irishness here described. This is the theme of Tom Garvin's *Preventing the Future: Why was Ireland So Poor for So Long?* (2004). In this he showed the Gaelic League, Catholic Church, small farmers, and politicians implementing a new order based on this sanctification of an Irishness developed at the turn of the century. Thus, in an educational system dominated by the Church, 'useful' subjects were squeezed out of the curriculums to accommodate compulsory Irish language-teaching, and criticism was considered anti-national. Education beyond primary level was not made available to the masses until 1967, and the poorly educated, unskilled emigrants poured into England in particular. Existing authoritarian tendencies in Catholicism were intensified by the political class's compliance. Yet however authoritarian the Church might appear, it could not normally continue in directions which did not command popular approval. Visitors to Ireland were astonished at the displays of Catholic fervour and loyalty to their Church. Churches were packed out not only on Sundays and holy days, but also for daily mass, first Fridays, novenas, 'missions', confraternities, and various other special devotions. The chapel was at the heart of most Irish people's lives, always open, always occupied, warm and comforting.

Garvin saw the real change in public attitudes starting when the collapse of the Mother and Child scheme in 1951 showed the bishops destroying a popular measure. The scheme, proposing free health care for mothers and children, ran foul of the Catholic Church's resistance to state interference in the family. What turned it into a cause célèbre was Taoiseach John A. Costello's public acceptance of the Church's rights to impose Catholic social teaching. 'I as a Catholic', he told the Dáil, 'obey my church authorities and will continue to do so.' The Health Minister, Dr Noel Browne, went on to publish the correspondence with the bishops. This was seized upon by the northern Unionist press as revealing 'the dominating influence of the Roman Catholic Church in Ireland', amply justifying fears for 'their civil and religious liberty' in a united Ireland (to which was added statistics for the declining numbers of Protestants in the South since partition).[65] There was internal criticism too, both within the Church and within the political elite. This new mood found an outlet in the clerical journals such as the *Furrow, Doctrine and Life*, and *Studies*, credited by Louise Fuller's in-depth analysis of Irish Catholic culture as important forces for change and prophetic in their warnings of the dangers of such an enclosed and uncritical religious culture. Many articles in these new journals reiterated Plunkett's criticisms half a century earlier, the Jesuit priest Fr John Kelly warning in 1959 that 'Too many people in Ireland today are trying to make do with a peasant religion when they are no longer peasants any more.'[66]

There is, however, another aspect to this which is often neglected: the pursuit of 'respectability'. I have seen it in train in Northern Ireland and much the same appears to have been happening in late nineteenth–early twentieth-century Ireland. D. P. Moran noted it, but dismissed it as snobbery and West Britonism. It works something like this: you live in a system where Protestants seem to have all the top positions and deem you inferior. So you push your children through education, not only to prove them wrong, but to break into those areas which most command respect, the professions, thereby attaining 'respectability'. That is what the newly rising Catholic middle class in Ireland was seeking and what their schools were promoting. In the eighteenth century, penalization and the revolutionary closure of its colleges on the Continent had bequeathed a relatively poor Catholic Church to the nineteenth century. It had not shown much interest in education beyond that for the priesthood until alarmed by the way the Second Reformation was targeting its poor. A popular thirst for education had sustained the hedge schools and made the free education offered by the proselytizing Bible schools attractive to poor Catholics. In consequence the state-funded non-denominational national schools (from the 1830s) were largely supported by the Catholic hierarchy. Mixed religious education, however, was fiercely resisted by the main Protestant Churches, turning the national schools into a largely Catholic Church preserve by the second half of the century.

Within Ireland the secondary sector had only really existed for Protestants until the Catholic religious orders set up their own fee-paying schools from the early nineteenth century. State-funded secondary education for all arrived only in the twentieth century, 1947 in the North, 1967 in the South. Until then the fee-paying schools were considered the training ground for future clerics and religious and the middle class who would take their place in various public offices. The 'informal consensus'[67] between Church and state after independence owed much to this shared education of lay and religious leaders of Catholic society and the social prestige which having a priest in the family had acquired by then. By 1901 there had been a 137 per cent increase in the numbers of priests and religious in Ireland since 1861 even though there had been a 27 per cent drop in population over the same period.[68] Teaching science or technology to the lower classes was not a priority for such professional preparation, though to be fair this trend was intensified by the Intermediate School Act 1878, which pegged funding to intensive competitive exams based on a narrow curriculum. The surge towards respectability was incremental thereafter, the numbers of Catholics in intermediate education almost tripling by 1911.

While successive British governments were sensitive to the hierarchy's protective and by now virtual control of Catholic education, it was also clear that Britain was gearing up for a major overhaul after the First World War. In 1899 new funding was made available for technical education, outside the Church's control and under the supervision of its *bête noire* Horace Plunkett. Government inquiries of 1904–5 showed Irish schools falling far behind those in England and Scotland, and all the signs were that the Church's stranglehold over Irish education was part of the reason. The Church responded by denouncing such moves as a return to 'penal days'. This was a British and Protestant conspiracy to take our schools as they once did our Churches, and statements to that effect were read at Sunday masses. The supportive *Freeman's Journal* put it even more bluntly: 'Catholic Ireland ... is not going to surrender them [its schools] to the domination of either Orange Toryism or Nonconformist Liberalism or Mugwump Agnosticism organised by any Government Department.'[69]

In independent Ireland the state fully accepted Catholic Church teaching that education was the sphere of the Church and the family and left it well alone. The Church had long resisted state inspection of its institutions, and we are only now learning about the consequences to vulnerable children and females. While there was good reason for the Catholic Church to suspect the state in times gone by, this had solidified by the twentieth century into a resistance to *any* lay interference, even by Catholics. Secondary schools were reserved for the rural lower-middle-class who stocked the clergy and the state departments. Ireland itself accepted that most Catholics were and would remain poor, and most could expect only primary education until the late 1960s.

In the pursuit of respectability before independence, the Catholic private schools had a head start (the Jesuits, true to their mission, setting up Clongowes Wood as early as 1814). Catholic public schools in England, such as Stonyhurst, Ampleforth, and Downside, also received increasing numbers of Irish Catholics, many going on to join the imperial civil service. It was the same story as of old: rather than overthrowing the establishment, Catholics wanted to join it.[70] These were Moran's main targets— Ireland's 'respectable class'—and although the term 'West Briton' had been used before, it was Moran who made it a fashionable slogan. He blamed what he saw as their double standards, the 'traders' of Cork and Tipperary fashionably subscribing to 'rebel' culture, then sending their sons to such schools to turn them into '*English* gentlemen' and get them into 'the Home and Indian service', which in public they denounced as that 'nefarious and bloodstained empire'.[71] In any other country, writes Moran, his success would be nationally celebrated, but in Ireland his pursuit of respectability consisted of aping old society and Anglicized ways. On the verge of ultimate success he made sure no one saw him and went into the Kildare Street Club, which in the past had been the preserve of the Protestant elite. He had become a 'shoneen', a little Englishman.[72] Moran's Irish Ireland turned on the newly successful Catholics and infused independent Ireland with a mean-spirited tendency to demean anything savouring of privilege, particularly among Catholics. But Moran was as critical as Plunkett of that inclination to see the poor peasant as the authentic Gael: 'the people who preserve in some degree the traditions of the Gael are the ignorant peasants. This state of affairs points to a rather hopeless outlook. Improve the condition of the peasants and you wipe out the traditions and the language . . . Truly there is something rotten in the state.'[73]

Social resentment of the 'have-nots' for the 'haves' is, of course, universal. In modern Irish history, however, this generally has had a religious element. Since the complementary myths of the down-trodden Gael and the progressive Protestant have served identity formation so well in the past, they are unlikely to disappear quickly. Catholic nationalist culture had been fashioned from negative and hostile views of both England and Protestantism. So it should not surprise that once in power it would protect itself from both. A prudish and joyless Catholicism was promoted in Ireland, the old tendency to overcompensate for Protestant put-downs continuing far into the twentieth century. Indeed, the Catholic journal *The Furrow* concluded in 1966 that if Vatican II had not come along, Catholic people would have rebelled. While 'our history' might explain why the Irish Church could be so inward-looking,

> The fact is that the Church here was leading a uniquely sheltered existence. This in turn partly explains some of the conservatism of the Irish Church, a conservatism shared alike by the clergy and by the laity. It was not difficult to find as conservative a hierarchy elsewhere. What was difficult to find was the combination of a conservative hierarchy and the virtually total acceptance by the laity of even the most extreme directives of that hierarchy . . . The

Catholic community in Ireland existed as a closed society for a very long time. And we would have remained a closed society... were it not that elsewhere this century has proved so revolutionary... [and] some of the backwash has overflown into our community in spite of the forlorn efforts of our native Canutes... We were all to blame for the creation and maintenance of this mutual admiration and were it not for the Council we would have gone on and on preening ourselves.[74]

8

'Beached': Religious Minorities in Partitioned Ireland

Division. All Ireland was divided, the border cut the north from the south, and the Mickeys from the Protestants, and at the Last Day, the goats would be divided from the sheep.

(Robert Harbinson, *No Surrender*)

The rights of the minority must be sacred to the majority.

(Edward Carson)

Partition in 1921 created two states, informed by the separate religious identities outlined in previous chapters. Protestants in the South and Catholics in the North felt abandoned. Southern Protestants, of course, had long experience of being a minority, and their economically privileged position remained, even if significantly reduced. The determination of successive southern governments to be seen to act even-handedly towards its minority also assisted pragmatic, if reluctant, Protestant acceptance of the new situation. But the prevailing Catholic and anti-English ethos of independent Ireland has caused real problems, and the claims that the Protestant minority has been treated well by the state rather ignores the fact that in that ethos Protestants had been considered England's 'garrison' and un-Irish, tolerated rather than totally accepted.

Although there would be common elements in the group psychologies and separate social structures of both minorities, there were huge differences and northern Catholics remained unreconciled to the new political situation. They formed the largest single religious denomination in the North, their numbers at the time of partition (34 per cent against the 7 per cent Protestant minority in the South) both gave them collective strength and made them a threat to the very survival of the state. Despite some early, though short-lived, efforts by the Unionist government at fair treatment, for the next forty years no further attempt was made to reconcile its aggrieved minority. Concessions, largely in the field of education, were handed out as unmerited gifts from 'our' state, rather than as equal treatment for all citizens.[1] In the South, Protestants had little choice but to accept reality. In the North, Catholics became a state within a state, their alternative social infrastructure rendering such pragmatic acceptance of realities unnecessary.

Southern Protestants

The two new states were born amidst sectarian violence, and for a while it looked as if southern Protestants might be made hostage for the killings of Catholics in the North. In his study of the Cork IRA in this period, Peter Hart has argued that behind the attacks on Protestants and their property was 'the quasi-millenarian idea of a final reckoning of the ancient conflict between settlers and natives'.[2] Many Protestants feared as much, and some 100,000 had left the Free State by 1926, by which time their numbers had declined from 10.4 per cent in 1911 to 7.4 per cent in 1926.[3] The decline in the number of Protestants in the early days of independence

is a very sensitive issue in Ireland, not least because Ulster Unionists at the time and since have made such propaganda out of it.
The suggestion that sectarianism may have been an issue in the
attacks on Protestants during Ireland's war of independence hits a
particularly raw nerve, given that Irish nationalism ignores, indeed
denies, any sectarianism in its makeup. The dust has not yet settled
from the recent controversy over the October 2007 Irish television
documentary (*Hidden History: The Killings at Coolacrease*) on the 1921
IRA killings of Protestants in County Offaly.[4] And yet, given the
land hunger, the resentment of Protestant privilege, and the
unusual numbers of impoverished young males in the country
because the First World War had closed off emigration, it would
have been surprising had sectarianism not been an element in the
burning down of almost 300 'big houses' during the war of independence and civil war 1919–23. Expectations raised by the Land
Acts had not been satisfied, and Sinn Féin exploited the sense of
grievance with its 'Back to the Land' campaign for land redistri-
bution. Protestant-owned estates were forcibly seized in the west
and midlands. Demesne walls were destroyed and cattle driven off,
and there were protests against such 'ascendancy' rural activities as
hunting and racing.[5] A number of murders of Protestants around
Clonakilty and Bandon in Cork resulted in the remainder of the
Protestant community there taking flight for England.[6] Other
areas where sectarian animosities had long been a feature also
witnessed a number of murders of Protestants.[7]

It is, of course, difficult to separate out sectarianism from economic and class envy. Also many of the attacks were for arms,
which tended to be more prevalent in the big houses of the gentry.
In County Clare, which witnessed less brutality, the shooting
parties and tennis parties of the gentry were objects of attack. At
the other end of the scale of IRA attacks on the big houses is David

Thomson's account of that on Woodbrook in County Roscommon. The group of young IRA men had awoken all the occupants and herded them into the bedroom of aged and deaf Aunt Nina, who, throughout the raid, shouted confused instructions at her eccentric Scottish companion. With the maids giggling in one corner, the stable-boys pulling faces at the strange scene in the other, and the IRA guard barely able to conceal his own mirth, it had all the traits of a stage farce.[8] In a wonderfully nuanced analysis of County Clare in these years, David Fitzpatrick also shows the Cork situation to have been unusual, and those pragmatic landed Protestants who did not take flight did rather well. But he also portrays most Protestants as refusing to step outside the 'shell' of old privilege, regarding the Catholic bishops as 'peasants' and even the non-violent nationalists as 'untouchables'. 'For many of the diehards . . . the social lowering entailed by the course of reconciliation was simply too cruel to bear.'[9]

Nervously, southern Protestant spokesmen denied that there was a religious war going on. Northern Unionists declared that there was. Their press proclaimed as much in bold headlines: 'War on Protestants', detailing every attack on southern Protestants and their property and slotting them into the Protestant story of persecution going back to 1641.[10] It was the killings in west Cork which prompted delegates attending the Church of Ireland Synod in May 1922 to ask the provisional government 'if they were to be permitted to live in Ireland or if it was desired that they should leave the country'. In fact, the attacks did not presage a general loss of Protestant property or any kind of punishment for the past, and in urban areas, where most Protestants lived, there had been more fear of the Black and Tans than of the IRA.[11] The eminent historian R. B. McDowell, whose own family had suffered harassment and attack, nevertheless concluded:

Compared with the thorough methods for dealing with unpopular minorities developed during the twentieth century in eastern and central Europe and elsewhere, the harassment of the Southern loyalists was not noticeably severe. Perhaps about sixty (including members of the RIC and Protestants in Cork) were killed after the Truce and a number were menaced, boycotted, bullied, frightened, plundered or deprived of their land. But the campaign against them was ill co-ordinated and sporadic. A number of those expelled returned after an interval, and most loyalists in Dublin, Cork city and the less disturbed parts of the countryside escaped unscathed.[12]

Michael Collins sought to reconcile southern Protestants, and their clergy urged acceptance of the Anglo-Irish Treaty on their people. Indeed, ultimately Protestants desperately wanted an end to the disorder in the country and were impressed at the speed with which the new Free State government achieved it. Former Unionists almost overnight became supporters of the pro-Treaty Cumann na nGaedheal party and their children of its successor, Fine Gael. Successive Irish governments were very anxious to show to Protestants in the North that their co-religionists did not suffer discrimination. The problem for Protestants in the new state was that they were a protected minority (rather like an endangered species) in a state which was now defiantly Catholic, and all those popish traits which they had so feared and despised were now part of the governing order. From the position of 'Lords of creation', admitted one commentator, we were now 'a shrunken timorous handful', and the 'role of underdog irked us'.[13] Would Protestants be punished for the sins of their ancestors? Certainly there was an undercurrent of this desire in Irish nationalism. When their worst fears did not materialize, however, Protestants became resigned, if resentful, to petty punishments, relieved that they were not worse.

The declining numbers of Protestants after independence is still a live issue, judging from a recent exchange in the *Irish Times* between Ian d'Alton (historian of the Protestants of Cork) and Garret Fitzgerald.[14] However, southern Protestants were often critical of the way their northern co-religionists made propaganda from their supposed plight, and a new generation of historians is questioning the 'disaster' interpretation of the decline and the tendency to over-concentrate on 'big house' Protestants. 'This decline in the Protestant population has been treated as a diaspora of the terrorised', writes Martin Maguire. 'In Northern Ireland this interpretation has been readily accepted, conflating as it does with a traditional narrative of siege and persecution stretching back to 1641.' There is little evidence of changed migratory behaviour after 1921, and no evidence of fear, at least in Dublin. Rather, there was an acceleration of trends already evident beforehand, added to which was the disproportionate Protestant loss of life in the First World War and the withdrawal of Crown forces after 1921. Some 21 per cent of all working-class Protestant males in Dublin were in the British armed forces in 1911, and over a third of Protestant marriages had been to soldiers. It was the decline in the working-class element that gives rise to belief that all Protestants were privileged. The Catholic population also declined, often through the same long-term trends, emigration and celibacy.[15] So the Protestant minority, while defensive, was 'by no means cowed', and some were quite prepared to challenge government publicly.[16]

On the whole, southern Protestants retained their privileged position in the private sector and the Church of Ireland itself remained a badge of status, quite unlike in Northern Ireland, where the Protestant poor were more likely to be Church of Ireland than Presbyterian. They lived disproportionately in the rich suburbs of Dublin, sending their children to English schools, speaking with posh (to many Irish ears, English) accents. The long-established (and Protestant-dominated) industries and businesses still tended to promote their own.[17] But their fall from landed privilege was sudden and permanent. As the Minister of Agriculture, Patrick Hogan, had rather threateningly summarized the mood of the electorate in 1923, 'a great change had come', the landlords were now 'a small minority, and an unpopular minority; that they could take the land from them for nothing if they wished', and if the government did not meet their demands, they would 'put in place another which would'.[18]

In the 1970s my family visited Lissadell in Sligo, the ancestral home to the Gore-Booths, celebrated in nationalist history as home to Countess Markievicz and retreat to William Butler Yeats, buried nearby in Drumcliff's Church of Ireland cemetery.[19] My father was a devout Catholic and nationalist in the Tone–Davis mould. This was not a Protestant 'big house' that we were visiting, but a monument to great Irish nationalists. It was in some disrepair and the elderly sisters who showed us around were bitter at how their family had been treated by the state. They were not alone. A patriotic past was no defence in the new order which saw the 'big house' as a reminder of an ascendancy past. Progressively sold or abandoned by owners who could no longer afford to maintain them, they were often demolished or left to fall into ruin by 'unsympathetic' government departments. Today only 10–15 per cent are in the hands of the original families.[20]

As noted earlier, social resentment was a fundamental part of Catholic sectarianism. Arthur Clery thought southern Protestants 'absorbable' once they had lost their privileged status. Were the faded graces of Lissadell part of that process? Another was Woodbrook in Roscommon, where John McGahern was given his love of books by the eccentric and intellectual Moroneys. The fact that the Moroneys were Protestants also helped save him from being removed from school by his otherwise philistine father. For McGahern senior thought well of Protestants. 'He considered them superior in every way to the general run of his fellow Catholics, less devious, morally more correct, more honest, better mannered, and much more abstemious.' Such positive Catholic stereotypes of Protestants were common, the *Church of Ireland Monthly Magazine* noting proudly in 1939 how they were valued for their honesty and good citizenship.[21] But the Moroneys had clearly seen better days. They lived as if they were landless, and there was great hilarity among the locals when Andy Moroney described himself as 'a gentleman farmer' on a radio programme. In time Andy Moroney became another statistic in the declining number of southern Protestants, for he too converted to Catholicism on marrying.

Much as in the past, the Protestant poor drifted into Catholicism. There were no clubs, private schools, or country houses for them to maintain their separateness, so that the 'neighbourliness' that Hubert Butler so advocated for his own class in their relations with Catholics was the norm for the poor. Lily O'Shea grew up in the Dublin tenements just north of the Liffey in the 1930s and 1940s. With little state help for the poor, big families, and unemployment, such neighbourliness spelt survival. The one tenement pram was shared out to carry turf from distant stores and transport injured children to hospital, as well as for more traditional uses. Lily and her sisters and brothers were products of a mixed marriage, though *Ne Temere* was not an issue, since her parents had married in her mother's Protestant church. Mrs O'Shea was readily involved in the many Catholic social practices which had seeped into popular culture and was always happy to give money to the children being paraded in their Holy Communion finery, knowing how hard it would have been for their families to pay for it all. On Sunday mornings Lily would wave at her friends and families (even the daddies) going to mass in their

Sunday clothes. Occasionally she wished she was Catholic like her playmates, though usually for practical reasons, such as the ready supply of serviceable chalk afforded Catholic children when those plaster statues which adorned even the poorest Catholic home frequently smashed.

Both the Catholic and Protestant charities afforded much-needed practical relief. Both exercised some pressure on which religion the children were to follow—though never as blatant as legend assumes. The Protestant minister visited regularly, and every week the Sunday school teacher would collect the five children and take them to church. On the way home Catholic children would pursue them with the ritual taunt 'Proddywoddy on the wall. Half a loaf'd feed ya all.' The parish was small and mostly 'well-to-do'. Lily had to stop her little brother from eating the fruit from harvest displays. The Protestant home to which they were all sent when their mother was in hospital was located in posh Dun Laoghaire, where the virtue of Protestant cleanliness was brutally enforced. The paternalism of 'Ould Willie', the kindly Church of Ireland rector who had looked after the poor of Robert Harbinson's Belfast, is absent from Lily's account.[22] As her mother lay dying, Lily ran in panic for help from their Catholic neighbour. She knew what to do, and prepared her mother for burial. 'Now Lily, listen to me! Go down and fetch your mother's minister . . . and ask him for the money for a habit for yer mammy so that she can be laid out properly.' The minister was abrupt. 'We Protestants do not wear habits like the Catholics do. You buy your mother a new nightdress.' The neighbours closed their curtains out of respect and attended the funeral, but would not enter the Protestant church (since that was a mortal sin), and hung back from the clergyman's prayers in the Protestant Mount Jerome cemetery. In fact such a prohibition had not existed in canon law since 1917. But no one, not even their priests, had thought to tell Irish Catholics and there were a number of very public occasions when Protestants were so snubbed, including the reinterment of William Butler Yeats in Sligo in 1948 and the funeral of Ireland's first President, Douglas Hyde, in 1949.[23] Ultimately Lily converted to Catholicism after pressure from her then fiancé. Later the real love of her life assured her that he would never have asked that of her.[24]

Of course, this rather better record of the Catholic Church towards the poor can be exaggerated, and its middle-class values created its own snobberies and made things difficult for the less well-off in its schools. Benedict Anderson recalls the anger of his mother in the Waterford of the 1940s–1950s at the way the Catholic Church's attitudes to sex so favoured the man and condemned poor women to endless, often life-threatening pregnancies. She saw young priests abusing their positions by jumping to the head of cinema queues, 'while barefoot little children, snots streaming from their noses, were pushed aside'.[25]

Whatever the more buoyant approach of recent commentaries on southern Protestantism, its character, as well as its numbers, had changed irrevocably from previous centuries. Outside Dublin, Methodism and Presbyterianism (together accounting for only 1 per cent of the southern population by 1961) had all but disappeared—giving quite a different feel to northern and southern Protestantism. The Church of Ireland was left as the dominant Protestant community in the South. But adjustment to the new reality was painful. Almost totally Unionist at the time of partition, and instinctively loyal to Britain and its forces of law and order, its members found themselves caught up in an Irish revolution which rejected everything British. Reluctantly they had come to accept the inevitability of Home Rule (it was after all on the statute book from 1914), only to find their Ulster co-religionists, including five bishops, calling for partition, which southern Protestants strenuously opposed. When it happened, it meant that the Church of Ireland was now a predominantly northern one (56 per cent in 1911, rising to some 75 per cent by 1961), even though its central organization remained in Dublin. Operating in different states, unsurprisingly northern and southern adherents progressively pulled apart over the next century.

Disproportionately the Church of Ireland had sent soldiers into the First World War, the long memorial lists in their churches and the British regiment flags further setting them apart in an independent Ireland which did not commemorate the many dead who had fought with British forces. All the changes have 'made me feel for the first time that I am myself essentially English not Irish', wrote one church member to Archbishop Bernard in 1921. 'A man is what he inherits . . . and for most of us protestants these things are ninety per cent English or Scotch . . . why I mainly fear . . . the new order . . . is not so much the material loss and annoyance as the tendency to cut us away from our roots, our civilisation.'[26] Reluctant changes were made in church services to accommodate political realities, falling short of the official Irish names for the new legislature, until 1949, when the new Republic was accepted. 'Many . . . will regret the loss of the familiar words,' declared Archbishop Gregg, 'but what other way is there? . . . For in our prayers above all, there must be reality.'[27]

However, they retained a strong attachment to Britain when anti-Britishness was central to the ethos of the new state and taunts of 'England's faithful garrison' were made at every level. Many later recalled the continuing loyalty to the British monarchy of their families and preference for British radio stations. By the 1960s the *Irish Times*—once the mouthpiece of Irish Protestantism—was critical of such lingering snobbery. In 1965 Michael Viney, the author of a series of articles on the minority, visited a wealthy Dublin suburb. He found both prosperous Catholics and Protestants living there, though at 25 per cent Protestants represented a significantly greater proportion than their (by now) 5 per cent of the population. 'I saw the last Union Jack hauled down in Ireland', recalled one of the residents, 'and thought the world had come to an end.' Reluctantly he had accepted the reality of the new Irish state, and only occasionally forgot himself and used the pre-independence name 'Kingstown' for the renamed Dublin suburb of Dun Laoghaire. But he wouldn't be seen dead in another wealthy suburb where prosperous Catholics tended to live. 'There are still a few people round here with a Union Jack rolled up in the drawer. But it's the maids who plaster the kitchen with Prince Philip. They're Catholics still, of course, when you can get them. All these blasted factories.'[28] In time, however, such emotional attachment to royalty and empire faded, despite initial shock at the declaration of the Irish Republic in 1948 and withdrawal of Ireland from the Commonwealth a year later.

Politically they were not seen as a fifth column by the state, as the far more numerous Catholics in the North were, and, just like Catholics under the penal laws, they were more likely to be insulted than persecuted. Insults directed at southern Protestants usually reminded them of their new powerlessness and numerical inferiority, many recalling, like Lily, the children's chants of 'Proddy, woddy on the wall' and ruder derivatives. Very many southern Irish Catholics could (indeed still can) go through life without ever encountering a Protestant, and such separation has led to a fearful fascination and all manner of strange notions. Paul Durcan captures this perfectly in his 1970s poem 'What is a Protestant Daddy?' Their clergymen dressed oddly and looked different. They scurried about in small black cars, unlike the stately processing of the Catholic clergy. Children thought them some kind of conspirators, 'Evilly flapping...about our virginal souls'. But you didn't see much of them. They dashed across deserted streets into vast, forlorn cathedrals, 'all silent and aloof'. There were no congregations and what there were, were octogenarian.

> Protestants were Martians,
> Light years more weird
> Than zoological creatures;
> But soon they would all go away
> For as a species they were dying out,
> Soon there would be no more Protestants...
> O Yea, O Lord,
> I was a proper little Irish Catholic boy
> Way back in the 1950s.[29]

Although numerically, socially, and politically there is no comparison in the situations of the northern Catholics and southern Protestants after partition, they shared many of the characteristics of aggrieved minorities. They looked for prejudice and insults even when they were absent; they kept their heads down and stuck together; they maintained separate educational, medical, and social institutions from those of the state; they would weigh up the religious affiliation of those they were talking to before they opened up; they were defensive, prickly, and defiant all at once; and, just like the Ulster Catholics, they often acted in ways which intensified the stereotypes. There are memories of lonely childhoods separated from Catholic friends as they were sent to different schools and from Protestant friends sent to England for education.

Most of all they felt isolated in a country whose ethos was now so demonstrably Catholic and whose national narrative bore so little relationship to their own. Protestants found themselves defined by a negative as 'non-Catholic'. Preaching in St Patrick's Cathedral on the opening of the 1922 General Synod, the Church of Ireland Bishop of Limerick urged Protestants to particularly resist this offensive appellation, which challenged their Irishness and classed them with all manner of unbelievers. 'We might form the church of a minority', he proclaimed. 'But our spiritual heritage went back to Patrick and the ancient Catholic Church.'[30] Once again the perceived values of Protestantism—individualism, freedom of conscience, honesty, and reliability—were emphasized, and the Church of Ireland went through another period of divesting itself of any signs of popery, and further 'Protestantizing' church services and clerical dress. Any cleric unhappy with these new canons had little chance of promotion, and Anglicanism's self-allusions to 'Catholic' or use of the term 'priest' were frowned upon. All of this was rigorously inculcated in the segregated schools through the General Synod examination, only finally abandoned in 1965.[31]

As in the North, the historically antagonistic Churches coexisted by keeping apart, and the sense that they were a tiny and receding island in a threatening sea of Catholicism made southern Protestants even more sensitive. The children's taunts reflected their own belief that their very survival was at risk. Archbishop Gregg spoke in 1946 about the Protestant and Catholic communities being 'outside one another'. 'It is a fact that we are outside the close-knit entity which the majority constitutes,' the smaller community declining because, 'on sociological grounds . . . Individuals transfer themselves to a more sympathetic environment.'[32]

If emigration affected every community, the 'mixed marriage' spelt annihilation for one whose island was less than 5 per cent and shrinking, unless protective measures were taken. The widely lampooned image of the Catholic priest denouncing 'company keeping' from the pulpit, and wandering the lanes of rural Ireland in search of courting couples, is replicated in the Protestant clergy's attempts at control over events where their young might meet Catholics and a future generation be lost to their faith. In west Cork, which had a higher concentration of Protestants than in most rural areas, there was a kind of 'parallel universe', as David Butler aptly terms it, where the Protestant young went to 'proddy hops', the entrance tickets having been signed by the church rector.[33] No Church liked mixed marriages. But in Ireland the Catholic Church's rulings are remembered with great bitterness by many Protestants and are held responsible (not entirely accurately[34]) for the progressive decline of the minority in the South. Protestants point repeatedly to the effects of the Catholic Church's *Ne Temere* decree, requiring the children of mixed marriages to be raised as Catholics, and although this was softened in 1970, Irish Catholicism traditionally took a hard line. Catholics and Protestants were repeatedly reminded of the dangers of such marriages by their clergy, and they were few. Even on holiday Protestants were warned to avoid the cinema and dance-hall as 'the first step on the road to a mixed marriage and the dreaded consequence of capitulation to Rome'.[35]

Catholic religious ceremonies regularly took over the thoroughfares, soldiers marching alongside. Bishop Michael Mayes recalled encountering a Corpus Christi procession in Dublin in 1958, and finding hundreds of eyes trained on him as he remained standing when all the Catholics went on their knees and said the rosary as the host passed. 'It was a strange, bewildering, sometimes frightening and very much a *foreign* world to be in... Here was power [i.e. of the Catholic Church] such as I had never experienced it before.'[36] You could feel very alone and awkward if a Protestant.

Apartness meant that Protestants and Catholics had developed different languages. Catholic phrases and customs had slipped into official culture, unnoticed by the majority, but for Protestants they were another factor making them feel like outsiders. The media tended to refer to *the* Church (meaning Catholic); state hospitals had holy statues and crucifixes, and priests recited the rosary in their wards; exclamations such as 'Jesus, Mary, and Joseph' (which for Protestants is blasphemy) or 'Holy Mother of God' were in general usage; the Angelus rang out twice a day in towns and villages and on the national radio station; landladies automatically told new guests the times of mass. The Donegal teacher May McClintock recalled the many holy pictures in the hotel where she lodged as a young teacher, when her family home only had embroidered pictures of biblical quotations. The Catholic Church was accorded a special place in the constitution and was seen to inform a number of major ethical decisions by the state, which then became part of Protestants' storehouse of victim lore, much as state sectarianism in the North was for Catholics. Indeed, given the core fears of popery outlined earlier, Church of Ireland clergy expressed outrage at the new state swearing allegiance to Rome. However, John Whyte concluded, in his pioneering 1971 study of the relationship between the Catholic Church and the Irish state, that the bishops interfered far less than legend allows. They did not need to. 'In a mainly Catholic country, the Catholic hierarchy has a weapon which no other interest possesses: its authority over men's consciences. Most politicians . . . are committed Catholics . . . recognise that the majority of the electorate are believers, and will act accordingly.'[37]

There were a number of notorious incidents in the 1950s which have become part of the Protestant folklore of victimhood, and shame on the part of the Catholic majority, as Ireland liberalized and secularized in later years. The Tilson case of 1950–1 was a reminder, if Protestants needed one, of the way in which Catholic mores pervaded Irish public life. Ernest Tilson, the Protestant father of three children, had on marriage to his Catholic wife agreed to raise the children as Catholic. He later changed his mind and removed the children when the marriage got into difficulties. The case came before Mr Justice George Gavan Duffy (member of the High Court 1936–46 and its President 1946–51), who had a history of overriding precedents developed under English law, to make Irish law more reflective of the country's Catholic ethos.

> The . . . Constitution affirms the indefeasible right of the Irish people to develop its life in accordance with its own genius and traditions. In a State where nine out of every ten citizens today are Catholics and on a matter closely touching the religious outlook of the people, it would be intolerable that the common law, as expounded after the Reformation in a Protestant land, should be taken to bind a nation which persistently repudiated the Reformation as heresy.[38]

In the Tilson case he ruled in favour of the Catholic mother, citing the special position of the Catholic Church in the constitution, which in his interpretation required judicial notice of canon law.[39]

In fact, this was one of a number of causes célèbres which seriously bothered many Catholics. Another was the Fethard-on-Sea boycott scandal of 1957, for which the Catholic Church felt compelled to apologize twenty years later, and a popular feature film (*A Love Divided*, 1998) portrayed the fault as lying entirely with the Church. In this small Wexford village, Catholics, apparently prompted by their parish priest, boycotted the entire Protestant community, thought to have supported the action of the Protestant mother in a mixed marriage, when she, like Eric Tilson, changed her mind about bringing the children up as Catholics and took them away to Belfast. Some Catholic bishops supported the boy-cott. But most, including the Archbishop of Armagh, Cardinal John d'Alton, refrained from public statement, showing an extra-ordinary lack of moral courage, even if, technically, canon law prevented one bishop from interfering in the diocese of another. Cardinal d'Alton, himself something of a liberal, nevertheless feared drawing the fire of northern Protestants; it came anyway. Even the local Church of Ireland bishop seemed anxious to play the episode down. But lay Catholics and Protestants alike were outraged. De Valera denounced the boycott in the Dáil. The historian John Whyte was told of Catholics travelling out of their way to shop at the boycotted Protestant businesses. But it was never formally called off by the Catholic bishops, who on mixed marriages, as on a number of other issues, were to find themselves out of line with Catholic Church leaders elsewhere in the world in the lead-up to Vatican II.[40]

Protestant intellectuals could be more forthright than their Church leaders. Foremost among them was the prolific essayist Hubert Butler. But he often told Protestants uncomfortable truths about themselves which they thought best left unsaid, and they came to fear his many public statements. To Catholics in general he appeared to talk with the same condescension and anti-popery as the old ascendancy. 'I am a child of the Reformation', he argued, proclaiming its legacy to Protestants of individual con-science against the control of the Catholic Church. He criticized his co-religionists for not accepting anti-Catholicism as part of the 'title-deeds' of their faith, and he saw their failure to mount a sustained attack on the intolerant Catholicism of Irish society as a betrayal of their natural role. He tore into Brian Inglis for his book *West Briton* (1962), for what he considered its apologetic tone for Protestants' past sins. And much as members of the Catholic middle class of the 1790s blamed the meek gratitude of their hierarchy for scraps of reform, so he criticized the way twentieth-century Catholics spoke of toleration and Protestants accepted it, repeating the 1790s argument that tolerance was the other side of intolerance.

Paradoxically he often found more support among Catholic intellectuals than Protestants, particularly during the so-called Papal Nuncio incident in 1952. With significant personal knowledge of Yugoslavia, he had criticized the Catholic Church's one-sided emphasis on Communist persecution by writing extensively about Catholic massacres of Serbs and forced conversions in Croatia. The papal legate walked out of a meeting in the Shelburne Hotel at which Butler challenged the speaker, who had spoken only of Communist mistreatment of the Catholic Church. There was uproar in the press, and protests about a papal representative having been insulted 'in a Catholic country' substituted for real debate. Butler found himself ostracized. His home county council, Kilkenny, called a special meeting to discuss his actions, at which the chairman made a characteristic, though self-defeating, effort to deny that they were in any way sectarian. As Robert Tobin's masterly study of Butler concludes, more was involved than what he had said about the Catholic Church in Croatia. Rather, 'he had upset a delicate balance in Kilkenny whereby Catholics generously affirmed the principle of toleration so long as Protestants ensured its actual practice remained unnecessary. By voicing his dissent publicly on such a sensitive topic, Butler had put an end to this charade, leaving Catholics sounding curiously defensive even as they spoke of how offended they were.'[41] It was the traditional propensity of Irish Catholics and Irish Protestants to look for insults and feel satisfied at their prejudices being confirmed when they apparently found them. Butler perceptively saw the pettiness in it all. 'I think all this pious indignation is a fake from start to finish', but—and he told of how one farmer, a long-term renter of one of his fields, sought a rent reduction—it is 'a wonderful excuse for exploiting the sinner'.[42]

Although Butler is considered one of the intellectuals who helped bring Ireland out of its self-imposed obscurantism, it is hard not to have some sympathy with the fear of his co-religionists that his outspokenness would simply 'get us into trouble'.[43] For while many Catholics agreed with him, much of what he said could be interpreted as Protestant condescension towards 'priest-ridden Ireland'. Even his call to his own community to assert their proper role in Irish society could sound like Protestants claiming the right to lead the slavish Catholics, much as their ancestors had done in the past.

Not surprisingly, when ecumenism spread elsewhere in world Christianity, Ireland moved slowly. At the Second Vatican Council the Irish Catholic bishops, with their talk of reconciling 'dissenters' to the true Church of Christ, seemed to come from a different era.[44] Hans Kung thought Vatican II had come too late for the rest of the world, but not for Ireland.[45] The new ice age of the 1950s began to melt in the 1960s, largely through overtures from Rome itself to the other Churches, resulting in 1960 in the first meeting since the Reformation between a pope and an archbishop of Canterbury. Thus was opened a dialogue for Christian unity which has continued in fits and starts to the present. The Catholic Archbishop of Dublin, John Charles McQuaid, was not enthusiastic, stating in 1966: 'Non-Catholics represent to us the people who deliberately strove for centuries to destroy the one true Faith, who till very recently occupied the dominant position in our economic and cultural life and who to-day stand for the English remnant that still holds a very great share of the sources of economic life.'[46] Archbishop McQuaid was of the same revolutionary generation as the men who led the state, but new men and new attitudes were coming to the fore in the Catholic Church. The same was happening in the Protestant Churches, those who had taken decades to recover from the 'psychological trauma' of finding themselves on the losing side after the 1920s giving way to new leadership. Then came the Troubles, revealing the continuing strength of religious divisions, and not just in the North.

Catholics in Northern Ireland after Partition

Arthur Clery had a knack, along with his hero D. P. Moran, for telling 'awkward truths'.[47] Unlike the anti-Treatyites, of which he was one, he supported partition—though along a line from Newry to Derry, which would still leave majority Catholic areas with the South. He anticipated the question: But what about the Catholics left behind, particularly in Belfast? His response: Why should the rest of Ireland be held hostage to the 'crawling' Ulster Catholic, already infected by the settler culture surrounding them? And, with malicious humour, he wondered whether there could be reciprocal arrangements for the Catholics of Belfast and the Protestants of Dublin, 'setting-off of the Falls Road against Rathmines'—working-class Catholic against middle-class Protestant. Then, he added, expressing another awkward truth, 'we shall have made the boundary of our country coincide with that of our people'.[48] Lack of sympathy for northerners of any hue, while maintaining the one-nation, reunification rhetoric, would be a feature of southern Irish politics for the next fifty years.[49] Little wonder that northern Catholics were confused.

For northern Catholics, particularly those in predominantly nationalist areas, it was hard to comprehend rule by their old enemies in Belfast, after centuries from Dublin and a Dublin now in *their* control. It had all been very sudden. In the last parliamentary elections held in a united Ireland (1918), Sinn Féin withheld its seventy-three new MPs from the parliament in London and set up the first Dáil in Dublin, leaving a tiny rump of largely northern nationalist MPs to fight unsuccessfully against partition. With some justification bitter northern nationalists would chide Sinn Féin for following a purely southern agenda, thereby contributing to the partition of the country.[50] With the boundary of the new state still to be permanently decided (1925), nationalists boycotted the Northern Ireland parliament (set up in 1921) and every other state body. While abstention and ambivalence were not quite the same as active resistance, and Unionism never gave credit to the predominance of non-violent nationalism in Ulster Catholicism, republican violence in the early days of the new state, and intermittently thereafter, fed the old stereotype of Catholics as rebels. The northern IRA had compensated for lack of numbers and arms by staging spectacular assassinations and burning of buildings. In the retaliation it was Belfast Catholics who paid the price for republican violence, and they figured disproportionately among those killed and expelled from their homes and workplaces in the years 1920–2. Father John Hassan, curate of St Mary's in central Belfast (and author of *Belfast Pogrom*, detailing the violence), did not blame ordinary Protestants, for they too had felt compelled to flee their homes.[51] But the movement into one-religion ghettos had been largely that of the city's Catholics. A quarter of its entire Catholic population, some 23,000, had fled for safety, adding to a hothouse of resentful communal memories built up from the many previous sectarian attacks which had made Belfast the most riot-torn city in Europe. Four years after the end of the violence, Patrick Shea described the atmosphere:

The Catholics, large numbers of them crowded into streets along the Falls Road, were cowed and dispirited; they had seen riots and death, the burning of homes and business premises, the violent expulsion of their men from the shipyards and factories and building sites. They had stories of murder and cruelty, of the wild exploits of the Special Constabulary, the bigoted outbursts of political leaders. The Protestants had something to say about the involvement of the IRA in the city's troubles but the Catholics discounted any allegations that blame lay on their side. They feared their Protestant neighbours with the anger of a people who had been subdued by force and left without any means of retaliating against their persecutors.[52]

At the time of partition Catholics were divided: those in border areas were more supportive of Sinn Féin and non-recognition of the new state, while those in Belfast and the eastern counties, long used to operating in a majority Protestant environment, supported the more moderate Nationalist Party. While aspiring to future reunification, the Nationalist Party sought to work with the new government. But the Catholic Bishop of Down and Connor and future primate (1928–45) Joseph MacCrory chose to work through Michael Collins rather than the northern Nationalist leader, Joseph Devlin. In retrospect this very public association of Ulster's Catholics with Sinn Féin was a disastrous misjudgement and was unrepresentative of majority Catholic opinion. In 1925 Devlin (with a huge West Belfast personal vote, which included working-class Protestants) led the Nationalist MPs into the northern parliament. But those early crucial years when they might have exercised some influence within the state had been lost. Given that most Catholics, like most Protestants, would have preferred continued rule from London to partition, it is surprising how quickly the Unionist state, with its large and unreconciled minority, settled into the status quo. In the early days there *were* Catholics willing to work with the new state and there was clear confusion about how to react to partition. Many commentators agree that they might have responded more positively had there been greater generosity on the part of Unionists.[53] However, political Protestantism had assumed the role of vigilant loyalism centuries earlier, and little had convinced it to change its tune. We should never lose sight of the fact that politicians were more often than not at the more extreme ends of their constituent groupings and there was never a decade when moderate Protestants did not challenge their bigoted statements. Indeed, successive Unionist Ministers for Home Affairs tried to act fairly and banned Orange parades through Catholic areas, only to be toppled from their posts. Alas, their stand was not remembered.[54]

The problem for the southern Protestant minority was the power of the Catholic Church and the intertwining of Catholicism with nationality. The problem for the northern Catholic minority, ironically, was the same, but they did not realize it. They did not realize it because political Protestantism translated Catholics' religious identity into other terms, 'disloyalists', 'scroungers', 'whingers', and any number of other insulting epithets. It is important to recall here the various elements in Protestant anti-popery, noted earlier, and the historical reasons for the concentration of ultra-Protestantism in Ulster. Put these together with high levels of segregation, the generally lower economic and social status of northern Catholics, the existence of a new Catholic state in the south (causing fear among Protestants and expectations of triumph among Catholics), and dismal political and religious leadership, and this was a pretty nasty cocktail. In Northern Ireland there were two communities fated to live together, their leaders determined to show how very reluctantly they were doing so.

Catholics in Northern Ireland were alternatively baffled and resentful at shows of anti-popery, the burning of the Pope in effigy on countless Twelfth bonfires, the numerous gable walls urging onlookers to 'F—— the Pope'. When this was explained (all too infrequently, for most people, conscious of their prejudices, tried to avoid giving offence), Catholics were startled and hurt. Patrick Shea put it eloquently:

> To many of my colleagues [in the Northern Ireland civil service after 1926] Catholics were strange animals of which they had astonishingly little knowledge ... I learned their beliefs about the power of the Pope and his clergy and no words could persuade them that I was not subject to malevolent direction by black-robed priests to whom Rome had entrusted its master plan for world domination ... under a Nationalist government [they believed that] the Pope would require his obedient Irish flock to banish the Protestants from the land.[55]

The issue for Protestants then was the Catholic Church itself. What Catholics could have done about that is difficult to see. It still is. They were rather unfortunate in the calibre of some of their Church leaders at the time, all of course firmly nationalist and opposed to partition. The Archbishop of Armagh, Cardinal Michael Logue, had condemned the violence and with the other bishops had excommunicated the anti-Treaty republicans. But he declined an invitation to the royal opening of the new parliament in 1921 and boycotted the official side of the Northern Ireland state, much to Devlin's distress. The state returned the insult by sending no representative to his funeral in 1924, though the King did. Bishop, later Cardinal, MacRory of Down and Connor (1915–28), then as Archbishop of Armagh (1928–45), made a number of injudicious statements in these years, which were pounced upon by vigilant Protestants as signs of 'the unchanging bigotry of Rome'.[56]

Catholics read reports of Unionist leaders denouncing their Church and themselves at Orange rallies, and with the sectarian attacks, notably in the 1930s, which often followed such rallies, these also became stored in Catholic folklore and reinforced the image, often repeated by the clergy, of the Church's and the people's struggle being one and the same.

While there was considerable diversity within the northern Catholic community and social interaction with Protestants on a number of levels, there were two common elements which united Catholics. Firstly, institutional Catholicism defined their lives and their politics and suffused their entire identity. Secondly, they knew that political Protestantism considered them inferior in every way. And the two were interconnected. Since it was for their religion that they were pilloried, there was pride in a strong Catholic Church and a publicly defiant commitment to it. Criticism, even anything other than total commitment, was unthinkable. For that would be giving in to the other's prejudices and your own community had imbibed all the Moran-like insults to silence you. And since Protestantism's long-standing fears of the Catholic Church had long ago been translated into the mindset 'We're on top because we're better', or cleaner, or more industrious, there was not much incentive to Catholics to understand. Indeed, it is only very recently that Protestant Church leaders have been willing to talk publicly about the anti-popery at the heart of their theology. So it is perhaps understandable why ordinary Catholics saw it purely and simply as bigotry. Protestant and Unionist anti-papist pronouncements reacted upon and reinforced the very object of their fears, the Catholic Church. As increasingly the Catholic Church became the visible representative of northern Catholics, so increasingly that was the very issue that made Protestants react in such a blatantly sectarian manner and why the Orange Order was so politically powerful. The obsession with the Catholic Church, noted earlier in the Unionist press and later in loyalist assumptions that it really was behind the IRA, was not so very different from that of ordinary Protestants, even though few carried it to such murderous extremes.

After partition northern Catholic society turned in on itself and, like the Protestant minority in the South, developed a parallel universe to the majority one. The separate social structures run by the Church were already there. Most Catholics read separate newspapers, often shopped in different shops, used Catholic professionals, and attended Catholic schools—stereotypes remaining undented by the lack of a need to interact at such basic levels. In nationalist areas Catholic religious festivals and processions took over the streets and roads in a pale imitation of loyalist ones, which dominated public spaces everywhere else. Tens of thousands would turn out for bishops' funerals, confraternities, and special high masses (120,000 attending that for the Catholic Truth Society in Belfast in 1934). Those for the Catholic emancipation centenary in 1929 and the Eucharistic Congress in 1932, linking into all-Ireland demonstrations of Catholic power, unnerved northern Protestants, for they coincided with a return to political power of anti-Treaty republicans and de Valera's election victory of 1932. Loyalists responded by attacking buses and trains taking the pilgrims to Dublin, particularly ugly scenes occurring in Ballymena.[57]

In the absence of a significant Catholic middle class and strong secular nationalist politics, after the death of the charismatic Joe Devlin in 1934, the clergy appeared increasingly as the main leaders of the Catholic community, fuelling existing Protestant beliefs about sinister priestly influences over their flocks. Much as in the past, politics appeared to be conducted at the church gates. This was considered the easiest way to 'canvass' constituents, when attendance at mass was almost 100 per cent and politics so religiously polarized. Church and people, nationalism and Catholicism, seemed as one. Devlin's successors as leaders of the Nationalist Party were all clerically connected and abstained from Stormont more often than not (when he had been so very critical of abstentionism). The closeness of the clergy to the Catholic community often worked well for Catholics. But it also meant that the Church felt that it alone spoke for that community. Indeed, in 1945 Bishop Neil Farren of Derry said as much in the fierce debate about the absence of lay members on Catholic school authorities.[58] They were also very effective in keeping alive the idea of the past persecution of the Church and relating it to the ongoing battle to retain separate denominational education in Northern Ireland.

Catholic culture settled into a largely passive sense of grievance, drawing on the already well-established traditions of the downtrodden and dispossessed Gael and suffering Church. Catholic print culture conveyed and sustained the victim psychology outlined in previous chapters. Almost every issue of the main Catholic newspaper, the *Irish News*, carried examples and complaints about discrimination, news about church services and celebrations, uncritical reports about the South, and frequent references to the Penal Laws—usually headlined 'Our Darkest Days'—and variations on how Catholics continued to be persecuted. There is the standard view of Protestants as planters, but also the apparently contradictory argument that they should accept their Irishness and join with the rest of Ireland. Another standard nationalist belief was that all Ireland's problems came from English tyranny. Yet there were frequent appeals to a perceived British sense of fair play and glowing reports when royal visitors came to Catholic establishments. Throughout there was a marked resistance to referring

to the northern state by any term other than the 'six counties'—
thereby refusing a legitimacy which the legal term 'Northern
Ireland' would afford. And within this fairly closed community,
super-nationalists watched for signs of slippage. 'Treason' it was
not, and London was critical of the way any discussion of an end of
partition was deemed a crime by Unionists.[59] However, Catholics
would not accept the legitimacy of the Unionist state, half-participated
in politics, shunned new institutions, then sulked when not invited
to state events. It was all very muted in comparison to that
expressed by militant republicans, petty even, but always enough
to keep the idea of 'a fifth column' alive.

Given the peculiar nature of Ulster society, discussed earlier,
and its concentration of ultra-Protestantism, the old issue of
whether Catholics could be 'loyal' to a Protestant state acquired
new relevance. Whether a part of twentieth-century Britain
should have been proclaiming itself 'a Protestant state', as Unionist leaders did, was not sufficiently addressed by the sovereign
power, even if it is entirely explicable in terms of the traditions
embedded in Ulster's religious culture and was usually a reaction
to southern politicians' rhetoric about Ireland as a 'Catholic
nation'. By invoking images of the long-perceived insidiousness
of popery—the Catholic state south of the border, its imperialistic
Church, its people infiltrating the north and taking Protestant
jobs—Unionist leaders fed the embattled triumphalism of populist
Unionism.

Catholics believed such attacks on their religion were just an
excuse for discrimination. A celebrated 1940 pamphlet, *The Persecution of Catholics in Northern Ireland*, by 'Ultach' (J. J. Campbell, a
moderate nationalist, future Queen's University professor and
BBC governor), called for a British inquiry into the treatment of
the North's minority. The problem was not partition as such, he

argued, but the existence of a one-party state, whose gerrymandering and abolition of proportional representation meant that any other party (even smaller Unionist ones) had little chance of gaining or sharing power. He cited all the statements of Unionist leaders (including two prime ministers) about Catholic disloyalty invariably made to Orange rallies and during elections called and fought on the one issue of partition. He added that he did not blame the ordinary Orangeman. He was told by authorities whom he trusted 'hair-raising stories about the tyranny of Rome' (and he cited speech after speech of leading Orangemen to this effect). Hatred of Rome was instilled from childhood. 'They are taught, too, all the scandalous stories about the Church that in other parts of the world have been relegated to a shameful past. "Maria Monk" is made live again', inspection of convents still called for, 'lurid' experiences recounted by 'ex-priests' and 'ex-nuns', and the young warned of 'a specially-trained troop of sirens' to lure Protestants into mixed marriages. 'He lives in real and constant fear of Rome', and he expects to be 'swamped' in a united Ireland. Predictably such attacks made Catholics defensive and protective of their Church.

'Ultach', like other nationalists, considered the 'disloyal' accusation an excuse for religious discrimination and argued that discrimination on religious grounds was something Britain would not tolerate. This is why Unionists dressed it up as 'disloyalty', and he quoted Sir Basil Brooke's defence of his controversial 1933–4 statements that Catholics were disloyal and should not be employed. Brooke, the future Prime Minister of Northern Ireland, declared himself astonished that 'these people appear rather hurt because of my utterances', and he denied ever having attacked any man because of his religion. But, he added in good political Protestant style, 'when that religion is so politically minded, and is out to destroy us as a body, it does concern us'.[60] Examine almost any 'defence', argued 'Ultach', and one would see that it all turned on the question of 'loyalty'.

> To the ordinary Englishman, and indeed, to outsiders generally the word loyalty... conveys a notion of loyalty to the King of England, to the flag, and to the Empire. The Six Counties is a 'loyal' area and it is natural sometimes that 'disloyalists' should get hurt. Riots 'break out' in 'disloyal' areas. 'Disloyalists' fail to get jobs. And so on. 'Well they must expect it if they are "disloyal"', says the outsider. But then the outsider does not know that the words 'loyalist' and 'disloyalist' have a meaning all their own in Northern Ireland.[61]

Many Protestants denied that there was discrimination against Catholics in employment, housing, electoral boundaries, and a host of other areas. But Lord Brookeborough (Northern Ireland premier, 1943–63) had bluntly explained the rationale: if Catholic numbers grew, they would vote us into a united Ireland. Keeping them out would encourage emigration—as it did. Mixed marriages were far more unpopular in Protestant than Catholic society, for, given Catholic Church rulings, the Protestant partner was considered lost anyway and the children certainly were. Watching Protestant decline in the South was more than mere propaganda—though it worked at that level too. 'We'll outbreed them yet' was indeed a factor in Catholic thinking, not just the extremes.[62] Census reports, as in the past, were scoured for signs of the inexorable rise of Catholic numbers, and there was considerable alarm when the 1951 census figures suggested a 'disloyal majority by 2000'.[63] By 1991 the rising numbers of Catholics seemed unstoppable, up to 42.5 per cent from 32.2 per cent in 1971. The census triggered a frightening escalation of loyalist murders of Catholics, even though its findings were challenged and partly discredited shortly afterwards.[64] It was sometimes difficult for Catholics to see the fears behind this.

The way the carnage in the First World War was added to the scales of Protestant loyalty was challenged by Catholics. Catholic ex-soldiers protested at their expulsion from the shipyard as 'disloyalists' and made a submission to the Boundary Commission to counter the Unionists' 'loyalty'-based case for partition. The *Irish News* conducted an informal survey of Catholic families in one street. It found that in twenty-one families, sixty-five members had served in the armed forces and ten had died on active service.[65] In the South, however, parades on Armistice Day (Remembrance Sunday after the Second World War) had been attacked by republicans, and from the 1930s Irish state support was progressively whittled down. It has taken a long time for any official move towards reconciliation, the Irish President attending a Remembrance Sunday service for the first time only in 1993. As Jane Leonard has pointed out, such ambivalence by the Irish state 'deeply scarred' Irish war veterans and war-bereaved, and was one of the many aspects of southern Irish culture feeding northern Protestant fears about a united Ireland.[66]

Catholic ex-servicemen continued to parade in some parts of the North, but they too were progressively ignored by the Catholic press and clergy.[67] By the time of its 1987 Remembrance Day massacre of eleven civilians, the IRA could be sure that only Protestants would be killed, exposing its flawed claim that it only targeted instruments of the state. However, in this, as in other areas, there was an element of self-fulfilling prophecy. Catholic ex-servicemen—like the Stormont gardener dismissed in 1934 in response to Orange complaints—could expect little recognition from the Unionist state. The only Northern Ireland person to be awarded a VC after the Second World War, seaman James

Magennis, was ostracized by Protestants because he was a Catholic and by Catholics because he was a British serviceman and had to settle in England. Popular Unionism had assumed service and sacrifice in Britain's armed forces into its origin-myth. Gerry Fitt, who had served in the merchant navy in the Second World War, was abused by Protestants in York Street, en route to Belfast City Hall, for VJ day celebrations in 1945.

> They weren't too friendly and shouted insults about me being a Catholic and about Irish neutrality. I remember looking at all the Union jacks that were being waved about. I had served under it during the war and had been glad to do so but I realised that day that here it was a Protestant flag, a unionist flag, and it looked different to me then.[68]

Nationalist ambivalence about the legitimacy of the state also helped perpetuate that old Protestant belief that this was 'our' state, tolerating an 'ungrateful' minority. Patrick Shea observed that when Unionists talked about how Catholics fared in Northern Ireland, 'they talk as though the Protestant community has been sharing its wealth with the less well-deserving' and every decade of the twentieth century provided any number of examples of Unionist people saying as much.[69] The generally lower economic status of Catholics informed a long-standing Protestant stereotype of Catholics as spongers and whingers. This attitude was intensified by the arrival of the British-sponsored welfare state. Once again, the very real benefits to Catholics—which should have been making them feel less dissatisfied—became mired by political rhetoric and causes célèbres such as the exclusion of the Catholic Mater Hospital from the National Health Service, even though it catered to the local, largely working-class population, irrespective of religion. Instead it had to be self-funded through door-to-door collections, raffles, and other Church fundraising events, sustaining the traditional image of priest and people still struggling together.

New welfare legislation also allowed the idea of the lazy Taig living off the dole and diddling the state to be added to the myth of the Protestant work ethic, though this has since been exploded by sociological studies showing little difference between Protestant and Catholic attitudes to work. Whatever the causes and attitudes, unemployment became a way of life in some Catholic working-class areas, notably in Belfast and Derry, and was a factor in sending young males into the IRA. Eamonn McCann recalled how the army regularly arrested young rioters at the Unemployment Exchange in 1970. 'The irony of that was not missed. "The only place you can be certain of finding a Derry rioter is at the dole." '[70] Every analysis since the outbreak of the Troubles has found evidence of much higher unemployment rates among Catholic males (30 per cent in 1981 against 12 per cent Protestant). By 1993 it was still 24 per cent against 10 per cent, though between 52–60 per cent in areas of Derry and Belfast considered republican strongholds. Fierce controversies have raged over these figures, focusing largely on whether (if they were true) the cause was the lower skills among Catholics rather than discrimination. Working-class Protestants in Derry and Belfast, believing their own community in decline, have simply rejected these statistics, and since the Good Friday Agreement in 1998 the highly visible improvement in the economic status of Catholics (largely driven by the final arrival of a Catholic middle class) has deeply unnerved those working-class Protestants who have not moved on from the insidiousness-of-popery traditions of popular Protestantism.

The post-war welfare reforms fed into an improved climate of community relations in Northern Ireland and there were signs that the minority community was becoming reconciled. There was, by now, some understanding of why most Protestants feared reunification. 'The border is not merely a geographical division', wrote Bishop Eugene O'Callaghan of Clogher in 1957, denouncing the renewed IRA campaign of 1956–62. 'It is a spiritual division of minds and hearts which physical force cannot heal, but only aggravate.'[71] By the early 1960s the old men of the revolutionary era were leaving the stage in the North as well as the South. Terence O'Neill replaced the much disliked Brookeborough as Unionist Prime Minister in 1963. The northern bishops William Conway (Archbishop of Armagh, 1958–77) and William Philbin (Down and Connor, 1962–82) brought a new spirit to the Catholic hierarchy and were noted as the most forward-looking of the Irish bishops in the era of Vatican II. Unionists responded to this wave of reform of worldwide Catholicism under Pope John XXIII by flying the Union flag at half-mast on his death in 1963, over the often notoriously anti-Catholic City Hall in Belfast. An Irish Taoiseach (Lemass) came north on an official visit, the first since partition. The northern Nationalist Party declared itself the official opposition at Stormont, thereby providing the recognition which it had withheld for nearly half a century. There were many more signs of Catholics responding to the apparently changed climate by abandoning decades of negativity, all of which was reflected in the *Irish News*'s enthusiastic support for O'Neill's premiership.

In hindsight historians have queried O'Neill's genuine reformism. But that was not how many saw it at the time and there was a real sense of optimism abroad in the second half of the 1960s. The virulent anti-popery of Paisleyism seemed from another age and many simply incorporated it into that sectarian humour which flourishes in religiously divided societies. When some took the trouble to actually read his *Protestant Telegraph* or attend his sermons at his Martyrs' Memorial Church in Belfast, they concluded that this was Unionism with the lid off (to coin Conor Cruise O'Brien's description of Irish cultural nationalism). But at the time, his campaign against O'Neill and any Protestant institutions showing signs of weakening towards popery increased Catholic support for O'Neillism. Many Catholics were now making it through to university and had become somewhat dismissive of the folk memories of their parents' generation. It was, after all, 1968. Students marched out from Queen's University singing 'We shall overcome', believing, in a confused kind of way, that we were part of that same struggle for civil rights bringing students out halfway round the world. But things went very suddenly and disastrously wrong and the pessimists (or realists) said 'we told you so'.

The signs were already there. The fiftieth anniversary of the 1916 Easter rising in 1966 (unfortunately coinciding with that of the Somme) witnessed demonstrations and commemorative events in nationalist areas all over Northern Ireland. Extreme loyalists responded, as they had always done, by attacking Catholics. The feel-good factors which were allowing Catholics to identify more with the state were creating those tensions with which poorer Protestants had always reacted to signs of Catholics prospering. With the heavy industries in free-fall, where in the past they had been assured jobs, working-class Protestants refused to believe that Catholics were still disproportionally disadvantaged and every overdue reform was treated as popery closing in. After all, that is what they continued to be told by their leaders. Civil rights marchers were treated like the rebels they had always been told about. Another irritation was the sight of Catholic university students on perceived 'handouts' from 'their' state, when there was little tradition of the Protestant working class going through higher education. The brutal attack by Paisleyites and B Specials on student marchers at Burntollet in January 1969, and the subsequent riot by Royal Ulster Constabulary reserves in Derry, set the tone for the year.

The parading season had been quiet for some years. But with Unionism falling apart and critics baying for O'Neill's blood, no one in power seemed to think that perhaps in these months all parades and marches needed some controlling. Loyal parades became the opportunity of showing papists who really was in control, much as they had been in the past. Fifteen thousand loyalists descended on Derry for the annual Apprentice Boys' march of 12 August 1969. Throwing pennies down from the walls into the Catholic Bogside district below had been a feature of these parades in the past. But in the tinderbox conditions of 1969, it was this act which seems to have sparked the explosion that effectively marked the beginning of the Troubles. Once again, as in the nineteenth century, as in the 1920s and 1930s, the Catholic working classes of Belfast paid the price. Catholic teenagers taunted angry Protestant crowds by singing the Irish national anthem and hurled petrol bombs at the police. Protestants from the Shankill Road torched Catholic homes in the streets adjoining the Falls. Over the next few years 60,000 people were intimidated out of their homes in Belfast, almost 50,000 of them Catholic. Everyone seemed to be behaving as the stereotypes said they would. Even the Dublin government, so dismissive of northern Catholics in the past, made noises, which, much to the dismay of civil rights leaders like John Hume, gave rise to a belief that the Irish army was about to invade.[72] It was the need for defence of the Catholic ghettos which called the IRA back into existence, and this time it was a new, more Catholic brand of the IRA than before, more informed by the communal history of northern Catholicism.

The future broadcaster and journalist Malachi O'Doherty, a Falls Road Catholic in 1969, was walking his Protestant girlfriend to the bus stop on the evening of 13 August on the second night of rioting in Belfast. They looked up Divis Street at the rioters attacking the police station. She was contemptuous. He tried to explain that there was a background to it.[73] Others, too, recalled a sudden awareness of the different religion of friends, neighbours, girlfriends, and boyfriends. In working-class areas it could become positively dangerous not to share the religious identity of the area, and further religious segregation (enforced and voluntary) became one of the earliest and most lasting consequences of the Troubles. O'Doherty went on to be a frequent critic of republicanism and nationalism alike. But his recollection of August 1969 underlines an important factor in the Northern Ireland Troubles: Protestant and Catholic origin-myths put them into context. You knew where they came from. It took tremendous courage, particularly on the part of public figures, to see the flaws in those origin-myths. The atrocities carried out in their name by their extremes came to invalidate their rights to the moral heights of victimhood, though it is far too early to expect those who really have been victims to recognize as much. They have also made it difficult to show how unrepresentative the murderous republicans and loyalists actually have been of the communities from which they came.

Certainly all Catholics and Protestants would have imbibed the ideas of the other religious culture discussed in this book, and yes the friendship and neighbourliness may have been across the divide. But Northern Ireland never descended into civil war, even during the Troubles. The 'whatever you say, say nothing' syndrome of different communities, living together in genuine friendship and respect, is sometimes mocked. But although soft sectarianism underlay such mutual agreement to avoid things which would divide, there was often a polite gentleness and a genuine cross-community neighbourliness which may take decades to rebuild, if at all. Most people can tell endless stories of how daily life operated perfectly reasonably between the extremes. But one of my favourites is that by the former Ombudsman Dr Maurice Hayes, who recounts having to take the oath of loyalty before a magistrate in the 1950s before embarking on a teaching career. Other Catholics sought a Catholic magistrate who would under-stand their reluctance. But he was having no such equivocation. He declared his allegiance before a Protestant JP and his determination to return to tell him if he ever felt impelled to withdraw it. 'He looked at me with mounting horror and said he did not think that would be necessary, that it was no part of his function and that, in such a case, he would be better not knowing. We had a pleasant discussion about the novels he remembered from his Edwardian schooldays, and the proprieties had been attended to.'[74]

Recent commentators have pointed to a widening of the gulf between North and South, a growing identification between Cath-olic and Protestant in the South and a weakening of links with their co-religionists in the North.[75] The northern versions of their reli-gious identities are unwelcome reminders of a past sectarianism which people in the Irish Republic would prefer to forget. Patrick Williams's 'barbarians' are now on the north side of the border. Southern Protestants told interviewees for a 2002 book that they thought the northerners 'crazy people' and things would be far worse for them if Ireland were to be reunited (when Protestants would be 20 per cent instead of 3 per cent).[76] The annual Orange riots at Drumcree Church of Ireland church from 1996 alienated southern Protestants and seem to have effectively partitioned the Church of Ireland, the one Protestant Church with an all-Ireland ethos, the one-time common movement of clergy between North and South having already dried up.[77] Most northern Protestants did not go south anyway and the heightened criticism in these years from their southern co-religionists made little difference (except to the difficult position of the leader of the Church of Ireland, Archbishop Robin Eames). The end of the Troubles and the declining role of the Catholic Church has allowed southern Protestants to speak more openly about what it felt like being a small and endangered minority after partition. Although causing great offence at the time, David Trimble's 2002 reference to the Irish Republic as a monocultural sectarian state was echoed by the Revd John Faris, a Presbyterian minister in Cork: 'I sense residual sectarianism in the Republic, with insufficient "closure" on the sectarian violence connected with the foundations of this State', and he was upset at the 2001 state funerals accorded some of the IRA men executed by Britain during the war of independence eighty years earlier.[78] Even in the Irish Republic healing has still some way to go.

The pace of change in Northern Ireland has surpassed everybody's expectations. However, unlike southern Protestants, it is too early for northern Catholics to reassess their past with quite such honesty. And even though opinion polls show very high percentages of Protestants and Catholics looking to a greater mixing of communities, it remains an aspiration.[79] We still await another in-depth study of attitudes such as Fionnuala O Connor's 1993 study of Catholics' reassessment of their identity after twenty-five years of violence. Then, there was considerable reluctance not to 'rehash it all', a consciousness that the grievances charted by the civil rights movement sounded old hat and much catalogued. But they could not deny what shaped them, and older Catholics spoke of how inferior and humiliated they had been made to feel in the Northern Ireland state. I found these feelings to be widespread among Catholics in research into my *Catholics of Ulster* (2000), informing its concluding chapter, 'A Resentful Belonging'.[80]

IRA violence, however, had caused a major rethink among northern Catholics about their identity. There was recognition (and considerable bitterness) at the way in which the South had often kept alive their hopes of reunification in the past, then seemed more favourably disposed towards Unionists than themselves. Many Fionnuala O Connor spoke to, particularly republicans, thought southern lack of sympathy was all part of a new snobbery radiating out from 'Dublin 4'. This use of the trendy liberal part of Dublin city has become another slogan to denounce any new thinking on the national issue. Dislike of the northerner was given a new life by the Troubles, rather than the expected identity of suffering which shared nationalist traditions had taught northerners to assume. 'You consider yourselves far too new-fashioned to be old-fashioned', wrote Sinn Féin's publicity officer Danny Morrison to the *Irish Times* in April 1993. 'In your sophistication, your smugness, your aloofness, your hypocrisy and your forgetfulness, you are as guilty for prolonging this conflict as I am of participating in it.'[81] He had a point, but the object of his criticism was too narrow. Rather it should have been directed at the entire national origin-myth to which most Irish Catholics continue to subscribe while airily dismissing its manifestation in the Troubles as northern sectarianism. In Northern Ireland the religiously based and conflicting world-views which I have endeavoured to unscramble in this book were left to fester, largely dismissed by the two states whose forebears had created them in the first place.

But there are increasing numbers of people resisting the 'Which religion?' question in census and other official forms. The march of secularism and the retreat of religion to the private sphere might further the Northern Ireland peace process. South of the border it has certainly halted the apparently inexorable decline of Protestantism.

There are some interesting parallels. Just as southern Protestants fell suddenly from a position of power and developed a sense of victimhood before they could accept the new reality, so northern Protestants' sense of a lost golden past and like claims to victimhood may presage a similar pragmatism. Also the much anticipated 2001 census took the heat out of the idea of demographic creep by those fecund papists towards a united Ireland, and, as Kevin Bean argues, dealt 'a blow to one of the main assumptions underpinning Sinn Féin strategy'.[82] With results showing only small changes (the Northern Ireland populace 44 per cent Catholic, 53 per cent Protestant) and Catholic–Protestant birth rates starting to equalize, the idea that Catholics in time would be the majority has faded. The belief that they would vote the North into a united Ireland has been flawed in any case, referendums consistently indicating that up to a third might not so choose, given that choice. There is also some evidence of return migration by Protestants who left during the Troubles. This message has not trickled through to some working-class Protestant communities, programmed to see every Catholic advance as their loss. Time will tell whether the removal of the political threat will see this transmute into a class rather than a sectarian issue. But we should not be in too much of a hurry. It took their southern brethren half a century to get where they are now, and even they are still angry at continuing signs of political popery, though disguised as modern nationalism. Here changes within Catholicism will be as important in the North as they have been in the South, particularly since the Catholic minority, beached early last century, has finally been given that stake in Northern Ireland which was partly withheld and partly rejected for much of its existence.

Afterword

> And I envy the intransigence of my own
> Countrymen who shoot to kill and never
> See the victim's face become their own
> Or find his motive sabotage their motives...
> And one read black where the other read white, his hope
> The other man's damnation:
> Up the Rebels, To Hell with the Pope,
> And God save—as you prefer—the King or Ireland....
> And each one in his will
> Binds his heirs to continuance of hatred.

In this bleak poem, 'Autumn Journal', Louis MacNeice returns to one of his common themes, his 'love–hate relationship with Ireland' and 'the inescapability' of its 'polarities'.[1] These 'polarities' have also been the subject of this book. Why did I choose this subject for the Ford Lectures? Was it unfinished business, mopping up elements which I had left loose in many previous works? Or was it some kind of personal mission to answer questions which still disturbed me? Certainly the exploration of the theology behind anti-popery fell into that category, as did the continuing frustration at the way in which so many people failed to see that their religion could sometimes be a source of evil as well as good and how, given multiple choices, they had chosen the most negative to cling onto. And I can only apologize to some of my audience back then, who had wanted to hear a rosier 'the war is over' story. Perhaps it is—though it is too early to say. But I am a historian and I always want to know where things have come from. I also know that there is never one side to a story.

Much of what I have written here will make for uncomfortable reading, but I will be very surprised if there are not twinges of recognition. We were perhaps more ready to recognize our complicity in these attitudes during the Northern Ireland Troubles (which exposed the more extreme consequences of Irish nationalism and Ulster unionism and loyalism). We seem less so now. There are endless self-congratulatory meetings about how peace was achieved. We are even trying to show the world how we did it. Are we also trying to show how the murderousness happened in the first place?

Every people develops origin-myths, and the idea of a nation can be a benign solvent, bringing a common good out of diversity. The problem in Ireland is that there were two 'peoples' whose origin-myths have been based on extremely negative views of each other and, because these were religiously based, the clerics had far more power than they should have had. 'Irishness' has not been a broad church; its characteristics, defined by hostile outsiders and embittered insiders, have been narrow and sectarian. It found a way of disguising its sectarianism by embracing anti-Britishness and focusing in on Wolfe Tone's 'common name of Irishman' ideal. 'Catholicity', however, infused it, and the institutional Catholic Church was at its heart. There is no 'icity' in Protestant culture, which depended less on religious institutions than on anti-popery and exclusive political power as its gels. This will certainly pose a problem as the institutional Churches retreat.

None of this can be approached in 'sound-bites', which explains why it frequently seems as if the sloganizing extremists, looking for offence, have occupied centre stage. The less extreme are effectively censored by such baiting, knowing that every incautious word will be pounced upon. So their own culture remains unchallenged from within. A century ago George Birmingham commented on how this brought a superficial 'stability' to Irish society: 'We have attained a religious stability which would be simply impossible in a people deeply interested in religion.'[2] It was a label one was born with. Few gave much thought to the elements behind the brand description, but emphasized its exclusivity and were as resistant to sharing it as any modern commercial company. And yet, some historical awareness reveals more than just godliness behind the creation and perpetuation of the sectarianized identities here discussed. The elites did rather well out of them.

As I close this book I recall a visit with a friend to the Catholic church where her parents and grandparents had worshipped. It is one of those truly magnificent structures that one encounters in Ireland, frequently towering over or juxtaposed against crowded, poor communities, much as Plunkett or McCarthy had so critically described them a hundred years ago. Their mushrooming throughout Ireland (and beyond) in the late nineteenth–early twentieth centuries was a visible and popular token of Catholicism's re-emergence as a powerful institution after centuries of being the underdog. I understood this, have written about it, and had much sympathy for it. But I also know that the pennies of the poor played a major part in such restored magnificence. As we looked at the dazzling golden sunburst surrounding the Madonna on a side altar, she told me how a call went out for parishioners to donate items of gold to be melted down to create the magnificent altarpiece, and how her father had donated her grandmother's wedding ring, the only material object which linked him to the mother he never knew because she had died in childbirth. She was visibly upset. Like Bridie Steen and the Protestant family Bible, this was her forebears somehow locked up in an institutional religion which put a distance between them and herself. This may pale into insignificance beside the great lordly estates and ancestral homes, built on lands which Catholics believed stolen from their ancestors—though resting on the labours and rents of the poor of all denominations. I end this book with these thoughts, because I have only obliquely been able to touch on the consequences of the religious policies of the elites for the bulk of Irish people in the past and I can put it no better than did my friend Owen Dudley Edwards when returning an early draft of this book, which he had just read:

> My Dear Marianne,
> I went with a group to Chatsworth of Ducal ownership . . . and after seeing how Bess of Hardwick and her successors bled their countrymen white, the miserable contestants for scratched livings in Ulster seem noble and virtuous by comparison. In your conclusion there would be much to be said for an act of respect for past generations on both sides, who however mutually rapacious and murderous, were still figures of greater integrity than the lords of human kind who ruled and racked them, be such rulers clerical or lay.

Amen

Notes

Preface

1. Amin Maalouf, *On Identity* (London, 2000), 36.

1. Irish Christians *Again*

1. This was used as the frontispiece to D. H. Akenson, *Small Differences: Irish Catholics and Irish Protestants, 1815–1922. An International Perspective* (Dublin, 1991).
2. Sean O'Faolain, *The Irish* (West Drayton, 1947), 6.
3. Marilyn Silverman and P. H. Gulliver (eds), *Approaching the Past: Historical Anthropology through Irish Case Studies* (New York, 1982), 8–11, gives a good example of this happening in County Kilkenny. See also discussion of how 'political entrepreneurs' use the past to invent the traditions of group identity in Joseph L. Soeters, *Ethnic Conflict and Terrorism: The Origins and Dynamics of Civil Wars* (Abingdon, 2005), 83–6.
4. Patrick Clancy, Sheelagh Drudy, Kathleen Lynch, and Liam O'Dowd (eds), *Irish Society: Sociological Perspectives* (Dublin, 1995), 14–17.
5. Robert Benjamin Tobin, 'The Minority Voice: Hubert Butler, Southern Protestantism and Intellectual Dissent, 1930–72', D.Phil. thesis (Oxford University, 2004), 151: Butler's criticism of people like Patrick Kavanagh, who dismissed the Literary Revival legacy as 'the foul aftertaste of the Anglo-Irish Ascendancy', while working for the BBC and the British Council.
6. R. F. Foster, *Luck and the Irish: A Brief History of Change c.1970–2000* (London, 2007), 6; Nicholas Canny, 'Why the Reformation Failed in Ireland: *Une Question mal posée*', *Journal of Ecclesiastical History*, 30 (1979), 423–50.

7. D. H. Akenson, *Intolerance: The E-Coli of the Human Mind* (Canberra, 2004), 60.

8. R. Scott Appleby, *The Ambivalence of the Sacred: Religion, Violence and Reconciliation* (Lanham, Md., 2000), 69.

9. Joseph Liechty and Cecilia Clegg, *Moving beyond Sectarianism: Religion, Conflict, and Reconciliation in Northern Ireland* (Dublin, 2001), 31–2, 39; John Fulton, *The Tragedy of Belief: Division, Politics and Religion in Ireland* (Oxford, 1991), 117, on the inability of religious people to see the link between religion and sectarianism.

10. Liechty and Clegg, *Moving beyond Sectarianism*, 114–17.

11. Interview in the 1980s with O'Donnell, in Ronnie Munck and Bill Rolston, *Belfast in the Thirties: An Oral History* (Belfast, 1987), 183–4. See *Irish News*, 28 Mar. 1932: the march was to Milltown cemetery and had been banned by the Minister of Home Affairs. A priest led the marchers as they recited the rosary in Irish. The protest passed off peacefully. 'Secular Republican', *An Phoblacht*, 12 Apr. 2007, complains of the same. An interesting survival of the rosary as protest is recorded in Tom Inglis, *Global Ireland: Same Difference* (New York, 2008), 251–2, when protesters against the Shell gas pipeline in Mayo in September 2006 successfully resisted dispersal by the Garda by maintaining the recitation of the rosary over many hours.

12. Seamus Heaney, *North* (London, 1975), 53.

13. Sigmund Freud, *Civilization and its Discontents* (New York, 1989), 72.

14. J. J. Lee, *Ireland 1912–1985: Politics and Society* (Cambridge, 1989), p. xiv.

15. Micheál MacGréil, *Prejudice in Ireland Revisited* (Maynooth, 1996), 102, 118, 121, 244–32. In terms of ethnic preferences, the Northern Irish came sixth, behind the British, Scottish, and Americans.

16. Tariq Modood and Pnina Werbner (eds), *The Politics of Multiculturalism in the New Europe: Racism, Identity and Community* (London, 1997), 175, and 10, 13, 169–71, 178, on essentialism. A very good survey of the problems can be found in Máiréad NicCraith, *Culture and Identity Politics in Northern Ireland* (Basingstoke, 2003), 1–13.

17. Amin Maalouf, *On Identity* (London, 2000), 21–31, 36.

18. MacGréil, *Prejudice in Ireland Revisited*, 102–3.

19. Anton Blok, 'The Narcissism of Minor Differences', *European Journal of Social Theory*, 1/1 (July 1998), 33–55, and the focus of Akenson's *Small Differences*, which has inspired much of the present book.

20. Tone's first memorial on the present state of Ireland, Feb. 1796, original in the Archives Nationales, Paris, AF IV 1671/88–92, printed in T. W. Moody, R. B. McDowell, and C. J. Woods (eds), *The Writings of Theobald Wolfe Tone, 1763–98*, ii (Oxford, 2001), 64.

21. *The Sunday Show*, RTE, Nov. 2004.

22. Henry Glassie, *Passing the Time in Ballymenone* (Bloomington, Ind., 1995), 18.

23. Peter McDonald, *Mistaken Identities: Poetry and Northern Ireland* (Oxford, 1997), 82.

24. Benedict Anderson, 'Selective Kinship', *Dublin Review* (Spring 2003), 5–29; my thanks to Roy Foster for bringing this to my attention.

25. Fionnuala O Connor, *In Search of a State* (Belfast, 1993), 246.

26. Joep Leerssen, 'Monument and Trauma: Varieties of Remembrance', in Ian McBride (ed.), *History and Memory in Modern Ireland* (Cambridge, 2001), 215–17.

27. Liechty and Clegg, *Moving beyond Sectarianism*, 65; *The Report of the Working Party on Sectarianism: A Discussion Document for Presentation to the Inter-Church Meeting* (Belfast, 1993). The omitted history of sectarianism was published as a separate pamphlet: Joseph Liechty, *Roots of Sectarianism in Ireland: Chronology and Reflections* (Belfast, 1993).

28. Toíbín may well have had in mind the real-life case of Mr Justice George Gavan Duffy, who, as President of the High Court in 1946–51, played a significant part in ensuring Ireland's law reflected her Catholic character; see J. H. Whyte, *Church and State in Modern Ireland, 1923–1970* (Dublin, 1971), 167–9.

29. Desmond Fennell, *The Changing Face of Catholic Ireland* (London, 1978), 24.

30. Stephen Mennell in Colin Murphy and Lynne Adair (eds), *Untold Stories: Protestants in the Republic of Ireland, 1922–2002* (Dublin, 2002), 3.

31. 'The Religious Angle in Irish Life', cited in Jack White, *Minority Report: The Anatomy of the Southern Irish Protestant* (Dublin, 1975), 161.

32. MacGréil, *Prejudice in Ireland Revisited*, 27, on 'vicious-circle' and 'self-fulfilling' theories.

33. Andy Pollak, Torkel Opsahl, et al., *A Citizens' Inquiry* (Dublin, 1993), 412.

34. *Irish Times*, 29 May 2000; Liechty and Clegg, *Moving beyond Sectarianism*, 277; Tobin, 'Minority Voice', 169–70, on Protestant belief that the Reformation introduced critical thinking to religion, whereas Catholics really didn't have to think (the Church of Ireland Primate, Archbishop John Gregg (d. 1961), says this towards end of his life).

35. See e.g. 1968 interview with the Unionist MP William Kennedy on a new estate for Protestants so that they would not suffer 'deterioration' in 'positively filthy' Catholic estates; cited in Marc Mulholland, 'Why did Unionists Discriminate?', in Sabine Wichert (ed.), *From the United Irishmen to Twentieth-Century Unionism: A Festschrift for A. T. Q. Stewart* (Dublin, 2004), 191–2.

36. Padraic Fiacc, *The Wearing of the Black: An Anthology of Contemporary Ulster Poetry* (Belfast, 1974), 15.

37. Michael Viney, *The Five Per Cent: A Survey of Protestants in the Republic* (Dublin, 1965), 16; repr. from the *Irish Times*.

38. Malachi O'Doherty, 'A Bit of a Nuisance', in Mark Carruthers, Stephen Douds, and Tim Loane (eds), *Re-imagining Belfast: Manifesto for the Arts* (Belfast, 2003), 76.

39. George A. Birmingham, *An Irishman Looks at his World* (London, 1919), 119–20.

40. The Oxford historian the late Revd Jack McManners, cited in Nicholas Atkin and Frank Tallett, *Priests, Prelates and People: A History of European Catholicism since 1750* (London, 2003), 5.

41. I owe this thought to fellow discussants at the October 2004 Salzburg Seminar, particularly Alan McCully.

42. BBC NI, *Sunday Sequence*, 3 Oct. 2004.

43. The process has been examined in R. F. Foster, *Luck and the Irish: A Brief History of Change 1970–2000* (London, 2007), 64–5, 106–8, 115–16. The earliest major statement of this new thinking was by Conor Cruise O'Brien, *States of Ireland* (London, 1972).

44. *Irish Times*, 28 Sept. 1981.

2. Irishness at the Altar

1. Colin Murphy and Lynne Adair (eds), *Untold Stories: Protestants in the Republic of Ireland, 1922–2002* (Dublin, 2002), 69–70.

2. Marianne Elliott, *Wolfe Tone: Prophet of Irish Independence* (London, 1989), 1–2, 310–12.

3. 'A New Song for Nationalist Heroes', in 'Micíbocht', *Dance to Democracy: A Collection of Broadsides with Insights into our Present Troubles* (Belfast, n.d.), Linenhall Library, NI Political Collection.

4. Barry Raftery, 'The End of Prehistory', in Howard B. Clarke, Jacinta Prunty, and Mark Hennessy (eds), *Surveying Ireland's Past: Multidisciplinary Essays in Honour of Anngret Simms* (Dublin, 2004), 1–12.

5. John Richardson, *A Proposal for the Conversion of the Popish Natives of Ireland to the Establish'd Religion* (London, 1712), 101–4.

6. Marianne Elliott, *The Catholics of Ulster: A History* (London, 2000), 12, 171, 202–4, 273–6. It is important to note, however, that some bawdy poetry *was* retained, most notably Brian Merriman's *Cuirt an Mheán-Oíche* ('The Midnight Court', *c.*1780).

7. Poem by Aodh MacDomnhaill, 'An Ghorta' ('The Famine', 1846), in Énri Ó Muirgheasa, *Dhá Chéad de Cheoltaibh Uladh* (Dublin, 1934), 369.

8. *Brief of Paul V to the Irish People* (*c.*1607), in John Hagan (ed.), 'Miscellanea Vaticano-Hibernica', *Archivium Hibernicum*, 3 (1914), 260–4; Patrick J. Corish, *The Irish Catholic Experience: A Historical Survey* (Dublin, 1985), 95.

9. *maol*—bald, bare, naked—possibly a reference to clean-shaven, shorn, cropped hair, singling them out from the bearded and long-haired Irish. The term also appears in United Irish ballads; see Georges-Denis Zimmermann, *Songs of Irish Rebellion: Political Street Ballads and Rebel Songs 1780–1900* (Dublin, 1967), 142–3; this from Wexford in 1798.

10. As pointed out by Jeffrey Dudgeon, *Irish Times*, 25 Apr. 2006.

11. Vincent Morley, 'Views of the Past in Irish Vernacular Literature, 1650–1850', *Proceedings of the British Academy*, 134 (2006), 174–98; Énri Ó Muirgheasa, *Céad de Cheoltaibh Uladh* (Dublin, 1915), 165; Anna Heusaff, *Filí agus Cléir san Ochtú hAois Déag* (Dublin, 1992), 56. Fr Phelim O'Neill (much respected by the poets) transcribed Keating, 'An Síogaí' and 'Tuireamh na hÉireann', in the 18th century.

12. Cited in Michael J. F. McCarthy's very anti-Catholic *Priests and People in Ireland* (Dublin, 1902), 273; Ruth Fleischmann, *Catholic Nationalism in the Irish Revival: A Study of Canon Sheehan, 1852–1913* (New York, 1997), 139.

13. Tomás Ó Fiaich, *Art Mac Cumhaigh: Dánta* (Baile Átha Cliath, 1981), 83–7, 113, 133.

14. Conor Cruise O'Brien, *Ancestral Voices: Religion and Nationalism in Ireland* (Dublin, 1994), 37.

15. R. V. Comerford, *Ireland* (London, 2003), 188.

16. Zimmermann, *Songs of Irish Rebellion*, 174.

17. Revd William Corkey, *The Church of Rome and Irish Unrest: How Hatred of Britain is Taught in Irish Schools* (Edinburgh, 1918).

18. The Christian Brothers, *Irish History Reader* (Dublin, 1916), 145–6.

19. Marianne Elliott (ed.), *The Long Road to Peace in Northern Ireland* (Liverpool, 2007), 177.

20. A point made perceptively by Owen Dudley Edwards.

21. Donnchadh Ó Corráin, 'Nationality and Kingship in Pre-Norman Ireland', in T. W. Moody (ed.), *Nationality and the Pursuit of National Independence* (Belfast, 1978), 31–2.

22. F. X. Martin, *No Hero in the House: Diarmait Mac Murchada and the Coming of the Normans to Ireland* (Dublin, 1975), 5.

23. A recent example: Eoghan Rice, 'English Invasion of Ireland in 12th Century based on "Sexed-up Dodgy Dossier": Henry II fiddled document to make it seem he had unqualified papal approval to launch 800 years of misery', *Sunday Tribune*, 30 July 2006.

24. Michael Richter, *Medieval Ireland* (Dublin, 2005), 128; Seamus Deane (ed.), *The Field Day Anthology of Irish Writing*, 3 vols (Derry, 1991), i. 143; Steven Ellis, 'Nationalist Historiography and the English and Gaelic Worlds', *Irish Historical Studies*, 25 (May 1986), 1–18.

25. James Lydon, 'The Middle Nation', in Lydon (ed.), *The English in Medieval Ireland* (Dublin, 1982), 15; Art Cosgrove (ed.), *A New History of Ireland*, ii: *Medieval Ireland 1169–1534* (Oxford, 1987), pp. l–liii, lxi, and Martin, *No Hero in the House*, pp. l–liii, for the various terms. For criticism of the term 'Anglo-Irish' for 'the Englishry of Ireland', see Ellis, 'Nationalist Historiography and the English and Gaelic Worlds', 1–18.

26. Eleanor Knott (ed.), *The Bardic Poems of Tadhg Dall Ó hUiginn*, Irish Texts Society, 2 vols (London, 1921), i. p. xlvii—Ó Dálaigh had used the words 'Goill' and 'Gall', translated as 'English' by the editor.

27. J. C. Beckett, *The Anglo-Irish Tradition* (London, 1976), 36.

28. Ibid. 42; S. J. Connolly, *Religion, Law and Power: The Making of Protestant Ireland 1660–1760* (Oxford, 1992), 115. Sir William Petty said much the same in 1672.

29. Elliott, *Catholics of Ulster*, 79; Joep Leerssen, *Mere Irish and Fíor-Ghael: Studies in the Idea of Irish Nationality, its Development and Literary Expression prior to the Nineteenth Century* (Cork, 1996), 274–7; Bernadette Cunningham, *The World of Geoffrey Keating: History, Myth and Religion in Seventeenth-Century Ireland* (Dublin, 2000), 226.

30. Lennox Robinson, *A Young Man from the South* (Dublin, 1917), 70.

31. Marianne Elliott, 'Hyphenated Hybrids: Irishness, Englishness and Religious Identities in Britain and Ireland', in *Britain and Ireland: Lives Entwined II* (Dublin, 2006), 48–62.

32. Elliott, 'Religion and Identity in Northern Ireland', in Elliott (ed.), *Long Road to Peace in Northern Ireland*, 170–1.

33. Jack White, *Minority Report: The Anatomy of the Southern Irish Protestant* (Dublin, 1975), 17; Norman Vance, *Irish Literature: A Social History*, 2nd edn (Dublin, 1999), 11–12.

34. Beckett, *Anglo-Irish Tradition*, 11; see also his 'Literature in English, 1691–1800', in T. W. Moody and W. E. Vaughan (eds), *A New History of Ireland*, iv: *Eighteenth-Century Ireland, 1691–1800* (Oxford, 1986), 425–6.

35. Beckett, *Anglo-Irish Tradition*, 125–30, on how they lost all influence, and on how they were moving towards extinction as he wrote (152).

36. David Hayton, 'Anglo-Irish Attitudes: Changing Perceptions of National Identity among the Protestant Ascendancy in Ireland, *ca.*1690–1750', *Studies in Eighteenth-Century Culture*, 17 (1987), 151–2, and 147 for how 1690 was referred to as 'the overthrow of the Irish'; Toby Barnard, 'Protestantism, Ethnicity and Irish Identities, 1660–1760', in Tony Claydon and Ian McBride (eds), *Protestantism and National Identity in Britain and Ireland, c.1650–c.1850* (Cambridge, 1998), 207–8. However, see Connolly, *Religion, Law and Power*, 123–4, about the dangers of over-tight categorizations. David Hayton's article also deals with their resentment at being thought inferior Irish by the English.

37. William Molyneux, *The Case of Ireland's being Bound by Acts of Parliament in England, Stated* (Dublin, 1698; repr. 1977), 88.

38. Beckett, 'Literature in English, 1691–1800', 425.

39. Deane (ed.), *The Field Day Anthology*, i. 433.

40. Ian McBride, ' "The Common Name of Irishman": Protestantism and Patriotism in Eighteenth-Century Ireland', in Claydon and McBride (eds), *Protestantism and National Identity in Britain and Ireland*, 261.

41. Beckett, *Anglo-Irish Tradition*, 108; Emyr Estyn Evans, 'The Irishness of the Irish', in *Ireland and the Atlantic Heritage: Selected Writings* (Dublin, 1996), 32, 41.

42. See also Revd John M. Barclay, 'Being Protestant', in James McLoone (ed.), *Being Protestant in Ireland* (Dublin, 1985), 8, saying much the same.

43. Joseph Spence, 'The Philosophy of Irish Toryism, 1833–52', Ph.D. thesis (University of London, 1991), 334.

44. A recurrent theme throughout Spence, 'The Philosophy of Irish Toryism', e.g. 361–76; D. George Boyce, 'Trembling Solicitude: Irish Conservatism, Nationality and Public Opinion', in D. George Boyce, Robert Eccleshall, and Vincent Geoghegan (eds), *Political Thought in Ireland since the Seventeenth Century* (London, 1993).

45. Spence, 'The Philosophy of Irish Toryism', 165.

46. Ibid. 111.

47. Alvin Jackson, *Home Rule: An Irish History 1800–2000* (London, 2003), 24.

48. Spence, 'Philosophy of Irish Toryism', 298.

49. Ibid. 328–9; *Dublin University Magazine*, 3 (Apr. 1834), 456–78.

50. Timothy G. McMahon, *Grand Opportunity: The Gaelic Revival and Irish Society, 1893–1910* (Syracuse, N.Y., 2008), 4–6, 114–18, 135–7.

51. Ibid. 119–24.

52. R. B. D. French, 'J. O. Hannay and the Gaelic League', *Hermathena: A Dublin University Review*, 102 (Spring 1966), 26–52; Brian Taylor, *The Life and Writings of James Owen Hannay (George A. Birmingham) 1865–1950* (Lampeter, 1995), 55–69.

53. David W. Miller, *Church, State and Nation in Ireland, 1898–1921* (Dublin, 1973), 34–5, 133, 235–7; McMahon, *Grand Opportunity*, 68–70.

54. *The Seething Pot* (London, 1932), 9–10, 29, 276–82.

55. *Irish Independent,* 26 June 1929.

56. Fleischmann, *Catholic Nationalism in the Irish Revival,* 136–9; Sheehan's *The Intellectuals* (1911) recommends discussion between Catholic and Protestant intellectuals. But when serialized in the *Irish Rosary,* the sales dropped so badly that the editor had to stop printing it (whether through its intellectual–academic nature or lack of interest).

57. Catherine Candy, *Priestly Fictions: Popular Irish Novelists of the Early 20th Century* (Dublin, 1995), 79.

58. Ibid. 75.

59. John Mitchel, *Jail Journal* (Dublin, n.d), 408.

60. Fleischmann, *Catholic Nationalism in the Irish Revival,* 69–70, 82; see also James H. Murphy, *Catholic Fiction and Social Reality in Ireland, 1873–1922* (Westport, Conn., 1997), 40.

61. Fergus O'Ferrall, *Catholic Emancipation: Daniel O'Connell and the Birth of Irish Democracy* (Dublin, 1985), 58; Elizabeth Bowen, *Bowen's Court* (Cork, 1998), 266–7.

62. Elliott, *Catholics of Ulster,* 293, 279–84; Desmond Bowen, *The Protestant Crusade in Ireland 1800–70* (Dublin, 1978), 262–72, on Cullen's intense anti-Protestantism.

63. S. J. Connolly, *Priests and People in Pre-Famine Ireland, 1780–1845* (Dublin, 1982), 110.

64. A good example of how 'Palesman' entered Catholic insult vocabulary can be found in Éamon Ó Doibhlin, *Domhnach Mór (Donaghmore): An Outline of Parish History,* 2nd edn (Dungannon, 1988), 171–3, in this case to denounce the accommodating attitude of the Old English archbishop (and future saint) Oliver Plunkett towards Protestant gentry and government. I discuss this in my *Catholics of Ulster,* 144–5.

65. D. P. Moran, *The Philosophy of Irish Ireland,* ed. Patrick Maume (Dublin, 2006), pp. viii–ix; R. F. Foster, *W. B. Yeats: A Life,* i: *The Apprentice Mage* (Oxford, 1997), 240.

66. *The Leader,* 2 Jan. 1903; McMahon, *Grand Opportunity,* 29.

67. *The Independent,* 21 June 1929; Revd Myles V. Ronan, *Catholic Emancipation Centenary Record* (Dublin, 1929).

68. J. H. Whyte, *Church and State in Modern Ireland, 1923–1970* (Dublin, 1971), 58–9.

69. *Northern Ireland House of Commons*, vol. xvi (1933–4), col. 1095.

70. John Bowman, *De Valera and the Ulster Question, 1917–1973* (Oxford, 1982), 152–4.

71. Dermot Keogh, 'Catholicism and the Formation of the Modern Irish Society', in *Irishness in a Changing Society*, Princess Grace Irish Library Series (Gerrards Cross, 1988), 161–9, 175.

72. James M. Smith, *Ireland's Magdalen Laundries and the Nation's Architecture of Containment* (Notre Dame, Ind., 2007), 5–10, 46–7, 150, makes a powerful case for this.

73. E. R. Norman, *The English Catholic Church in the Nineteenth Century* (Oxford, 1985), 217; Nicholas Atkin and Frank Tallett, *Priests, Prelates and People: A History of European Catholicism since 1750* (London, 2003), 228.

74. Norman, *English Catholic Church*, 323–4.

75. Fr Robert Culhane, 'Irish Catholics in Britain', *The Furrow*, 1 (1950), 387–8; also 395–420 for responses to the article; Enda Delaney, *The Irish in Post-War Britain* (Oxford, 2007), 37, 138, 160–1.

76. *The Furrow*, 1 (1950), 395, response to Culhane by Canon T. F. Duggan of Cork.

77. Padraig O'Malley, *Biting at the Grave: The Irish Hunger Strikes and the Politics of Despair* (Belfast, 1990), 176–7.

78. O'Ferrall, *Catholic Emancipation*, 40–2.

79. Jane Leonard, 'The Catholic Chaplaincy', in David Fitzpatrick (ed.), *Ireland and the First Word War* (Dublin, 1986), 1–14.

80. Keogh, 'Catholicism and the Formation of the Modern Irish Society', 156–9; Jacqueline Hill, 'Protestant Ascendancy Challenged: The Church of Ireland Laity and the Public Sphere, 1740–1869', in Raymond Gillespie and W. G. Neely (eds), *The Laity and the Church of Ireland, 1000–2000* (Dublin, 2002), 162–3.

81. Andy Pollak, Torkel Opsahl, et al., *A Citizens' Inquiry* (Dublin, 1993), 410.

3. Protestantism and the Spectre of Popery

1. Quoted in Robert Benjamin Tobin, 'The Minority Voice: Hubert Butler, Southern Protestantism and Intellectual Dissent, 1930–72', D.Phil. thesis (Oxford University, 2004), 269, from *Twentieth Century*, 154 (Oct. 1953), 291–2.

2. Robert Harbinson, *No Surrender: An Ulster Childhood* (London, 1960), 121–3.

3. John Dunlop, *A Precarious Belonging: Presbyterians and the Conflict in Ireland* (Belfast, 1995), 31.

4. *The Bodley Head Bernard Shaw Collected Plays with their Prefaces*, [ed. Dan H. Laurence], ii (London, 1971), 821–3; Revd V. G. B. Griffin, *Anglican and Irish: What we Believe* (Dublin, 1976), 7.

5. Alan Ford, *James Ussher: Theology, History, and Politics in Early-Modern Ireland and England* (Oxford, 2007), 114, and for the 1615 Articles, 93–4, 99–100; id., 'A Puritan Church', in Alan Ford, James McGuire, and Kenneth Milne (eds), *As by Law Established: The Church of Ireland since the Reformation* (Dublin, 1995), 57–8; Joseph Liechty, *Roots of Sectarianism in Ireland: Chronology and Reflections* (Belfast, 1993), 14.

6. This from Alan Ford, who recalls being challenged by a Free Presbyterian on this very point.

7. David Hempton, *Religion and Political Culture in Britain and Ireland* (Cambridge, 1996), 144. Peter Lake describes well how 'the identification of the pope as Antichrist, provided the central organising principle for a whole view of the world' ('The Significance of the Identification of the Pope as Antichrist', *Journal of Ecclesiastical History*, 31 (1980), 161).

8. John Brady, *Catholics and Catholicism in the Eighteenth-Century Press* (Maynooth, 1965), 70; *A Test of Roman Catholic Liberality, submitted to the consideration of both Roman Catholicks and Protestants. By a Citizen of London-Derry* (Londonderry, 1792). Even this liberal Protestant feared that were Catholics to be given power they might close Protestants' churches and schools and persecute their religion.

9. Thomas MacKnight, *Ulster As It Is, or, Twenty-Eight Years' Experience as an Irish Editor*, 2 vols (London, 1896), i. 8.

10. Harbinson, *No Surrender*, 121.

11. Toby Barnard, 'Improving Clergymen, 1660–1760', in Ford et al. (eds), *As by Law Established*, 147.

12. Revd Charles Stuart Stanford, *A Handbook to the Romish Controversy: Being a Refutation in Detail of the Creed of Pope Pius the Fourth on the Grounds of Scripture and Reason* (Dublin, 1864), p. ix.

13. Alan Acheson, *A History of the Church of Ireland* (Dublin, 1997), 182.

14. Stanford, *Handbook to the Romish Controversy*, 35; also 50, 61.

15. BBC NI, *Sunday Sequence*, 8 Oct. 2006.

16. 'Second Letter from an Orangeman', *Dublin University Magazine*, 6 (1835), 272.

17. Diarmaid MacCulloch, *Reformation: Europe's House Divided 1490–1700* (London: Allen Lane, 2003), 248–9.

18. Stanford, *Handbook to the Romish Controversy*, 89–130.

19. MacCulloch, *Reformation*, 119–26, 150–1, 241–2, 250–1. Stanford, *Handbook to the Romish Controversy*, 37–48, bases his case on the same biblical texts.

20. Patrick Mitchel, *Evangelicalism and National Identity in Ulster, 1921–1998* (Oxford, 2003), 154–6, 185–6; Acheson, *History of the Church of Ireland*, 131; David Hayton, 'Did Protestantism Fail in Early Eighteenth-Century Ireland? Charity Schools and the Enterprise of Religious and Social Reformation, *c*.1690–1730', in Ford et al. (eds), *As by Law Established*, 176–7.

21. Quoted in Steve Bruce, *God Save Ulster: The Religion and Politics of Paisleyism* (Oxford, 1986), 269–70; John Whyte, *Interpreting Northern Ireland* (Oxford, 1990), 107–8; Mitchel, *Evangelicalism and National Identity*, 186, sees Paisleyism's definition of 'God's people' as even narrower, synonymous with the Free Presbyterian Church.

22. Ian Green, ' "The necessary knowledge of the principles of religion": Catechisms and Catechizing in Ireland', in Ford et al. (eds), *As by Law Established*, 79; Raymond Gillespie, 'Lay Spirituality and Worship, 1558–1750: Holy Books and Godly Readers', in Raymond Gillespie and W. G. Neely (eds), *The Laity and the Church of Ireland, 1000–2000* (Dublin, 2002), 133.

23. D. H. Akenson, *God's Peoples: Covenant and Land in South Africa, Israel, and Ulster* (Ithaca, N.Y., 1992), 124.

24. Jonathan Swift, *A Tale of a Tub*, 2nd edn, ed. A. C. Guthkelch and D. Nichol Smith (Oxford, 1958), 190–8; also Seamus Deane (ed.), *The Field Day Anthology of Irish Writing*, 3 vols (Derry, 1991), i. 331–5.

25. *Calvin: Institutes of the Christian Religion*, ed. John T. McNeill, 2 vols (London, 1961), ii. 1052; Stanford, *Handbook to the Romish Controversy*, 151.

26. MacCulloch, *Reformation*, 280.

27. Harbinson, *No Surrender*, 121–3; Desmond Bowen, *History and the Shaping of Irish Protestantism* (New York, 1995), felt the need to intertwine the history of Irish Protestantism with a detailed history of the papacy from its earliest centuries.

28. Ian McBride's aptly named *Scripture Politics: Ulster Presbyterians and Irish Radicalism in the Late Eighteenth Century* (Oxford, 1998), 63, 103–4; David W. Miller, 'Presbyterianism and "Modernization" in Ulster', *Past and Present*, 80 (1978), 66–90.

29. McBride, *Scripture Politics*, 81.

30. John Gamble, *Sketches of History, Politics, and Manners, taken in Dublin and the North of Ireland* (1811), 217–18.

31. *Orange Standard* (Glasgow, n.d.), 4–5; Georges-Denis Zimmermann, *Songs of Irish Rebellion: Political Street Ballads and Rebel Songs 1780–1900* (Dublin, 1967), 295–320. Likewise, Ulster loyalist publications, particularly the most successful, the UVF *Orange Cross*, often had very witty sectarian humour sections, favourite themes being the confessional, and Blackpool-postcard-like scatological humour about the marital lives of Catholic politicians. See too *WDA News*, 5 July 1975, 14 June 1976. At times commentary is more sinister, where company-keeping with 'rebels' singled out victims for particularly vicious punishment—most notably the case of Senator Paddy Wilson of the Social Democratic and Labour Party (SDLP) and his Protestant assistant Irene Andrews (*Loyalist News*, 2 and 16 Sept. 1972). Both were brutally murdered the following year. See Jack Holland, 'The Voices of Loyalist Extremism', *Hibernia*, 27 June 1975.

32. MacCulloch, *Reformation*, 285.

33. John Foxe, *Foxe's Book of Martyrs* (Peabody, Mass., 2004), 314.

34. Colin Haydon, *Anti-Catholicism in Eighteenth-Century England, c.1714–80: A Political and Social Study* (Manchester, 1993), 44–5, is a good account of this.

35. My thanks to Diarmaid MacCulloch for pointing this out to me.

36. Harbinson, *No Surrender*, 132–3.

37. Ralph Lambert, *A Sermon Preach'd to the Protestants of Ireland, now residing in London at their anniversary meeting on Oct. xxiii 1708 in commemoration of their deliverance from the barbarous massacre committed by the Irish papists in the year 1641* (London, 1708), 1.

38. B. M. Walker, '1641, 1689, 1690 and All That: The Unionist Sense of History', *Irish Review*, 12 (1992), 58.

39. A. T. Q. Stewart, *The Narrow Ground: Aspects of Ulster* (London, 1977), 49.

40. T. C. Barnard, 'Crises of Identity among Irish Protestants 1641–1685', *Past and Present*, 127 (1990), 39–83.

41. Ibid. 64.

42. H. Jones, *A Remonstrance of Divers Remarkable Passages concerning the Church and Kingdome of Ireland* (London, 1641), 1.

43. Barnard, 'Crises of Identity among Irish Protestants', 56.

44. Raymond D. Tumbleson, *Catholicism in the English Protestant Imagination: Nationalism, Religion and Literature, 1660–1745* (Cambridge, 1998), 89, citing George Fox's list of Irish atrocities in his *Arraignment of Popery* (London, 1667).

45. Toby Barnard, '1641: A Bibliographical Essay', in Brian MacCuarta (ed.), *Ulster 1641: Aspects of the Rising* (Belfast, 1993), 180–1.

46. Lambert, *Sermon Preach'd to the Protestants of Ireland*, 1–3, 12.

47. <http://www.ianpaisley.org>.

48. Jacqueline Hill, '1641 and the Quest for Catholic Emancipation 1691–1829', in MacCuarta (ed.), *Ulster 1641*, 159–71; the 1812 edition carries the subtitle 'Now reprinted for the perusal of all Protestants, as the most effectual warning-piece to keep them upon their guard against the encroachments of popery'.

49. Giraldus Cambrensis, *Topographia Hibernica* ('The History and Topography of Ireland'; Harmondsworth, 1988), 107–9.

50. 'Sons whose sires with William bled', *Orange Standard*, 3.

51. Andy Pollak, Torkel Opsahl, et al., *A Citizens' Inquiry* (Dublin, 1993), 37.

52. 'O'Croly on Popery in Ireland', *Dublin University Magazine*, 7 (1836), 80.

53. A 2008 web search showed 6.5 million entries, with new editions in 2006 and 2007, selling on all the main bookselling web sites, including Tesco's, and given a five-star booksellers' rating on the very popular AbeBooks.

54. Marianne Elliott, *The Catholics of Ulster: A History* (New York, 2001), 354; *Report of the Commission of Inquiry into . . . the Riots in Belfast, in July and September, 1857*, HC 1857–8 [2309], 8, 2, 124; *Dublin University Magazine*, 10 (1837), 210–11.

55. MacKnight, *Ulster As It Is*, i. 7–9.

56. Sean O'Casey, *I Knock at the Door: Swift Glances back at Things that Made Me* (London, 1943), 35.

57. Ken Heskin, *Northern Ireland: A Psychological Analysis* (Dublin, 1980), 28–30; Whyte, *Interpreting Northern Ireland*, 106–7.

58. Quoted in Tobin, 'The Minority Voice', 268.

59. Quoted in S. J. Connolly, *Religion, Law and Power: The Making of Protestant Ireland 1660–1760* (Oxford, 1992), 35.

60. Gamble, *Sketches*, 218.

61. See e.g. Revd Ian Meredith and Revd Brian Kennaway, *The Orange Order: An Evangelical Perspective* ([Belfast?], 1993), 22; Bruce, *God Save Ulster*, 144; John Fulton, *The Tragedy of Belief: Division, Politics, and Religion in Ireland* (Oxford, 1991), 118.

62. Brady, *Catholics and Catholicism in the Eighteenth-Century Press*, 69–73. See Mitchel, *Evangelicalism and National Identity*, 162, for similar beliefs held by members of the Orange Order about freedom in Protestant states.

63. Francis Joseph Bigger, *The Ulster Land War of 1770* (Dublin, 1910), 101.

64. *A Letter to a Member of Parliament concerning the Laws which Disable Papists from Purchasing in this Kingdom* ([Dublin or Derry], 1751).

65. MacCulloch, *Reformation*, 334.

66. *Dublin University Magazine*, 10 (1837), 632–6; 12 (1838), 183–95.

67. Patrick Fagan, *Divided Loyalties: The Question of an Oath for Irish Catholics in the Eighteenth Century* (Dublin, 1997), 11, 174; Elliott, *Catholics of Ulster*, 168–70; Connolly, *Religion, Law and Power*, 17–24, 156–9, 189.

68. Cited by Hill, '1641 and the Quest for Catholic Emancipation 1691–1829', 169.

69. Marianne Elliott, *Watchmen in Sion: The Protestant Idea of Liberty* (Belfast, 1985), 14–15; also Harbinson, *No Surrender*, 120, on recollection of the gable wall in the 1940s. The ultimate refinement of 'God's people' occurs in the common loyalist slogan 'We are the People', analysed in Peter Shirlow and Mark McGovern (eds), *Who are 'the People'? Unionism, Protestantism and Loyalism in Northern Ireland* (London, 1997).

70. Dunlop, *Precarious Belonging*, 135; he adds, 'We could do with some new interpretative models.'

71. Ian McBride, *The Siege of Derry in Ulster Protestant Mythology* (Dublin, 1997), 28–9.

72. *The Journal of the Rev. John Wesley*, 4 vols (London, 1895), ii. 67.

73. Ibid. ii. 424; also iii. 11, 412, 414.

74. David Hempton and Myrtle Hill, *Evangelical Protestantism in Ulster Society, 1740–1890* (London, 1992), 41; this was Gideon Ouseley.

75. Asenath Nicholson, *Ireland's Welcome to the Stranger*, ed. Maureen Murphy (Dublin, 2002), 331.

76. Elliott, *Catholics of Ulster*, 272–5; Janice Holmes, *Religious Revivals in Britain and Ireland 1859–1905* (Dublin, 2000), 31.

77. Mitchel, *Evangelicalism and National Identity*, 10.

78. Nicholson, *Ireland's Welcome to the Stranger*, 245.

79. Jacqueline R. Hill, 'Artisans, Sectarianism and Politics in Dublin, 1829–48', *Saothar* (1981), 20–3.

80. Martin Maguire, 'The Church of Ireland and the Problem of the Protestant Working-Class of Dublin, 1870s–1930s', in Ford et al. (eds), *As by Law Established*, 196; R. B. McDowell, *Crisis and Decline: The Fate of the Southern Unionists* (Dublin, 1997), 37–8.

81. Meredith and Kennaway, *The Orange Order*, 8.

82. Ibid. 24.

83. Earl Storey, *Traditional Roots: Towards an Appropriate Relationship between the Church of Ireland and the Orange Order* (Dublin, 2002).

84. Mitchel, *Evangelicalism and National Identity*, 248.

85. Dunlop, *Precarious Belonging*, 60.

86. Patrick Shea, *Voices and the Sound of Drums: An Irish Autobiography* (Belfast, 1981), 39–41.

87. Kyla Madden, *Forkhill Protestants and Forkhill Catholics, 1787–1858* (Liverpool, 2005).

88. Zimmermann, *Songs of Irish Rebellion*, 311–13; Elliott, *Catholics of Ulster*, 351; *The Illustrated Orange Song Book* (Belfast, n.d.), 10, purchased in Sandy Row in 2007.

89. R. M. Sibbett, *Orangeism in Ireland and throughout the Empire*, 2 vols (London, 1938), i. 5, 229–30, 276, 387.

90. Ian d'Alton, *Protestant Society and Politics in Cork 1812–1844* (Cork, 1980), 202–10; K. Theodore Hoppen, *Elections, Politics and Society in Ireland,*

1832–1885 (Oxford, 1984), 319–32; Maguire, 'The Church of Ireland and the Problem of the Protestant Working-Class of Dublin', 195–203.

91. *Orange Standard*, 13; *Illustrated Orange Song Book*, 7; Ian R. K. Paisley, *The Massacre of St. Bartholomew: A Record of Papal Terror and Protestant Triumph in France in the Sixteenth Century* (Belfast, 1972).

92. *Protestant Telegraph*, 16 May 1981, on 'the Church of Rome' behind the hunger strikes and the violence. Tony Parker, *May the Lord in his Mercy be Kind to Belfast* (London, 1993), 293, found the same statements being made by ordinary loyalists.

93. *Orange Cross*, no. 29, [17] June 1973.

94. *Orange Cross*, no. 18. Also John D. Brewer with Gareth I. Higgins, *Anti-Catholicism in Northern Ireland, 1600–1998: The Mote and the Beam* (London, 1998), 177–8, for the totemic nature of 1641 in political Protestantism.

95. *Orange Cross*, no. 77.

96. *Loyalist News*, 25 Nov. 1972.

97. Harbinson, *No Surrender*, 53–4. Information on its American origins courtesy of Don Akenson.

98. *Loyalist News*, 6 Nov. 1871.

99. *Orange Cross*, no. 30—to be purchased from the Scottish Protestant Union in Edinburgh.

100. *Orange Cross*, no. 33.

101. Mitchel, *Evangelicalism and National Identity*, 133–70.

102. Frank Wright, 'Protestant Ideology and Politics in Ulster', *Archives Européennes de Sociologie*, 14 (1973), 245; Mitchel, *Evangelicalism and National Identity*, 144–5.

103. Earl Storey, *Traditional Roots: Towards an Appropriate Relationship between the Church of Ireland and the Orange Orders* (Blackrock, 2002), 38. See also Revd Brian Kennaway, *The Orange Order: A Tradition Betrayed* (London, 2006), a powerful critique by a one-time insider of the Order today, though a denial that it was ever sectarian in the past.

104. Storey, *Traditional Roots*, 83.

105. Bruce, *God Save Ulster*, 222.

4. The Church of Ireland as Establishment

1. W. G. Neely, 'The Laity in a Changing Society, 1830–1900', in Raymond Gillespie and W. G. Neely (eds), *The Laity and the Church of Ireland, 1000–2000* (Dublin, 2002), 224.

2. Alan Ford, *The Protestant Reformation in Ireland, 1590–1645* (Frankfurt am Main, 1987), ch. 8.

3. Alan Ford, James McGuire, and Kenneth Milne (eds), *As by Law Established: The Church of Ireland since the Reformation* (Dublin, 1995), 57; Alan Ford, *James Ussher: Theology, History, and Politics in Early-Modern Ireland and England* (Oxford, 2007), 23–4.

4. Jacqueline Hill, 'Protestant Ascendancy Challenged: The Church of Ireland Laity and the Public Sphere, 1740–1869', in Gillespie and Neely (eds), *The Laity and the Church of Ireland*, 166.

5. David Hempton, *Religion and Political Culture in Britain and Ireland* (Cambridge, 1996), 3.

6. A. P. W. Malcolmson, *Archbishop Charles Agar: Churchmanship and Politics in Eighteenth-Century Ireland* (Dublin, 2002), 184. The foreignness can be overplayed: of serving clergy in Cork in 1837, most were local and only 1.6 per cent were English-born; Ian d'Alton, *Protestant Society and Politics in Cork 1812–1844* (Cork, 1980), 66.

7. Richard Lord Bishop of Cloyne, *The Present State of the Church of Ireland: Containing a description of it's [sic] precarious situation; and the consequent danger to the public*, 7th edn (London, 1787).

8. *Dublin University Magazine*, 7 (Apr. 1836), 436.

9. *Dublin University Magazine*, 2 (Oct. 1833), 410. In an effort to staunch the British parliament's dismantling of its position as an arm of the state, Archbishop Whately argued that the Church of Ireland was an English colony requiring support from the legislature; see D. H. Akenson, *The Church of Ireland: Ecclesiastical Reform and Revolution, 1800–1885* (New Haven, 1971), 211.

10. Thomas MacKnight, *Ulster As It Is, or, Twenty-Eight Years' Experience as an Irish Editor*, 2 vols (London, 1896), i. 39.

11. George Birmingham, *The Seething Pot* (1905; London, 1932), 134–5.

12. Akenson, *Church of Ireland*, 274; *Primate Alexander, Archbishop of Armagh: Memoir*, ed. Eleanor Alexander (London, 1913), 173.

13. D. H. Akenson, *Small Differences: Irish Catholics and Irish Protestants, 1815–1922. An International Perspective* (Dublin, 1991), 138.

14. Ford, *James Ussher*, 66–76, also showing the fierce independence of the Church of Ireland in this period. Ussher had been a noted antiquarian and Irish-language scholar and was happy to share his findings with Counter-Reformation Catholic clerics since both were anxious to defend Ireland's reputation as the island of saints and scholars.

15. Martin Maguire, 'Churches and Symbolic Power in the Irish Landscape', *Landscapes*, 2 (2004), 102–5.

16. Clare O'Halloran, ' "The Island of Saints and Scholars": Views of the Early Church and Sectarian Politics in Late Eighteenth-Century Ireland', *Eighteenth-Century Ireland*, 5 (1990), 7–20; Ford, *James Ussher*, 126–7.

17. Joseph Spence, 'The Philosophy of Irish Toryism, 1833–52', Ph.D. thesis (University of London, 1991), 60, 159–61, 177–9. James Godkin, *Ireland and her Churches* (London, 1867), 22–83, also says it is taught to divinity students in Trinity College Dublin.

18. *Irish Independent*, 21 June 1929.

19. Revd William Bell and Revd N. D. Emerson (eds), *The Church of Ireland A.D. 432–1932: The Report of the Church of Ireland Conference held in Dublin, 11–14 October, 1932* (Dublin, 1932), 235–6; Martin Maguire, ' "Our People": The Church of Ireland and the Culture of Community in Dublin since Disestablishment', in Gillespie and Neely (eds), *The Laity and the Church of Ireland*, 286–7 (special sermons on the Church of Ireland's historical claims were preached in the Dublin parishes, tours organized of historic locations, and special lectures arranged, including for children); Robert Benjamin Tobin, 'The Minority Voice: Hubert Butler, Southern Protestantism and Intellectual Dissent, 1930–72', D.Phil. thesis (Oxford University, 2004), 288.

20. W. A. Phillips (ed.), *History of the Church of Ireland*, 3 vols (Oxford, 1933–4), vol. i, pp. v–ix.

21. V. G. B. Griffin, *Anglican and Irish: What we Believe* (Dublin, 1976), 7–8.

22. Denis Carroll (ed.), *Religion in Ireland, Past, Present and Future* (Dublin, 1999), 29–39.

23. Toby Barnard, 'Protestantism, Ethnicity and Irish Identities, 1660–1760', in Tony Claydon and Ian McBride (eds), *Protestantism and National Identity in Britain and Ireland, c.1650–c.1850* (Cambridge, 1998), 227–35.

24. Alexander, *Primate Alexander*, 7. For terms used, see *Some Observations and Queries on the Present Laws of this Kingdom, relative to Papists, by a True Church of England-Man*, 2nd edn (Dublin, 1761); 'The Church Establishment in Ireland', *Dublin University Magazine*, 2 (Oct. 1833), 402–10. There is a good discussion by Kenneth Milne, 'The Protestant Churches in Independent Ireland', in James P. Mackey and Enda McDonagh (eds), *Religion and Politics in Ireland at the Turn of the Millennium* (Dublin, 2003), 79.

25. Finlay Holmes, *The Presbyterian Church in Ireland: A Popular History* (Blackrock, 2000), 118.

26. Énri Ó Muirgheasa, *Dánta Diadha Uladh* (Dublin, 1936), 376.

27. Alan Acheson, *A History of the Church of Ireland* (Dublin, 1997), 202–3.

28. J. C. Beckett, *The Anglo-Irish Tradition* (London, 1976), 108.

29. R. B. McDowell, *The Church of Ireland, 1869–1969* (London, 1975), 2–6; Akenson, *Church of Ireland*, 215–16; Godkin in 1867 estimated that 'the blood of the Anglican bishops has been the seed of the Irish aristocracy' (*Ireland and her Churches*, pp. xix, 527). However, Tadhg O'Sullivan, 'Burke, Ireland and the Counter-Revolution, 1791–1801', in Seán Patrick Donlan (ed.), *Edmund Burke's Irish Identities* (Dublin, 2007), 176–7, has a number of examples of Church of Ireland clergy taking up the cause of the poor.

30. John Tunney, 'The Marquis, the Reverend, the Grandmaster and the Major: Protestant Politics in Donegal, 1868–1933', in William Nolan, Liam Ronayne, and Mairead Dunlevy (eds), *Donegal History and Society: Interdisciplinary Essays on the History of an Irish County* (Dublin, 1995), 675–95.

31. Desmond J. O'Dowd, *Changing Times: The Story of Religion in Nineteenth-Century Celbridge* (Dublin, 1997), 34. The best pews—some with their own fireplaces—were acquired by the major landowners.

32. D. H. Akenson, *A Protestant in Purgatory: Richard Whately, Archbishop of Dublin* (Hamden, Conn., 1981).

33. Thomas Moore, *Memoirs of Captain Rock*, 4th edn (London, 1824), 19.

34. Godkin, *Ireland and her Churches*, 342–3.

35. D'Alton, *Protestant Society and Politics in Cork*, 71, also 59, 66, 80–1.

36. Godkin, *Ireland and her Churches*, 5, 164–7, 282, 312.

37. Acheson, *History of the Church of Ireland*, 108–9; Patrick Comerford, 'An Innovative People: The Church of Ireland Laity, 1780–1830', in Gillespie and Neely (eds), *The Laity and the Church of Ireland*, 174–5; McDowell, *Church of Ireland*, 24; W. H. Crawford and B. Trainor (eds), *Aspects of Irish Social History* (Belfast, 1969), 112–13.

38. Asenath Nicholson, *Ireland's Welcome to the Stranger*, ed. Maureen Murphy (Dublin, 2002), 15–16.

39. Ibid. 379, 161, 177.

40. Birmingham, *The Seething Pot*, 269, also 212; O'Dowd, *Changing Times*, 36–7; all the main landowners were members of the select vestry.

41. Birmingham, *The Seething Pot*, 37, also 40, 67–8; Spence, 'Philosophy of Irish Toryism', 70. O'Dowd, *Changing Times*, 6–57, also shows that where there were Protestant landowners, there was little unemployment among lower-class Protestants as they tended to get jobs as servants and gardeners.

42. D'Alton, *Protestant Society and Politics in Cork*, 71; Comerford, 'An Innovative People', 174–5.

43. O'Dowd, *Changing Times*, 61–4.

44. Maguire, ' "Our People": The Church of Ireland and the Culture of Community since Disestablishment', in Gillespie and Neely (eds), *The Laity and the Church of Ireland*, 287–8.

45. Lily O'Connor, *Can Lily O'Shea Come Out to Play?* (Dingle, 2000). I am grateful to Martin Maguire, who introduced me to this magical book.

46. Akenson, *A Protestant in Purgatory*, 138.

47. Jack White, *Minority Report: The Anatomy of the Southern Irish Protestant* (Dublin, 1975), 65; Beckett, *Anglo-Irish Tradition*, 44–5, 65. Edith Newman Devlin, *Speaking Volumes: A Dublin Childhood* (Belfast, 2000), 116–19, recalls similar teaching by her father.

48. Akenson, *Church of Ireland*, 266.

49. Alexander, *Primate Alexander*, 183. See also White, *Minority Report*, 64, on disestablishment: the 'established' nature of the Church had been 'a psychological bulwark'; now, with priests increasingly in politics and in 1870 the doctrine of infallibility declared, their fears sharpened.

50. Beckett, *Anglo-Irish Tradition*, 110–11.

51. Carroll (ed.), *Religion in Ireland*, 31.

52. Alexander, *Primate Alexander*, p. xiii. This middle-way aspect of the Church of Ireland is often emphasized by its clergy; see e.g. V. G. B. Griffin, *Anglican and Irish: What we Believe* (Dublin, 1976), 27, 45, 48.

53. Alexander, *Primate Alexander*, 32.

54. D'Alton, *Protestant Society and Politics in Cork*, 70–3, 84 n. 84.

55. Alexander, *Primate Alexander*, 65–6, 70–7, 261.

56. Hempton, *Religion and Political Culture in Britain and Ireland*, 151.

57. David Hempton and Myrtle Hill, *Evangelical Protestantism in Ulster Society, 1740–1890* (London, 1992), 122.

58. Alexander, *Primate Alexander*, 76–7.

59. Paul Larmour and Stephen McBride, 'Church Building from Medieval to Modern', in Gillespie and Neely (eds), *The Laity and the Church of Ireland*, 345; also Neely, 'The Laity in a Changing Society', 203; Akenson, *Church of Ireland*, 302–9.

60. Godkin, *Ireland and her Churches*, 163, 328, 342–3, 390; J. D. A. Sirr, *A Memoir of Power: Le Poer Trench, Last Archbishop of Tuam* (Dublin, 1845), 541. Sirr gives no date for the visit; Trench was Archbishop of Tuam in 1819–39.

61. Akenson, *Church of Ireland*, 165, 210; T. W. Moody, F. X. Martin, and F. J. Byrne (eds), *A New History of Ireland*, ix (Oxford, 1984), 72; d'Alton, *Protestant Society and Politics in Cork*, 57.

62. 'Emigration of the Protestants of Ireland', *Dublin University Magazine*, 4 (July 1834), 4–5; Jacqueline R. Hill, 'Artisans, Sectarianism and Politics in Dublin, 1829–48', *Saothar* (1981), 15–16. See also John Brady, *Catholics and Catholicism in the Eighteenth-Century Press* (Maynooth, 1965), 167, for similar worries and complaints in 1774.

63. T. C. Barnard, 'Parishes, Pews and Parsons: Lay People and the Church of Ireland, 1647–1780', in Gillespie and Neely (eds), *The Laity and the Church of Ireland*, 91–3.

64. Malcolmson, *Archbishop Charles Agar*, 281.

65. Akenson, *A Protestant in Purgatory*, pp. x–xi.

5. The 'Outlanders' of Ulster

1. *Orange Cross*, no. 50 [May 1974].

2. Arthur Clery, 'The Outlanders of Ulster', *New Ireland Review* (1905), in *The Idea of a Nation*, ed. Patrick Maume (Dublin, 2002), 86. Ian McBride suggests this is a possible take on the Boers' term 'Uitlanders' for the English settlers in South Africa.

3. South Armagh, just west of Newry.

4. Clery, *The Idea of a Nation*, 86–97.

5. R. F. Foster, *W. B. Yeats: A Life*, ii: *The Arch-Poet 1915–1939* (Oxford, 2003).

6. Historically the bulk of Presbyterians were in Ulster, with smaller numbers elsewhere, particularly in Cork and Dublin (D. H. Akenson, *Small Differences: Irish Catholics and Irish Protestants, 1815–1922. An International Perspective* (Dublin, 1991), 153–7; Ian d'Alton, *Protestant Society and Politics in Cork 1812–1844* (Cork, 1980), 74–6). See D. H. Akenson, *God's Peoples: Covenant and Land in South Africa, Israel, and Ulster* (Ithaca, N.Y., 1992), 186, on how Presbyterianism has infused Protestant culture in the North: the 'cultural hegemony that the Ulster-Scots held over the entire Protestant population of the north of Ireland'.

7. Barry Sloan, 'William Carleton: Protestants and Protestantism', in Gordon Brand (ed.), *William Carleton: The Authentic Voice* (Gerrards Cross, 2006), 247; Norman Vance, *Irish Literature: A Social History* (Dublin, 1999), 147–8.

8. Patrick Mitchel, *Evangelicalism and National Identity in Ulster, 1921–1998* (Oxford, 2003), 182–3, lists them. See also Alan J. Megahey, *Irish Protestant Churches in the Twentieth Century* (Basingstoke, 2000), 132, on Paisley's background.

9. Quoted in Mitchel, *Evangelicalism and National Identity in Ulster*, 178.

10. Steve Bruce, *God Save Ulster: The Religion and Politics of Paisleyism* (Oxford, 1986), 249–50; id., *The Edge of the Union: The Ulster Loyalist Political Vision* (Oxford, 194), 18–19.

11. Akenson, *God's Peoples*, 26–32.

12. Quoted in Marianne Elliott, *Watchmen in Sion: The Protestant Idea of Liberty* (Belfast, 1985), 10.

13. John Wilson Foster, *Forces and Themes in Ulster Fiction* (Dublin, 1974), 8–9; Mitchel, *Evangelicalism and National Identity in Ulster*, 208. See also R. M. Sibbett, *Orangeism in Ireland and throughout the Empire*, 2 vols (Belfast, 1914), 126–7, 175–6.

14. Finlay Holmes, *The Presbyterian Church in Ireland: A Popular History* (Blackrock, 2000), 24–6; Revd Patrick Adair, *A True Narrative of the Rise and Progress of the Presbyterian Church in Ireland*, ed. W. D. Killen (Belfast, 1866).

15. James Godkin, *Ireland and her Churches* (London, 1867), 57–61; Andrew R. Holmes, *The Shaping of Ulster Presbyterian Belief and Practice, 1770–1840* (Oxford, 2006), 27, on the Presbyterian sense of 'rootedness' in Ulster.

16. Thomas MacKnight, *Ulster As It Is, or, Twenty-Eight Years' Experience as an Irish Editor*, 2 vols (London, 1896), ii. 379–80; *Dublin University Magazine*, 6 (July 1835), 42–50.

17. James Seaton Reid, *The History of the Presbyterian Church in Ireland*, 3 vols (Edinburgh, 1834), ii. 31.

18. Finlay Holmes, *About Being a Presbyterian* (Belfast, 1993).

19. Akenson, *God's Peoples*, 112.

20. R. Gardiner (ed.), *The Constitutional Documents of the Puritan Revolution, 1625–1660*, 3rd edn (Oxford, 1906), no. 58 (<http://www.constitution.org>).

21. W. T. Latimer, *A History of the Irish Presbyterians* (Belfast, [1893]), 53; Reid, *History of the Presbyterian Church in Ireland*, ii. 31.

22. Marianne Elliott, *The Catholics of Ulster: A History* (London, 2000), 253–9.

23. *Ulster Presbyterians and Irish Radicalism in the Late Eighteenth Century* (Oxford, 1998), 73–5.

24. *The Journal of the Rev. John Wesley*, 4 vols (London, 1895), iii. 201.

25. Ibid. 263.

26. Latimer, *History of the Irish Presbyterians*, 163, 160.

27. McBride, *Scripture Politics*, 214, from *Belfast Monthly Magazine*, 7 (1811), 488–9.

28. Peter Brooke, *Ulster Presbyterianism: The Historical Perspective 1610–1970* (Dublin, 1987), 194.

29. R. Finlay Holmes, *Henry Cooke* (Belfast, 1981), 148.

30. Godkin, *Ireland and her Churches*, 83.

31. *Letters to the Presbyterians of Ulster, by a Member of the Synod of Ulster*, 2nd edn (Belfast, 1835); Julie Louise Nelson, ' "Violently Democratic and Anti-Conservative"? An Analysis of Presbyterian "Radicalism" in Ulster, *c.*1800–1852', Ph.D. thesis (University of Durham, 2006), 60–1, 100–39; Godkin, *Ireland and her Churches*, 83; Holmes, *Shaping of Ulster Presbyterian Belief and Practice*, 40.

32. Nelson, 'Violently Democratic', 12, 58–66, 190; David W. Miller, 'Did Ulster Presbyterians have a Devotional Revolution?', in James H. Murphy (ed.), *Evangelicals and Catholics in Nineteenth-Century Ireland* (Dublin, 2005), 49.

33. Latimer, *History of the Irish Presbyterians*, 225, commenting that the Established Church received £8 million in compensation in contrast to the Presbyterian Church's £586,000.

34. Ian McBride, *The Siege of Derry in Ulster Protestant Mythology* (Dublin, 1997), 27–32, on resentment at Walker's statue. In Latimer's 1893 *History of the Irish Presbyterians*, 109–112, dislike and contempt jump off the page: 'But his story, having got the start, was believed by the world, and some, even now, have magnified this miserable old meddler into a military genius and a hero.'

35. Latimer, *History of the Irish Presbyterians*, 140.

36. Ulster Folk and Transport Museum, Holywood, Co. Down, Collectors' Books V12/1.

37. J. C. Beckett, *Confrontations: Studies in Irish History* (London, 1972), 89.

38. *The Paralel* [*sic*], *or, Persecution of Protestants: The Shortest Way to Prevent the Growth of Popery in Ireland* (Dublin, 1707), 3.

39. McBride, *Scripture Politics*, 223, shows validity of Presbyterian marriages still being debated 1840. Because of the lack of landed wealth, Presbyterians were still under-represented in national and local government (224).

40. McBride, 'Presbyterians in the Penal Era', *Bullán*, 1–2 (Autumn 1994), 73–86; J. C. Beckett, *Protestant Dissent in Ireland 1687–1780* (London, 1948), *passim*. On the road from Newtown Stewart in 1810 Dr John Gamble encountered a Presbyterian couple. They were emigrating to America and told him 'there's nae hard landlords nor prude vicars there to take the poor man's mite' (John Gamble, *Sketches of History, Politics, and Manners, taken in Dublin and the North of Ireland* (1811), 274).

41. B. M. Walker, *Ulster Politics: The Formative Years, 1868–86* (Belfast, 1989), 17–25.

42. Reid, *History of the Presbyterian Church in Ireland*, i. 130–1.

43. Latimer, *History of the Irish Presbyterians*, 36–43.

44. Ibid. 74–80; Ian Adamson, *The Identity of Ulster: The Land, the Language and the People*, 2nd edn (Belfast, 1987), 24–31.

45. Holmes, *Shaping of Ulster Presbyterian Belief and Practice*, 44.

46. Alexander, *Primate Alexander*, 115, 35–7.

47. Gamble, *Sketches*, 228, 168; *Letters Written by John O'Donovan, relating to the History and Antiquities of the County of Down in 1834* (Dublin, 1909), 66, on how Presbyterians and Roman Catholics pronounced place names differently. See also the excellent article by Graham Walker on this: 'Ulster Unionism and the Scottish Dimension', in William Kelly and John R. Young (eds), *Ulster and Scotland, 1600–2000: History, Language and Identity* (Dublin, 2004), 33–42.

48. W. S. Kerr, Bishop of Down, *Who Persecuted? Episcopalian and Presbyterian in Ulster* (Belfast, 1947); Revd Prof. R. L. Marshall and Revd Principal J. E. Davey, *'Presbyterians and Persecution': Replies to Dean Kerr's Recent Pamphlet* (Belfast, [1947?]).

49. Nelson, 'Violently Democratic', 68; McBride, *Scripture Politics*, 224; Holmes, *Shaping of Ulster Presbyterian Belief and Practice*, 212–16.

50. Elliott, *Catholics of Ulster*, 130–1, 179, 340–1.

51. Latimer, *History of the Irish Presbyterians*, 238.

52. Holmes, *Shaping of Ulster Presbyterian Belief and Practice*, 119. The Wesleyan minister the Revd William Arthur made much the same point; *Shall the Loyal be Deserted and the Disloyal Set Over Them? An Appeal to Liberals and Nonconformists* (London, 1886).

53. See Megahey, *Irish Protestant Churches in the Twentieth Century*, 24, for a summary.

54. Raymond M. Lee, 'Intermarriage, Conflict and Social Control in Ireland: The Decree *Ne Temere*', *Economic and Social Review*, 17 (1985), 23; Eoin de Bhaldraithe, 'Mixed Marriages and Irish Politics: The Effect of *Ne Temere*', *Studies*, 77 (1988), 284–99; Revd William Corkey, *The McCann Mixed Marriage Case*, 2nd edn (Edinburgh, 1911). The Revd Corkey was Mrs McCann's minister in Belfast.

55. Revd William Corkey, *The Religious Crisis in Ireland* (London, 1914), 5–7.

56. Patrick Buckland, *Irish Unionism 1885–1923: A Documentary History* (Belfast, 1973), 78–9.

57. *Belfast News Letter*, 30 Sept. 1912; McBride, *Scriptural Politics*, 226; Mitchel, *Evangelicalism and National Identity in Ulster*, 220.

58. The *Ulster Herald*, 10 June 1916, says as much; see John B. Dooher, 'Tyrone Nationalism and the Question of Partition, 1910–25', M.Phil. thesis (University of Ulster, 1986), 185.

59. Mitchel, *Evangelicalism and National Identity in Ulster*, 236.

60. Anne Crone, *Bridie Steen* (Belfast, 1984), 55.

61. Mitchel, *Evangelicalism and National Identity in Ulster*, 235–6.

62. D. W. Miller, *Queen's Rebels: Ulster Loyalism in Historical Perspective* (Dublin, 1978), 136, an excellent account of how this operated in terms of policies towards the minority.

63. Marc Mulholland, *The Longest War: Northern Ireland's Troubled History* (Oxford, 2002), 29–30, 38–9.

64. T. Hennessey, *A History of Northern Ireland* (Dublin, 1997), 11.

65. A. C. Hepburn, *The Conflict of Nationality in Modern Ireland* (London, 1980), 155.

66. Alvin Jackson, *Home Rule: An Irish History, 1800–2000* (London, 2003), 219–24.

67. *Northern Ireland House of Commons*, vol. i, col. 308.

68. Revd William Corkey, *The Church of Rome and Irish Unrest: How Hatred of Britain is Taught in Irish Schools* (Edinburgh, 1918), 23.

69. Dennis Kennedy, *The Widening Gulf: Northern Attitudes to the Independent Irish State, 1919–49* (Belfast, 1988), 138.

70. Elliott, *Catholics of Ulster*, 436–7.

71. Rodgers, 'The Character of Ireland', in *Collected Poems*, ed. Dan Davin (London, 1971), 131; I was introduced to this splendid poem in John Dunlop's *A Precarious Belonging: Presbyterians and the Conflict in Ireland* (Belfast, 1995).

72. Robert Harbinson, *Song of Erne* (Belfast, 1988), 17–18; also (as Robin Bryans) his *Ulster: A Journey through Six Counties* (Belfast, 1964), 35–6. These books were very popular in 1960s with both communities. We have always been able to laugh at our prejudices, at least in the right company.

73. Harbinson, *Up Spake the Cabin Boy*, 2nd edn (Belfast, 1988), 228–30.

74. Crone, *Bridie Steen*, 229–30.
75. Rosemary Harris, *Prejudice and Tolerance in Ulster: A Study of Neighbours and 'Strangers' in a Border Community* (Manchester, 1972), 175–81.
76. Daithí Ó Corráin, *Rendering to God and Caesar: The Irish Churches and the Two States in Ireland, 1949–73* (Manchester, 2006), 32.
77. *The Presbyterian Church in Ireland: Reports of the General Assembly* (June 1980), 1–6; *Irish News*, 1 Oct. 1979; Maria Power, *From Ecumenism to Community Relations: Inter-Church Relationships in Northern Ireland 1980–2005* (Dublin, 2007), 34.
78. Power, *From Ecumenism to Community Relations*, 61–2.
79. Ibid. 31–2; Megahey, *Irish Protestant Churches in the Twentieth Century*, 158–61.

6. 'Our Darkest Days': Religious Persecution and Catholic Identity

1. Desmond Fennell, *The Changing Face of Catholic Ireland* (London, 1968), 33.
2. Eamonn McCann, *War and an Irish Town* (Harmondsworth, 1974), 69–70.
3. Joseph Guinan, *The Island Parish* (Dublin, 1908), 96–7; Catherine Candy, *Priestly Fictions: Popular Irish Novelists of the Early 20th Century* (Dublin, 1995), 98. Peter R. Connolly, 'The Priest in Modern Irish Fiction', *The Furrow*, 9 (1958), 790–1, found that so successful was this image of the Soggarth Aroon that no subsequent author had challenged it.
4. The Christian Brothers, *Irish History Reader* (Dublin, 1916), p. viii.
5. Colin Murphy and Lynn Adair (eds), *Untold Stories* (Dublin, 2000), 39.
6. Thomas Davis, *National and Historical Ballads, Songs and Poems* (Dublin, n.d.), 144–7, one of Duffy's National Library series, the hugely popular sixpenny books of national tales and song.
7. A. M. Sullivan, *The Story of Ireland* (Dublin, 1867), 477; R. F. Foster, *The Irish Story: Telling Tales and Making it up in Ireland* (London, 2001), 2–8.
8. The Treaty (1691) ending the Williamite war, whereby William granted favourable surrender terms to the Jacobite forces, including freedom of religion to all Catholics, 'consistent with the laws of

Ireland'. The largely Protestant Irish parliament refused to ratify this clause, and subsequent Catholic tradition saw the Penal Laws as a betrayal of the Treaty. 'Remember Limerick' became shorthand for persecution and betrayal.

9. Mrs Stephen Gwynn, *Stories from Irish History* (Dublin, 1904), 142–3.

10. Revd William Corkey, *The Church of Rome and Irish Unrest: How Hatred of Britain is Taught in Irish Schools* (Edinburgh, 1918), 31–3; *The Witness*, 8 May 1918.

11. Alan Ford, James McGuire, and Kenneth Milne (eds), *As by Law Established: The Church of Ireland since the Reformation* (Dublin, 1995), 4; Myles V. Ronan, *The Irish Martyrs of the Penal Laws* (London, 1935).

12. W. J. Lockington SJ, *The Soul of Ireland* (London, 1919), 40–9.

13. Henry Glassie, *Passing the Time in Ballymenone* (Bloomington, Ind., 1995), 124–6, shows that Carleton had entered oral tradition in Fermanagh.

14. Sullivan, *Story of Ireland*, 479.

15. William Carleton, *The Autobiography of William Carleton*, rev. edn (London, 1968), 43–4.

16. Marianne Elliott, *The Catholics of Ulster: A History* (New York, 2001), 200–1.

17. *Irish Independent*, 19–21 June 1929.

18. Christian Brothers, *Irish History Reader*, 240.

19. See D. Vincent Twomey, *The End of Irish Catholicism?* (Dublin, 2003), for an honest analysis of this from within the Catholic Church.

20. William Shaw, *Cullybackey: The Story of an Ulster Village* (Edinburgh, 1913), 132; Michael G. Quinn, 'Religion and Landownership in County Louth 1641–*c*.1750', MA thesis (University of Ulster, 1984), 7.

21. J. G. Simms, 'Irish Catholics and the Parliamentary Franchise, 1692–1728', in D. W. Hayton and Gerard O'Brien (eds), *War and Politics in Ireland, 1649–1730* (London, 1986), 224–34.

22. Ian McBride, 'The Penal Laws', unpub. paper delivered in Belfast, Mar. 2007.

23. *The Journal of the Rev. John Wesley*, 4 vols (London, 1895), ii. 67.

24. I look at this in my *Catholics of Ulster*, 174; there is also a good survey, reaching the same conclusion, in Revd P. Ó Gallachair, 'Clogher's Altars of the Penal Days', *Clogher Record*, 2 (1957–9), 97–130; 4 (1960– 1), 113–14; 9 (1976), 108–9. He found 150 sites in Clogher alone, and the list continued to grow as he was told of others.

25. Wesley, *Journal*, ii. 139.

26. Elliott, *Catholics of Ulster*, 190.

27. W. E. Vaughan (ed.), *A New History of Ireland*, v: *Ireland under the Union*, i: 1801–70 (Oxford, 1989), 106.

28. Marianne Elliott, *Wolfe Tone: Prophet of Irish Independence* (London, 1989), 181–6.

29. Ian d'Alton, *Protestant Society and Politics in Cork 1812–1844* (Cork, 1980), 35–6, 88–119; Jacqueline Hill, 'Protestant Ascendancy Challenged: The Church of Ireland Laity and the Public Sphere, 1740–1869', in Raymond Gillespie and W. G. Neely (eds), *The Laity and the Church of Ireland, 1000–2000* (Dublin, 2002), 161–4.

30. Allan Blackstock, *An Ascendancy Army: The Irish Yeomanry 1796–1834* (Dublin, 1998), 113–22.

31. James Godkin, *Ireland and her Churches* (London, 1867), 19.

32. Fergus O'Ferrall, *Catholic Emancipation: Daniel O'Connell and the Birth of Irish Democracy 1820–30* (Dublin, 1985), 256.

33. Nicholas Atkin and Frank Tallett, *Priests, Prelates and People: A History of European Catholicism since 1750* (London, 2003), 97; E. R. Norman (ed.), *Anti-Catholicism in Victorian England* (London, 1968), 131.

34. D. H. Akenson, *Intolerance: The E-Coli of the Human Mind* (Canberra, 2004), 56–7; Vaughan (ed.), *New History of Ireland*, v. 735.

35. Constantia Maxwell, *A History of Trinity College Dublin, 1591–1812* (Dublin, 1946), 190–1.

36. William Parnell, *An Inquiry into the Causes of Popular Discontent in Ireland by an Irish Country Gentleman* (London, 1804), 12.

37. Arthur Young, *Tour in Ireland (1776–1779)*, 2 vols (London, 1892), ii. 66.

38. John Brady, *Catholics and Catholicism in the Eighteenth-Century Press* (Maynooth, 1965), 13–14, 157, 168, 196–8, 208–9, 257.

39. Michael Brown, Charles I. McGrath, and Thomas P. Power (eds), *Converts and Conversion in Ireland, 1650–1850* (Dublin, 2005), 14–15.

40. Pierre Benoit, *Le Lac salé* (Paris, 1921), 168; my thanks to Dr Ian McKeane, Institute of Irish Studies, University of Liverpool, for alerting me to this work.

41. Tom Garvin, *Preventing the Future: Why was Ireland So Poor for So Long?* (Dublin, 2004), 37.

42. Elliott, *Catholics of Ulster*, 90.

43. See e.g. Bernadette Cunningham, 'Continuity and Change: Donnchadh O'Brien, Fourth Earl of Thomond (d. 1624), and the Anglicisation of the Thomond Lordship', in Matthew Lynch and Patrick Nugent (eds), *Clare History and Society: Interdisciplinary Essays on the History of an Irish County* (Dublin, 2008), 75–6.

44. There is a good survey in Terence Dooley, *The Big Houses and Landed Estates in Ireland: A Research Guide* (Dublin, 2007), 13–17; Elliott, *Catholics of Ulster*, 117; S. J. Connolly, *Religion, Law and Power: The Making of Protestant Ireland 1660–1760* (Oxford, 1992), 15–16.

45. J. C. Beckett, *The Anglo-Irish Tradition* (London, 1976), 48, 51; Godkin, *Ireland and her Churches*, 59.

46. Oliver MacDonagh, *States of Mind: A Study of Anglo–Irish Conflict 1780–1980* (London, 1983), 1.

47. John Bowman, *De Valera and the Ulster Question, 1917–1973* (Oxford, 1982), 140.

48. Kurt Bowen, *Protestants in a Catholic State: Ireland's Privileged Minority* (Dublin, 1983), 16, quoting the Census Commissioners in 1871: 'the acreage of land in protestant episcopalian ownership exceeds so largely the surface under all other proprietorship as to constitute the landed proprietory of the country', and he sees the economic discontent of Catholics at being 'a community of tenants in their own country' feeding into nationalism.

49. Andy Pollak, Torkel Opsahl, et al., *A Citizens' Inquiry* (Dublin, 1993), 409.

50. Dermot Keogh, 'Catholicism and the Formation of Modern Irish Society', in *Irishness in a Changing Society*, Princess Grace Irish Library Series (Gerrards Cross, 1988), 155.

51. Candy, *Priestly Fictions*, 98.

52. Robert Benjamin Tobin, 'The Minority Voice: Hubert Butler, Southern Protestantism and Intellectual Dissent, 1930–72', D.Phil. thesis (Oxford University, 2004), 10.

53. Marcus Tanner, Ireland's *Holy Wars: The Struggle for a Nation's Soul* (New Haven, 2001), 162–3.

7. The Poor are Always with us; the Poor are Always Catholic

1. D. P. Moran, *The Philosophy of Irish Ireland*, ed. Patrick Maume (Dublin, 2006), 123.
2. Edith Newman Devlin, *Speaking Volumes: A Dublin Childhood* (Belfast, 2000), 117.
3. J. C. Beckett, *The Anglo-Irish Tradition* (London, 1976), 109.
4. Joseph Spence, 'The Philosophy of Irish Toryism, 1833–52', Ph.D. thesis (University of London, 1991), 165.
5. John Brady, *Catholics and Catholicism in the Eighteenth-Century Press* (Maynooth, 1965), 68–73.
6. D. A. Chart (ed.), *The Drennan Letters* (Belfast, 1931), 215, 228.
7. Toby Barnard, *A New Anatomy of Ireland: The Irish Protestants, 1649–1770* (New Haven, 2003), 18–19; also his 'The Political Material and Mental Culture of the Cork Settlers, c.1650–1700', in Patrick O'Flanagan and Cornelius G. Buttimer (eds), *Cork, History and Society* (Dublin, 1993), 349–50; see also Martin Maguire, 'The Church of Ireland and the Problem of the Protestant Working-Class of Dublin, 1870s–1930s', in Alan Ford, James McGuire, and Kenneth Milne (eds), *As by Law Established: The Church of Ireland since the Reformation* (Dublin, 1995), 195–203.
8. David Hempton and Myrtle Hill, *Evangelical Protestantism in Ulster Society, 1740–1890* (London, 1992), 15.
9. George A. Birmingham, *The Seething Pot* (London, 1932), 79–80.
10. Brian Taylor, *The Life and Writings of James Owen Hannay (George A. Birmingham) 1865–1950* (Lampeter, 1995), 55.
11. Willard Potts, *Joyce and the Two Irelands* (Austin, Tex., 2000), 35.
12. Ibid. 120; James Joyce, *Portrait of the Artist as a Young Man* (London, 1992), 141–2, 183.
13. See e.g. *Irish Times*, 1 May 2004, on the case of Sandy Row, a block of £90,000 flats bought by Catholics at the university, dubbed Vatican

Square, and subjected to loyalist attacks; also 'Who's Got the Bling Here—Catholics or Protestants?', *Belfast Telegraph*, 18 June 2008.

14. Marianne Elliott, *The Catholics of Ulster: A History* (London, 2000), 190, 230.

15. Quoted in Daire Keogh, *'The French Disease': The Catholic Church and Radicalism in Ireland, 1790–1800* (Dublin, 1993), 149.

16. Catherine Candy, *Priestly Fictions: Popular Irish Novelists of the Early 20th Century* (Dublin, 1995), 98.

17. Ibid. 85–8.

18. Elliott, *Catholics of Ulster*, 464; Diarmaid Ferriter, *The Transformation of Ireland 1900–2000* (London, 2004), 361.

19. R. F. Foster, *Modern Ireland 1600–1972* (London, 1988), 453.

20. Geoffrey Keating, *History of Ireland*, 4 vols (London, 1902–14), i. 153.

21. Gerald of Wales, *The History and Topography of Ireland*, trans. John O'Meara (London, 1982), 106, 100–1.

22. Andrew Hadfield, 'Briton and Scythian: Tudor Representations of Irish Origins', *Irish Historical Studies*, 28 (1993), 390–408.

23. Edmund Spenser, *A View of the State of Ireland*, in James Ware (ed.), *Ancient Irish Histories*, 2 vols (Dublin, 1809), i. 135. Any number of English travellers in Ireland through the centuries commented on how negative were English perceptions of Ireland; see e.g. Charles Topham Bowden, *A Tour through Ireland* (Dublin, 1791), 33–4, and John Carr, *The Stranger in Ireland* (London, 1805), 33.

24. T. C. Barnard, 'The Political, Material and Mental Culture of the Cork Settlers, *c.*1650–1700', in O'Flanagan and Buttimer (eds), *Cork, History and Society*, 310; *New Anatomy*, 310; David Dickson, *Old World Colony: Cork and South Munster 1630–1830* (Cork, 2005), 57–8.

25. Finlay Holmes, *Henry Cooke* (Belfast, 1981), 132; R. L. McCartney, *Liberty and Authority in Ireland*, Field Day Pamphlet 9 (Derry, 1985), 23.

26. Jack White, *Minority Report: The Anatomy of the Southern Irish Protestant* (Dublin, 1975), 62.

27. Tom Garvin, *Preventing the Future: Why was Ireland So Poor for So Long?* (Dublin, 2004), 32–4, 148–9, while accepting a particular mindset, also argues other causes and sees the industrial prowess of the North as largely illusory by the 20th century. See also Cormac Ó Gráda, *Ireland: A New Economic History 1780–1939* (Oxford, 1995), 328–30, 348.

28. James Loughlin, 'Imagining "Ulster": The North of Ireland and British National Identity, 1880–1921', in S. J. Connolly (ed.), *Kingdoms United? Great Britain and Ireland since 1500: Integration and Diversity* (Dublin, 1999), 110–12; R. M. Sibbett, *Orangeism in Ireland and throughout the Empire*, 2 vols (Belfast, 1914), i. 118–20, citing Macaulay on the industriousness of the colonists.

29. D. H. Akenson, *Small Differences: Irish Catholics and Irish Protestants, 1815–1922: An International Perspective* (Dublin, 1991), 22–3; id., 'Hatred Maintenance Systems: Max Weber and the Irish Case', in *Intolerance: The E-Coli of the Human Mind* (Canberra, 2004), 45–61.

30. Thomas Davis, *National and Historical Ballads, Songs and Poems* (Dublin, n.d.), 146. Alice Stopford Green, *Irish Nationality* (New York, n.d.), 142, lists their achievements abroad: 'We may ask whether in the history of the world there was cast out of any country such genius, learning, and industry, as the English flung, as it were, into the sea.'

31. Susan McKay, *Northern Protestants: An Unsettled People* (Belfast, 2000), 172; A. C. Hepburn, *A Past Apart: Studies in the History of Catholic Belfast 1850–1950* (Belfast, 1996), 160; Marc Mulholland, 'Why did Unionists Discriminate?', in Sabine Wichert (ed.), *From the United Irishmen to Twentieth-Century Unionism: A Festschrift for A. T. Q. Stewart* (Dublin, 2004), 190–2.

32. McKay, *Northern Protestants*, 152.

33. The Revd Canon Sheehan, *My New Curate: A Story Gathered from the Stray Leaves of an Old Diary* (1899; 4th edn, Dublin, 1944), 35–7.

34. John Coakley, 'Religion, National Identity and Political Change in Modern Ireland', *Irish Political Studies*, 17 (2002), 10–11.

35. Akenson, *Small Differences*, 160–80.

36. Elliott, *Catholics of Ulster*, 362; also 545 n. 79.

37. Ibid. 354.

38. *Parliamentary Debates*, 5th ser., vol. xxxix, cols 1097–8 (13 June 1912); White, *Minority Report*, 65.

39. Frank McCourt, *Angela's Ashes* (London, 1996), 338. The phrase was also used to describe what would happen to northern Catholics in a partitioned country; see Eamon Phoenix, *Northern Nationalism: Nationalist Politics, Partition and the Catholic Minority in Northern Ireland 1890–1940* (Belfast, 1994), 32.

40. P. McNally, *Parties, Patriots and Undertakers* (Dublin, 1997), 28.

41. Marianne Elliott, 'Religion and Identity in Northern Ireland', in Elliott (ed.), *The Long Road to Peace in Northern Ireland*, 2nd edn (Liverpool, 2007), 180.

42. Énri Ó Muirgheasa (ed.), *Dánta Diadha Uladh* (Dublin, 1936), 276–7; Philip Robinson, *Plantation of Ulster* (Dublin, 1984), 189: report of the woodkerne hanging an Irishman because he had conformed, 1615.

43. Ibid. 363–4.

44. Thomas Moore, *Memoirs, Journal and Correspondence*, ed. Lord John Russell, 8 vols (London, 1853–6), iii. 275.

45. W. J. McCormack, *Sheridan Le Fanu and Victorian Ireland* (Oxford, 1980), 11.

46. *Travels of an Irish Gentleman in Search of a Religion . . . by the Editor of 'Captain Rock's Memoirs'*, 2 vols (London, 1833), i. 3–4.

47. Chart, *Drennan Letters*, 79.

48. The Christian Brothers, *Irish History Reader* (Dublin, 1916), 103.

49. As a correspondent says in a letter printed in his *Rome in Ireland* (London, 1904), 338. The antiquarian copy in my possession has a newspaper cutting pinned to its flyleaf, *Daily Mail*, 13 Aug. 1965, on the opening of Galway Cathedral, costing £1 million, donated by the parishioners over ninety years. Other works by McCarthy on the same theme are: *Five Years in Ireland* (1901) and *Priests and People in Ireland* (1902); Alan Megahey, *Irish Protestant Churches in the Twentieth Century*, 24; James H. Murphy, *Catholic Fiction and Social Reality in Ireland, 1873–1922* (Westport, Conn., 1997), 73 n. 3, 103 n. 12.

50. Horace Plunkett, *Ireland in the New Century* (1904; New York, 1970), 101–2.

51. Ibid. 116–17.

52. Michael O'Riordan, *Catholicity and Progress in Ireland* (London, 1906), 31.

53. Ibid. 21–2.

54. George Berkeley, *A Word to the Wise, or, The Bishop of Cloyne's Exhortation to the Roman Catholic Clergy of Ireland*, 4th edn (Waterford, 1750).

55. Ibid. 4–5; Andrew Sneddon, ' "Darkness must be Expell'd by Letting in the Light": Bishop Francis Hutchinson and the Conversion of Irish Catholics by Means of the Irish Language, *c.*1720–4', *Eighteenth-*

Century Ireland, 18 (2004), 38–9; Brady, *Catholics and Catholicism in the Eighteenth-Century Press*, 78 ff., also 131; W. E. H. Lecky, *A History of Ireland in the Eighteenth Century*, 5 vols (London, 1892), i. 229.

56. O'Riordan, *Catholicity and Progress in Ireland*, 164–6.

57. Ibid. 88.

58. Ibid. 271–5.

59. Ibid. 279.

60. Ibid. 148; Cormac Ó Gráda, *Ireland: A New Economic History 1780–1939* (Oxford, 1995), 328–30, 348. Liam Kennedy, *Colonialism, Religion and Nationalism in Ireland* (Belfast, 1996), pp. xiii–xiv, 103–34, plays this down, despite the Church's anti-industrialism.

61. James H. Murphy, *Catholic Fiction and Social Reality in Ireland, 1873–1922* (Westport, Conn., 1997), 115.

62. Ibid. 80–6; R. V. Comerford, *Ireland* (London, 2003), 176–7.

63. *James Joyce: Occasional, Critical, and Political Writing*, ed. Kevin Barry (Oxford, 2000), 62; my thanks to Frank Shovlin for drawing my attention to this.

64. R. B. D. French, 'J. O. Hannay and the Gaelic League', *Hermathena: A Dublin University Review*, 102 (Spring 1966), 37–8.

65. *Southern Ireland—State or Church*, Ulster Unionist Council pamphlet, printed by the *Belfast News Letter* (1951).

66. Fr John Kelly, 'Solid Virtue in Ireland', *Doctrine and Life*, 9 (Oct.–Nov. 1959), 120; Louise Fuller, *Irish Catholicism since 1950: The Undoing of a Culture* (Dublin, 2004), 61.

67. Dermot Keogh, 'Catholicism and the Formation of Modern Irish Society', in his *Irishness in a Changing Society*, Princess Grace Irish Library Series (Gerrards Cross, 1988), 161.

68. E. Brian Titley, *Church, State and the Control of Schooling in Ireland 1900–1944* (Dublin, 1983), 146 ff.

69. Ibid. 8–27, 62.

70. The best account of all this is Senia Pešeta, *Before the Revolution: Nationalism, Social Change and Ireland's Catholic Elite, 1879–1922* (Cork, 1999).

71. *The Leader*, 1 Sept. 1900; Pešeta, *Before the Revolution*, 39.

72. 'Politics, Nationality and Snobs', in his *The Philosophy of Irish Ireland*, 60–1. Catholics doing well also risked disapproval from other Cath-

olics; see Anthony D. Buckley, *A Gentle People: A Study of a Peaceful Community in Ulster* ([Holywood], 1982), 59.

73. 'Is the Irish Nation Dying?', in his *The Philosophy of Irish Ireland*, 9–10.

74. Dónall Ó Moráin, 'Ireland and the Church', *The Furrow*, 17 (1966), 429–32. Similar criticisms were made in Margaret McCarthy, 'Irish Catholicism: An Irish American's Impressions', *The Tablet* (25 July 1964), 829–30, and endorsed in a letter from an Irish priest on mission in Nigeria (*The Tablet*, 29 Aug. 1964), 980–1.

8. 'Beached': Religious Minorities in Partitioned Ireland

1. Though see Revd Brian Kennaway, *The Orange Order: An Evangelical Perspective* ([Belfast], 1993), 192–3, on how Protestants complained of Catholic educational institutions receiving funding, when specifically Protestant ones did not.

2. Peter Hart, *The IRA and its Enemies: Violence and Community in Cork, 1916–23* (Oxford, 1998), 288; id., 'Class, Community and the Irish Republican Army in Cork, 1917–23', in Patrick O'Flanagan and Cornelius G. Buttimer (eds), *Cork, History and Society* (Dublin, 1993), 970; Kurt Bowen, *Protestants in a Catholic State: Ireland's Privileged Minority* (Dublin, 1983), 23–4; Robert Benjamin Tobin, 'The Minority Voice: Hubert Butler, Southern Protestantism and Intellectual Dissent, 1930–72', D.Phil. thesis (Oxford University, 2004), 53, on how unusual Cork was; also David Fitzpatrick, *Politics and Irish Life, 1913–1921: Provincial Experience of War and Revolution* (Dublin, 1998), 54, 66–7. But Tobin does talk of the 'loneliness' of Protestants in the Free State. They had become 'outcasts'. J. C. Beckett, *The Anglo-Irish Tradition* (London, 1976), 70, sees the burnings as 'a warning that they were not wanted in the new Ireland that was emerging'.

3. John Coakley, 'Religion, Ethnic Identity and the Protestant Minority in the Republic', in William Crotty and David Schmitt (eds), *Ireland and the Politics of Change* (London, 1998), 89. By 1991 it had declined to 3.2 per cent of the Irish population (2.5 per cent Church of Ireland).

4. 'War of Independence Debate on Sectarianism Descends on Unassuming Offaly', <http://www.indymedia.ie>, accessed Apr. 2008. Most of the commentary and webmail totally denies that Irish republicanism could be sectarian, though the murders of these Protestants are justified by reference to their ancestors as Cromwellian settlers and 'the ethnic cleansing and colonising activities of the English state'. A more level-headed critique is that by Brian Hanley, 'Fear and Loathing at Coolacrease', *History Ireland*, 16 (Jan.–Feb. 2008), 5–6; Niamh Sammon, feature article on the Offaly killings, 'A True History of Violence', *Irish Times*, 20 Oct. 2007; various exchanges *Sunday Independent*, 9, 16, and 21 Oct., 11 and 18 Nov. 2007. See also accounts of IRA sectarianism in Longford in Liam Kennedy, *Colonialism, Religion and Nationalism in Ireland* (Belfast, 1996), 30.

5. *Meath Chronicle*, 25 Jan. 1919.

6. Marcus Tanner, *Ireland's Holy Wars* (New Haven, 2001), 292.

7. Terence Dooley, *The Plight of Monaghan Protestants, 1912–1926* (Dublin, 2000), 44–5; Natasha Claire Grayson, 'The Quality of Nationalism in Counties Cavan, Louth and Meath during the Irish Revolution', Ph.D. thesis (University of Keele, 2007), 300–3.

8. David Thomson, *Woodbrook* (London, 1991), 59–61. R. B. McDowell, *Crisis and Decline: The Fate of the Southern Unionists* (Dublin, 1997), 202, also recalls from his own 'loyalist' family 'a noticeable tendency to emphasize in conversation the humorous side of "the troubles" . . . and the strange inter-mixture of belligerency and normality that characterized the years 1919 to 1923 [and] nourished the incongruous and the comic'.

9. David Fitzpatrick, *Politics and Irish Life 1913–1921: Provincial Experience of War and Revolution* (Cork, 1977), 57.

10. Dennis Kennedy, *The Widening Gulf: Northern Attitudes to the Independent Irish State 1919–49* (Belfast, 1998), 49–55, 116–20; the *Irish Times*, 10 May 1922, report from the General Synod expressing fears that it would turn into a war of religion.

11. Martin Maguire, ' "Our People": The Church of Ireland and the Culture of Community in Dublin since Disestablishment', in Raymond Gillespie and W. G. Neely (eds), *The Laity and the Church of Ireland, 1000–2000* (Dublin, 2002), 282.

12. McDowell, *Crisis and Decline*, 135–6.

13. C.I.R., 'Gigmanity Uprooted', *The Bell*, 11/2 (Nov. 1945), 692.

14. *Irish Times*, 19, 24, 28 Apr. 2006.

15. Martin Maguire, 'A Socio-economic Analysis of the Dublin Protestant Working Class, 1870–1926', *Irish Economic and Social History*, 20 (1993), 35–61; id., 'The Organization and Activism of Dublin's Protestant Working Class, 1883–1935', *Irish Historical Studies*, 29 (May 1994), 65–87; id.,'Our People', 277–303. There is an excellent analysis of the decline in numbers in Coakley, 'Religion, Ethnic Identity and the Protestant Minority in the Republic', 88–93. Archbishop Gregg also blamed celibacy and late marriage; *Journal of the Church of Ireland General Synod* (1939), pp. lxvii–lxviii.

16. Maguire, 'Our People', 286; also Daithí Ó Corráin, *Rendering to God and Caesar: The Irish Churches and the Two States in Ireland, 1949–73* (Manchester, 2006), 70–114; Kenneth Milne, 'The Protestant Churches in Independent Ireland', in James P. Mackey and Enda McDonagh (eds), *Religion and Politics in Ireland at the Turn of the Millennium* (Dublin, 2003), 83; Robert Tobin, ' "Tracing again the Tiny Snail Track": Southern Protestant Memoir since 1950', *Yearbook of English Studies*, 35 (2005), 171–85, on 'plain' Protestants' annoyance at the idea of tragic decline, and the Big House reading of Irish Protestantism. This new work challenges Desmond Bowen's conclusion in *History and Shaping of Irish Protestantism* (New York, 1995), 436, suggesting that it was only in the 1970s that 'The long silence of a submerged intimidated people was coming to an end.'

17. Brian Inglis, *West Briton* (London, 1962), 23, 92, 147, 160–1.

18. Terence Dooley, *The Big Houses and Landed Estates in Ireland: A Research Guide* (Dublin, 2007), 58–9; but see also id., *'The Land for the People': The Land Question in Independent Ireland* (Dublin, 2004), who shows that it was not just the former 'ascendancy' which was to be replaced by small owner occupiers, but the grazier–rentier class.

19. R. F. Foster, *W. B. Yeats: A Life*, i: *The Apprentice Mage 1865–1914* (Oxford, 1997), 144; ii: *The Arch-Poet 1915–1939* (Oxford, 2003), 658.

20. Dooley, *Big Houses*, 136–41; Patrick J. Duffy, 'Writing Ireland: Literature and Art in the Representation of Irish Space', in Brian Graham (ed.), *In Search of Ireland: A Cultural Geography* (London, 1997), 71–4.

21. Maguire, 'Our People', 296.

22. 'Ould Willie' features regularly in Harbinson's multi-volume auto-biography, most movingly in *Up Spake the Cabin Boy* (Belfast, 1988), 228–30.

23. The ruling that Catholics could not attend Protestant services was not resolved until the 1960s (see Louise Fuller, *Irish Catholicism since 1950* (Dublin, 2004), 185), though related controversies regularly appear in the Irish press.

24. Lily O'Connor, *Can Lily O'Shea Come Out to Play?* (Dingle, 2000).

25. Benedict Anderson, 'Selective Kinship', *Dublin Review* (Spring 2003), 28.

26. R. B. McDowell, *The Church of Ireland 1869–1969* (London, 1975), 110.

27. Ibid. 112; *Journal of the General Synod* (1949), pp. lxxxiii–iv.

28. Michael Viney, *The Five Per Cent: A Survey of Protestants in the Republic* (Dublin, [1965]), 32.

29. Paul Durcan, *A Snail in my Prime* (London, 1999), 27–8; John F. Deane (ed.), *Irish Poetry of Faith and Doubt: The Cold Heaven* (Dublin, 1990), 172–3.

30. *Irish Times*, 10 May 1922.

31. McDowell, *Church of Ireland*, 134.

32. Alan Acheson, *A History of the Church of Ireland* (Dublin, 1997), 229.

33. David Butler, 'Still Separate After All These Years? Growing up in Protestant West Cork', paper delivered to the Conference of Irish Geographers at the Institute of Irish Studies, University of Liverpool, May 2008.

34. See Maguire, 'A Socio-economic Analysis of the Dublin Protestant Working Class', 51–2. Also id., 'The Church of Ireland in Dublin since Disestablishment', in Gillespie and Neely (eds), *The Laity and the Church of Ireland*, 285, which shows a real social mix and a staggering number of war dead in some parishes; he also examines reasons for demographic decline after partition (300).

35. Dean Victor Griffin, in Colin Murphy and Lynne Adair (eds), *Untold Stories: Protestants in the Republic of Ireland, 1922–2002* (Dublin, 2002), 97. See Tobin, 'Minority Voice', 255, for fears about how Protestants could 'replenish' themselves; Fuller, *Irish Catholicism since 1950*, 17–18, 182–5.

36. Murphy and Adair (eds), *Untold Stories*, 142.

37. J. H. Whyte, *Church and State in Modern Ireland, 1923–1970* (Dublin, 1971), 368. He also shows, however, that governments did not automatically defer to the bishops, despite the very damaging claim by Taoiseach Costello during the Mother and Child controversy that he did.

38. Ibid. 168, citing *Irish Law Times Reports*, 79 (1945), 116–21.

39. Whyte, *Church and State in Modern Ireland*, 167–71.

40. Fuller, *Irish Catholicism since 1950*, 183; Whyte, *Church and State in Modern Ireland*, 323; Ó Corráin, *Rendering to God and Caesar*, 187.

41. Tobin, 'Minority Voice', 231–2.

42. Ibid. 232 n. 40.

43. Dean Victor Griffin's interview with Tobin, 'Minority Voice', 230.

44. Fuller, *Irish Catholicism since 1950*, 106.

45. Seán MacRéamoinn (ed.), *The Church in a New Ireland* (Blackrock, 1996), 21; Ó Moráin, 'Ireland and the Church', *The Furrow*, 17 (1966), 429–32.

46. Ó Corráin, *Rendering to God and Caesar*, 205.

47. Patrick Maume, in his fine introduction to Clery's writings, *The Idea of a Nation* (Dublin, 2002), p. xiii.

48. Clery, *The Idea of a Nation*, 86–97.

49. John Bowman, *De Valera and the Ulster Question, 1917–1973* (Oxford, 1982), 281–7; Conn McCluskey, *Up off their Knees: A Commentary on the Civil Rights Movement in Northern Ireland* (Galway, 1989), 22; also discussed in R. F. Foster, *Luck and the Irish: A Brief History of Change c.1970–2000* (London, 2007), 99–146.

50. Eamon Phoenix, *Northern Nationalism: Nationalist Politics, Partition and the Catholic Minority in Northern Ireland 1890–1940* (Belfast, 1994), 335.

51. G. B. Kenna [Fr John Hassan], *Facts and Figures of the Belfast Pogrom 1920–1922* (Dublin, 1922).

52. Patrick Shea, *Voices and the Sound of Drums: An Irish Autobiography* (Belfast, 1981), 112.

53. Paul Bew, Peter Gibbon, and Henry Patterson, *Northern Ireland, 1921–1994: Political Forces and Social Classes* (London, 1995), 64–70; Henry Patterson, *Ireland since 1939: The Persistence of Conflict* (Dublin, 2006), 17–18; John Whyte, *Interpreting Northern Ireland* (Oxford, 1990), 169.

54. See *Fermanagh Herald*, 16 Feb. 1957, for good examples of how it is the blatantly sectarian actions and words of prominent Unionists that are recalled; Jonathan Bardon, *A History of Ulster* (Belfast, 1992), 608–9; Patterson, *Ireland since 1939*, 122–4; Henry Patterson and Eric Kaufmann, *Unionism and Orangeism in Northern Ireland since 1945: The Decline of the Loyal Family* (Manchester, 2007), 15, 47–9, 63–4—this book also brings out well the many opinions within Unionism and Orangeism.

55. Shea, *Voices and the Sound of Drums*, 113; also Opsahl Commission submission by Robert Dickinson and Focus Group reports, Protestants in Auchnacloy, Castledawson, and Londonderry (in the possession of the author, who sat on the Commission, and publicly available in the Linenhall Library Belfast).

56. Kennedy, *Widening Gulf*, 164–6; ibid. 31 and *The Witness*, 8 May 1918, for accusations that the Catholic Church was behind the violence.

57. *Belfast News Letter*, 27 June 1932; Marianne Elliott, *The Catholics of Ulster: A History* (London, 2000), 470, for similar mass gatherings in 1934, 1939, 1947, and 1958.

58. Elliott, *Catholics of Ulster*, 462; Dominic Murray, *Worlds Apart: Segregated Schools in Northern Ireland* (Belfast, 1985), 21.

59. Bowman, *De Valera and the Ulster Question*, 184.

60. 'Ultach', 'The Persecution of Catholics in Northern Ireland', *Capuchin Annual* (1940), 161–75; *Fermanagh Times*, 13 July 1933; *Northern Ireland House of Commons*, vol. xvi, cols 612–19.

61. 'Ultach', 'The Persecution of Catholics in Northern Ireland', 167.

62. *Irish News*, 4 Apr. 1939, doggerel 'Stormont'. There was also an element of this in the systematic murder by the IRA of border Protestants during the Troubles; see Andy Pollak, Torkel Opsahl, et al., *A Citizens' Inquiry* (Dublin, 1993), 411, with comments by Frank Curran, former editor of *Derry Journal*; Colm Tóibín, *Bad Blood: A Walk along the Irish Border* (London, 1994), 72, 144–7.

63. In response, Lord Brookeborough considered restricting family allowances to the first three children; his own MPs at Westminster discouraged him from this blatant piece of discrimination. See Patterson, *Ireland since 1939*, 126, 375; also Patterson and Kaufmann, *Unionism and Orangeism in Northern Ireland*, 14, 44–9, on the paranoia about 'peaceful penetration' by 'disloyalists' from the South.

64. Marianne Elliott, 'Religion and Identity in Northern Ireland', in Elliott (ed.), *The Long Road to Peace in Northern Ireland* (Liverpool, 2007).

65. 'Ultach', 'The Persecution of Catholics in Northern Ireland', 170; *Irish News*, 11 Nov. 1932, showing respect for the dead of the First World War; John B. Dooher, 'Tyrone Nationalism and the Question of Partition, 1910–25', M.Phil. thesis (University of Ulster, 1986), 526.

66. Jane Leonard, 'The Twinge of Memory: Armistice Day and Remembrance Sunday in Dublin since 1919', in Richard English and Graham Walker (eds), *Unionism in Modern Ireland: New Perspectives on Politics and Culture* (Dublin, 1996).

67. Brian Walker, *Past and Present: History, Identity and Politics in Ireland* (Belfast, 2000), 86.

68. *Irish News*, 5 May 1995.

69. Shea, *Voices and the Sound of Drums*, 196; Elliott, *Catholics of Ulster*, 433–4; John D. Brewer with Gareth I. Higgins, *Anti-Catholicism in Northern Ireland, 1600–1998: The Mote and the Beam* (London, 1998), 156; Revd William Corkey, *The Religious Crisis in Ireland* (London, 1914), 10.

70. Eamonn McCann, *War and an Irish Town* (Harmondsworth, 1974), 81.

71. *Fermanagh Herald*, 9 Mar. 1957, Lenten pastoral by the Bishop of Clogher. See also Fionnuala O Connor, *In Search of a State* (Belfast, 1993), 106, for the impact of rebel songs.

72. Barry White, *John Hume: Statesman of the Troubles* (Belfast, 1984), 84–5.

73. Malachi O'Doherty, *The Trouble with Guns: Republican Strategy and the Provisional IRA* (Belfast, 1998), 30–1.

74. Maurice Hayes, *Minority Verdict: Experiences of a Catholic Public Servant* (Belfast, 1995), 15.

75. Foster, *Luck and the Irish*, 120; John Coakley, 'Religion, National Identity and Political Change in Modern Ireland', *Irish Political Studies*, 17 (2002), 104–5; *Through Irish Eyes: Irish Attitudes towards the UK*, report commissioned by the British Council in Ireland ([Dublin], 2003), 43–5; Garret Fitzgerald, 'Only Openness Can Close the Widening North–South Gulf', *Irish Times*, 3 Apr. 1993.

76. Murphy and Adair (eds), *Untold Stories*, 15.

77. Bishop Richard Clarke, 'On Doing Things Differently: A Church of Ireland Glance at the Past', in Denis Carroll (ed.), *Religion in Ireland: Past, Present and Future* (Dublin, 1999), 38.

78. Murphy and Adair (eds), *Untold Stories*, 81.

79. *Northern Ireland Life and Times Survey, 2007*, <http://www.ark.ac.uk>, accessed summer 2008, and analysis by Robin Wilson in *Fortnight*, no. 460 (July–Aug. 2008), 7–8.

80. O Connor, *In Search of a State*, 152.

81. Ibid. 250; Dermot Keogh, 'Catholicism and the Formation of the Modern Irish Society', in his *Irishness in a Changing Society*, Princess Grace Irish Library Series (Gerrards Cross, 1988), 168. Keogh only ever found one file which took the North into account when making a decision.

82. Kevin Bean, *The New Politics of Sinn Féin* (Liverpool, 2007), 210.

Afterword

1. Michael Longley, in his introduction to *Louis MacNeice: Poems Selected by Michael Longley* (London, 2005), p. ix, from which the quotations from 'Autumn Journal' are also taken, pp. 35–41.

2. George A. Birmingham, *An Irishman Looks at his World* (London, 1919), 90.

Acknowledgements

We are grateful for permission to include the following extracts of verse in this book.

Paul Durcan: from 'What is a Protestant, Daddy?' from *Teresa's Bar* (The Gallery Press, 1976), copyright © Paul Durcan 1976, reprinted by permission of the author c/o Rogers, Coleridge & White Ltd, 20 Powis Mews, London W11 1JN.

Seamus Heaney: from 'Whatever You Say Say Nothing' from *North* (Faber 1975), reprinted by permission of the publishers, Faber & Faber Ltd and Farrar Straus & Giroux, LLC.

Louis MacNeice: from 'Autumn Journal' from *Collected Poems* (Faber 1949), reprinted by permission of David Higham Associates Ltd.

W. R. Rodgers: from the Epilogue 'The Character of Ireland' from *Poems* (The Gallery Press 1993), reprinted by permission of the Estate of W. R. Rodgers and The Gallery Press, Loughcrew, Old-castle, County Meath, Ireland.

Patrick Williams: from 'Cage Under Siege' first published in Padraic Fiacc (ed.), *The Wearing of Black: An Anthology of Contemporary Ulster Poetry* (Blackstaff, 1974).

We have made every effort to trace and contact all copyright holders before publication. If notified, the publisher will be pleased to rectify any errors or omissions at the earliest opportunity.

Index

Index